THE OYSTER WAR

# THE
# OYSTER
# WAR

## THE TRUE STORY OF A
## SMALL FARM, BIG POLITICS,
## AND THE FUTURE OF
## WILDERNESS IN AMERICA

**SUMMER BRENNAN**

COUNTERPOINT
BERKELEY

Copyright © 2015 Summer Brennan

Library of Congress Cataloging-in-Publication Data is available.

ISBN 978-1-61902-527-1

Cover design by Kelly Winton
Interior design by Megan Jones Design

COUNTERPOINT
2560 Ninth Street, Suite 318
Berkeley, CA 94710
www.counterpointpress.com

Printed in Canada
Distributed by Publishers Group West

10 9 8 7 6 5 4 3 2 1

For my father
Patrick William Brennan

Everything not saved will be lost.

—QUIT SCREEN MESSAGE, NINTENDO

# CONTENTS

# DRAMATIS PERSONAE

## RANCHERS, FARMERS & OTHER WORKERS OF THE LAND & WATER

Kevin Lunny, *rancher and owner of the oyster farm since 2005*

Nancy Lunny, *his wife*

Brigid Lunny, *their daughter*

Ginny Lunny Cummings, *Kevin's sister, manager of Drakes Bay Oyster Company*

Joe Lunny Jr., *Kevin and Ginny's father*

Oscar,* *an oyster worker*

Ignacio,* *an oyster worker*

Rosa,* *an oyster worker's daughter*

J.V. Mendoza, *a rancher*

Zena Mendoza, *his wife*

Joseph Mendoza, *their son*

"Little Joey" Mendoza, *their grandson*

Charlie Johnson, *owner of the oyster farm 1957–1992*

Makiko Johnson, *an oyster farmer, Charlie's wife*

Tom Johnson, *Charlie's son, owner of the oyster farm 1992–2004*

John Stillwell Morgan, *ship's captain, West Coast oystering pioneer*

Sophia Morgan, née Crellin, *his wife*

John Crellin, *oyster magnate*

*names changed

Thomas Crellin, *oyster magnate*

Larry Jensen, *an oyster farmer*

Oscar Johansson, *an oyster farmer*

Boyd Stewart, *a rancher and farmer*

Pat Quail, *biologist, artist, first person to farm oysters in Drakes Estero*

Millard "Doc" Ottinger, *a doctor and gentleman rancher*

Ambrose Gondola, *his employee*

## ENVIRONMENTAL ADVOCATES

Fred Smith, *Executive Director of the Environmental Action Committee of West Marin, 2007–2010*

Amy Trainer, *took over from Fred in 2010*

Gordon Bennett, *a Sierra Club spokesperson and activist*

Beula Edmiston, *an advocate for tule elk*

## NATIONAL PARK SERVICE STAFF & GOVERNMENT OFFICIALS

Ken Salazar, *Secretary of the Interior 2009–2013*

Sally Jewell, *Secretary of the Interior 2013–*

Jonathan Jarvis, *National Park Service Director, former director of Pacific West Region*

John Sansing, *Point Reyes National Seashore Superintendent 1970–1995*

Don Neubacher, *Point Reyes National Seashore Superintendent 1995–2010*

Cicely Muldoon, *Point Reyes National Seashore Superintendent 2010–*

Sarah Allen, *biologist, Point Reyes National Seashore Senior Science Advisor*

Ben Becker, *Point Reyes biologist*

Dave Press, *Point Reyes biologist*

Melanie Gunn, *Point Reyes administrator*

John Dell'Osso, *Point Reyes National Seashore spokesperson*

Tim Ragen, *head of the Marine Mammal Commission*

## OTHER SCIENTISTS

Corey Goodman, *neuroscientist and venture capitalist*

Deborah Elliott-Fisk, *a biologist, UC Davis*

Roberto Anima, *a biologist, U.S. Geological Survey*

Harriet Huber, *a biologist focusing on marine mammals*

David Ainley, *a biologist focusing on marine mammals*

Steven D. Emslie, *a biologist focusing on seabirds*

McCrea Cobb, *a biologist studying tule elk*

## POLITICIANS

Pete McCloskey, *California Congressman 1975–1983, Republican*

Phillip Burton, *California Congressman 1964–1983, Democrat*

Dianne Feinstein, *California Senator, Democrat*

Barbara Boxer, *California Senator, Democrat*

Lynn Woolsey, *California Congresswoman, Democrat*

Steve Kinsey, *a county supervisor, de facto "mayor of West Marin"*

## OTHER PLAYERS

Greg Sarris, *Indian chief, novelist, professor and casino owner*

Burr Heneman, *former director of the Point Reyes Bird Observatory*

David Weiman, *a lobbyist*

Robert Plotkin, *owner of the* Point Reyes Light *newspaper 2005–2010*

Tom Baty, *a fisherman, beachcomber and forager*

Unnamed sharpshooter, *wildlife population control specialist with White Buffalo Inc.*

The Sealers' Woman, *a ghost*

# San Francisco Bay Area

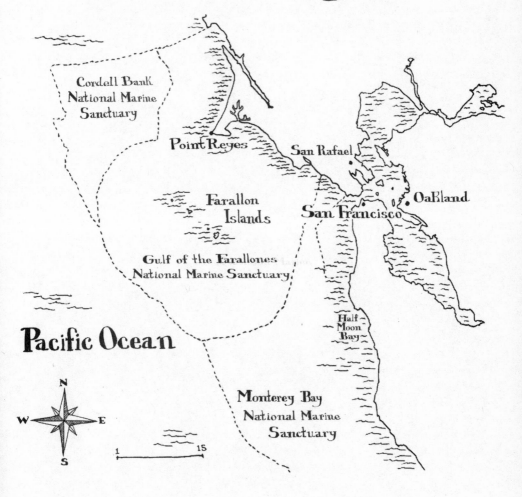

Cordell Bank
National Marine
Sanctuary

Point Reyes

San Rafael

Farallon
Islands

San Francisco

Oakland

Gulf of the Farallones
National Marine Sanctuary

Pacific Ocean

Half
Moon
Bay

N
W    E
S

1        15

Monterey Bay
National Marine
Sanctuary

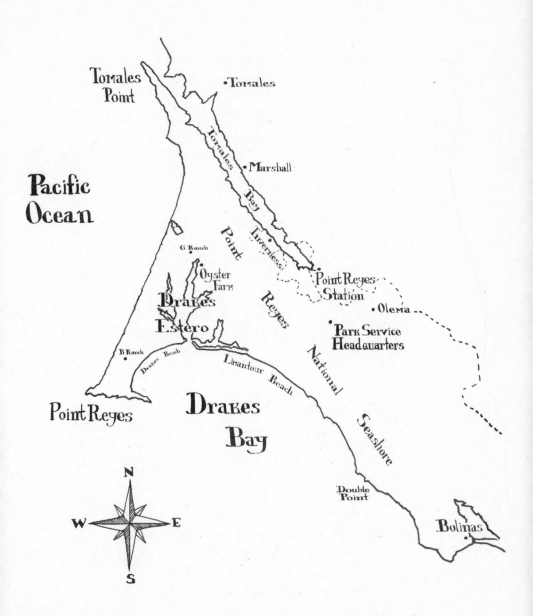

Point Reyes National Seashore

There is a pleasure in the pathless woods,
There is a rapture on the lonely shore,
There is society where none intrudes,
By the deep Sea, and music in its roar:
I love not Man the less, but Nature more.

—LORD BYRON

# PROLOGUE

THE SUMMER I spent as a reporter covering the war between the oysters and the wilderness, every night was a foggy one. The long days ended with a relief that arrived in two stages. The first came when the outstretched arm of Tomales Bay began to fill again in the late afternoons, submerging the gasping mud flats and exposed estuarine grasses as the little waves came lapping in, reaching high tide just as darkness fell. The second came when the fog made its way over the forested ridge from the sea, rolling wetly down hillsides, across meadows and into valleys. Still, as the clock ticked towards midnight, and then one, and then two, as I sat hunched over my desk night after night in the little newspaper office by the coast, I often wondered how it was that I found myself in the middle of all this.

It was a mess. There was no other word for it. The two camps had split the community, and it seemed that nearly everyone was passionately in favor of one side or the other. Lifelong neighbors stopped speaking. Family members who found themselves on opposite sides of the divide had finally, after much debate, agreed not to raise the topic at all. By the time I arrived, there had been so many scientific studies, and rebuttals and counter-rebuttals that even I, whose job it had become to know what was going on, had a hard time keeping everything straight. Some people would only meet with me about it in secret, too scared to email or talk about it on the phone. They squeezed clues and unsigned notes bearing unsolicited advice through the windows of my beater car if I left them rolled down a crack. Accusations were hurled from every direction, of fraud, scientific misconduct, environmental felony, lies, even "Tea Party Republicanism" and "Koch brothers' support"— grave insults to many in that largely liberal neck of the woods. Things were tense enough, and then the "hidden cameras" were discovered and then everything pretty much went to hell.

This isn't my story, and the part I play in it personally is small. Still, some things I can only tell through my own eyes, and for that I ask your indulgence. As far as sides go, I have tried my best to stay neutral. I was introduced to the conflict when I was hired by the *Point Reyes Light*, the rural weekly that has not been quiet about making its own position known. It was and remains staunchly in favor of the oyster farm. As my own research deepened, it was clear my approach and that of the *Light* were not in alignment, and we parted ways in September of 2012. Since then I have worked independently, funded by no one but myself, my modest book advance, and $3,541 raised on the crowdfunding site Indiegogo. I say that I have tried to stay neutral, but when presented with the facts, it's hard not to come to a conclusion. I'll let you decide for yourself. To those who have already taken a side, from you I would urge patience. Basically: Hear me out.

At least from a logistical perspective, the answer to how I found myself wedged between the National Park Service, wilderness advocates and their defenders on the one hand, and the Drakes Bay Oyster Company, the local agriculture community and *their* supporters on the other, was a fairly simple one. At the beginning of 2012 I realized I was tired of living in New York City and decided to move back to the rural

Northern California coast for a while. I'd been working since 2008 with the United Nations Department of Public Information, writing about the environment, decolonization, disarmament or the Israeli–Palestinian conflict. I'd sit in a grand but windowless room all day while various Arab diplomats raised their voices about alleged human rights abuses, and then the Israeli delegates would raise their voices back, and I'd write down a condensed version of it all. I liked the work quite a bit (in fact I still do) but as a country girl I was growing weary of the concrete and the New York weather, which seemed either torturously hot or criminally cold. One winter night after a mammoth day at the UN, while trudging home from the subway in the middle of a snowstorm, I thought to myself, *This is how Charles Dickens characters die.*

I grew up in the villages that border the Point Reyes National Seashore, just an hour north of San Francisco. But although it is one of the most visited national parks in the country, while playing in its surf or walking its beaches, camping in its forests or traipsing across its fields, I never thought much about any of that. To me it was just *outside*. It was where I belonged. And when I decided to move back, I didn't know I was about to find myself in the middle of a political and ecological battle, although that is exactly what happened.

During a gap between UN contracts I decided to pitch a freelance article to my old hometown newspaper, the *Light*. In a cursory online search I noticed that it had changed hands a few years back, but I didn't think too much of it. The paper was generally well-respected and had won a Pulitzer Prize the year that I was born for exposing a militant local cult. When the new editor, a woman about my age, offered me a full-time job as staff reporter, I accepted. Instead of refugees and lines of demarcation, I'd be writing about escaped dairy cows, local environmental issues and crop yields. This suited me just fine. New York colleagues commented that this sounded like the start of a romantic comedy. They imagined run-ins with old high school flames and hilarious hijinks involving livestock. But it didn't turn out that way.

Real wars have been fought over oysters, and I don't mean to diminish those by employing the language of battle here. From Chesapeake Bay to the Potomac, violent disputes flared between naval police and oyster pirates beginning in the middle of the nineteenth century, and the last recorded incidence of bloodshed there was as recent as 1959. But while there was no literal carnage over the Drakes Bay Oyster Company, calling what happening a "war" is truly the best way to describe it. Besides, gun-wielding oyster pirates do appear in these pages, after all.

The story of The Oyster War wound up being both bigger and smaller than I expected. I wanted to solve a specific scientific mystery, but found myself asking much broader questions instead. To answer them, I was obliged to set out on a journey that took me through the halls of Congress, Nixon's White House, the lawless oyster beds of Gold Rush San Francisco, the radical environmental activism of the 1970s to 1990s, and—of course—over the fog-soaked hills and into the misty forests of beautiful Point Reyes. Again and again I encountered two riddles. One, for a world that is in constant motion and overlap, how do we decide who belongs or doesn't belong? And two, when humanity has touched and changed every corner of the earth, what does it mean to be wild?

For much of the time I spent researching this story, if you asked me which side I believed and which I didn't, I honestly couldn't tell you. Who was telling the truth? That was what I was there to find out.

Newly back in town after almost ten years spent mostly away, it took a while to get my bearings. My life in the big city had been frenetic, and it was jarring to suddenly find myself one foggy spring night in Vladimir's, a dark Czechoslovakian pub on the edge of Tomales Bay, eating fish and chips with septuagenarian cowboys. Wild mustard was still growing tall along the roadsides, clustered white and purple against the weathered wood of old barns. Evenings came on blue and heavy from out over the Pacific. Some friends were skeptical of my decision to abandon the city, even if only temporarily. But outside, beyond the glow of Vlad's lanterns, the air was thick and wet and quiet, and it felt good to be home.

# PART I

## THE BROKEN SHORE

# 1

## THE OYSTER FARM

THE ROAD TO the oyster farm is paved with the moon-white grit of pulverized oyster shells. There is a gleam to it, and to drive it in the dusk of the dry summer months is to see the dust-coated leaves of the ditch plants take on the powdery luminosity of white moths.

Hugging the edge of the estuary's northernmost inlet, the narrow lane rises a little above a lush wetland dotted with egrets and blue herons, and then winds down again to the edge of a vast and shining body of water. This is Drakes Estero, what's been called "the heart of the park." The air feels different here. In winter or summer, heat or cold, there is an enlivening bite of freshness.

I was at the farm one evening in the late summer of 2013 to look for Oscar, one of the farm's workers. He had given me an unauthorized tour of the planting sites the month before, and I was worried that allowing him to do so had accidentally gotten him fired. Word on the street was that it had. I was initially shocked to hear this, but considering how contentious things had gotten, what with the legal battle and all the national media attention, I suppose I shouldn't have been surprised at all. For owners Kevin and Nancy Lunny, who by some estimates had already sunk more than a million dollars into their efforts to restore the farm and keep it open, the stakes could not have been higher.

Like many of the oyster workers, Oscar lived in one of the run-down buildings that made up the farm's small land-based compo-nent—a smattering of sheds, cottages, trailers and pre-fab homes. At least that is what he told me, though I didn't know if he still lived there. The buildings were scattered over just about an acre and a half, so I figured it wouldn't take too long to look.

I pulled up and parked my borrowed, mud-splattered 1991 Toyota station wagon in front of a weatherworn white building. A brightly painted sign exclaimed it to be the OYSTER SHACK. No more than six hundred square feet in total, it housed the retail portion of the business in front and the tiny hatchery in back, where the oysters were grown from spat (or "seed") the size of sand grains. On the wall of an adja-cent shed was pinned a large American flag.

The pop radio station I'd been listening to on the drive out had turned to white noise. I switched it off and got out of the car.

Outside, sagging on two legs, was an old lopsided National Park Service sign that was so weather-beaten it looked abandoned. Completely unreadable in places, I could nevertheless make out one of the blocks of text. It read:

> The tidal waters of Drakes Estero nurture a shellfish highly prized by local seafood lovers—the Drakes Bay Oyster. The oys-ters are grown and harvested here by Johnson Oyster Company under a special agreement with the California Department of Fish and Game and the National Park Service.

Yes, I thought, shaking my head. But maybe not for long.

I read on:

The oysters grow on wire "strings" hanging from wooden platforms. Here they receive nutrients carried in by the tide and are protected from starfish, crabs, stingrays and other enemies that lurk on the bottom. When the oysters are mature, oystermen collect them here for shucking, canning and marketing.

Looking around, I thought: *But where is* my *oysterman?*

Though the description of the farm's activities still fit, this wasn't the Johnson Oyster Company anymore. In early 2005 the Lunnys, a cattle ranching family from a half mile down the road, took over. Since then it had been the Drakes Bay Oyster Company—the infamous Drakes Bay Oyster Company, if you will, whose plight has garnered national media attention. Its opposing sides had brought together strange bedfellows, from anti-government militia groups to locavore celebrity chefs, and its fate had been debated heavily and contentiously across the country. Was the company causing environmental harm? Or had it been framed, the victim of government fraud? Why this sign hadn't been updated to reflect the change in ownership that took place nearly a decade prior will take the length of this book to tell.

The retail store was closed for the day, and the dock area was empty and quiet. The only sounds were the low whir of some unseen machinery and a static-y radio softly playing Mexican dance music. All were muffled by the blanket of fog that had already started rolling in. Surely this tiny, dilapidated enterprise couldn't be the big, bad "industrial" entity described by its detractors? That monster of privatization, befouling a pristine natural treasure that should be left alone for the benefit of all? Even though I'd been out to the farm many times before, I still couldn't help but ask myself, *Is this really it? Is this all?*

Covered in mud, oyster shells, bird droppings and bits of dried and wet seaweed, the waterside operations area could almost pass for something as long-abandoned as the outdated Johnson Oyster Company sign itself. Sand and shell grit escaped up from between the rotting wooden planks of the dock that sat under the rickety conveyer belt. Its concrete blocks were green with aquatic growth. The ground was slick in places with eelgrass that would be underwater again in just a few hours when the tide swelled. Off to the right was a half-sheltered wooden structure, bleached the pale gray of old driftwood, where the mature oysters were taken off of their hanging strings. There were overflowing crates of the black plastic spacers used to keep the oysters apart on the wires. Two small skiffs, one wooden and one fiberglass, were moored alongside a barge, or flatboat, not much bigger than the roof of a Volkswagen van. To the left, between the Oyster Shack and the shell-paved picnic area, stood open vats of aerated brackish water where the young oysters were grown until they were strong enough to be planted out in the deeper water. In the estuary itself, rods spackled with tiny growing oysterlings rocked gently in the lapping shallows. The empty picnic tables had white plastic cutting boards chained to the center for tourists to do their shucking. Now, the only visitors to brave the thickening evening fog were seagulls, searching the tables and ground for forgotten bits of food. They strutted along the low cliffs that stood above the six-foot mounds of discarded shells, and piles of stiff, black mesh planting bags tied together five or six at a time by lengths of yellow rope. Near the picnic tables, the blue plastic drums used as trash cans were decorated with the silvery paw prints of raccoons—the evidence of their nighttime theft left in oyster dust.

Deserted like this, the place seemed so ramshackle as to appear in danger of being reabsorbed by the landscape. I walked back towards the Oyster Shack, kicking shells as I went. They left white streaks on my black shoes. There were rusting tools left haphazardly on the ground, and a wall of blue and black crates stacked against a shed. In the gray light, the farm itself was not particularly charming to look at, though it had a kind of stark, honest beauty. Because though tourists came here—thousands every year—the farm was not a contrived tourist attraction. It was a real place where men and women worked, hauling bag after bag of the precious bivalves from the pristine estuary during every month of the year.

I had met Oscar late one morning, just before lunchtime, on a rare bright coastal day without even a lick of fog. I called Ginny—one of the Lunny siblings—about getting an official tour of the oyster farm and decided to drop by to see if she was available. As I drove up, I saw a man in a wetsuit running across the inlet of mudflats with a blue and white cooler carried on his shoulders. He left a trail of deep tracks behind him. On the far end, two more figures in wetsuits crouched beside a small cluster of triangular red flags. When he reached them, the man set the cooler down, jumped into a waist-deep trough of water and began to wrestle with something. There was shouting, but I couldn't make out what was being said.

"Do you know what's happening?" a man asked me as I got out of my car. He was standing by a minivan with three little girls hanging out of the windows and sliding door, trying to get a glimpse of the action. Beside us, a couple in their forties unloaded colorful plastic kayaks from the roof of their sport utility vehicle.

"I have no idea," I said.

I wondered if the people in wetsuits were doing something with the seals, thinking maybe one was sick or had gotten stuck in the mud or something. Out of curiosity, I asked the kayakers if they knew anything about harbor seals in the estuary, and whether tourists were allowed to paddle out at this time of year.

"Oh I don't know!" the man said. "But it seems okay though, right? I mean, there's no sign."

"There is, actually," I said, noticing it, and drew his attention to a small paper pinned to a bulletin board under glass at the edge of the parking lot gravel. "See, no kayaking here during pupping season. Looks like you're okay, though." The pupping season had just ended in June. The kayaker gave me a look as if to say "whatever."

The man with the cooler came back towards us and showed us his catch. The three little girls, their father and the kayakers all crowded around. Inside the cooler, a leopard shark lay curled, slowly seething in the shallow water. The man, it turned out, was a parasitology post-doc, and his group intended to take the animal back to their lab at UC Santa Barbara for dissection.

"This estuary is just teeming with parasites!" he said excitedly, as if this were a fascinating rather than a disgusting fact.

Not wanting to look too long at the doomed and apparently parasitic leopard shark, I went over to where an older tourist couple stood snapping photos of the activity down by the dock. Point Reyes National Seashore gets all kinds of visitors from a variety of demographics, including an increasing number of, dare I say it, hipsters.

(Somehow, between my childhood and my return, it seemed that Point Reyes had become "cool.") These two were regulation issue though: Caucasian, gray hair, visors, fanny packs. They watched as a dozen or more oystermen worked in the sunshine, lively *bachata* music playing on the radio. All of the workers were Latino. Some hurled bags onto the barge, while others hurled different bags off of it. The rest worked to separate the good oysters from the bad as they traveled down the rusty conveyor belt. One of the men waved hello. I waved hello back, and soon I was chatting with them in my terrible Spanish. Everyone seemed to be enjoying themselves, all smiles in the fresh air and sunshine.

"You want to go with?" one of the men asked me in English, pointing a thumb towards the little wooden boat.

"Of course!" I said. But as I stepped forward he laughed and put his hands up.

"No, no," he said. "*No puedo*. Sorry."

"It's okay," I said, though I was disappointed. I stood with the tourists and watched the activity for a few minutes, thinking I'd better go find Ginny. Then I heard a whistle. One of the workers closer to the water was motioning for me to approach.

"Hey, *mija*," he said, "*vamanos*," and threw me a muddy orange life vest.

I caught it, clasping it against my white shirt, which until a second ago had been clean. I wasn't prepared for something like this. I was wearing my favorite black jeans, not a pair I'd want to get dirty, but I tried not to think about that. He ushered me across a balanced plank that led to the moored motorboat where two men were loading the black mesh bags onto the barge tethered alongside. Both the boat and the barge were old, warped by weather and water away from their original symmetry. One of the men looked quite young; tall and lanky and barely out of high school. The other, who was older and stockier, offered me his outstretched hand and helped me climb aboard.

The younger man wore black trousers, a black knit cap and a black sweatshirt with the hood pulled up. The older man, in jeans, a gray sweatshirt and white baseball cap, had a broad smile and a luxurious dark mustache. Both wore thick gloves and rubber boots that reached to their thighs.

I sat down in the boat and put on my life vest. The raw wood was covered in black mud, streaks of oyster dust, crumbled shells, and smudges of bright green seaweed. Near my leg lay the pale body of a small, crushed crab.

I made my introductions and shook the men's hands. The tall one was named Ignacio, and the shorter one introduced himself as Oscar. The sun felt hot on the top of my head, and too late I remembered that not only did I not have a hat, but I wasn't wearing any sunscreen.

"Okay, *bonita*," Oscar said to me as he gunned the little engine with a wink. "Hold on."

"Are you sure this is okay?" I asked him as we motored out into the open water. Ignacio crouched on the barge while Oscar navigated. He smiled and squinted, tilting his head from side to side as if to say, *Who cares?*

"It's just that I don't want to get you in trouble," I said.

"It's okay," he said to me with a twinkle. "I will just say you are my girlfriend."

I was having misgivings about how okay this entire thing really was, but it was too late to turn back now. Six thin wooden posts, about thirty yards apart, pointed our way towards the ocean. Cormorants perched on them with their wings outstretched, drying their feathers in the sun. Gulls floated past, and a small flock of sandpipers swooped by, skimming low to the surface.

Oscar explained to me that we were going out to "plant" the bags of young oysters, which he said were about eight months old. He reached across to the barge and opened one of the bags, fishing out a handful to give to me. The wet, closed shells were only slightly larger than silver dollars. They were pearlescent and matte, pale and dark gray, green and black, smooth and rough.

I like oysters. I like how tasting their wild brininess makes me feel closer to the sea. When in Manhattan, I sometimes like to go to the Oyster Bar in Grand Central Station after work. On a cold night, there is nothing more comforting and warming than a piping hot bowl of New England clam chowder, with a dash of Tabasco stirred in. I'll sit at the bar and order oysters à la carte, charmed by their outlandish or lyrical names: Witch Duck and Moonstone, Pearl and Pemaquid, Gooseberry and Shinnecock. The tiny Oregon Kumamotos, bright and tender, which though famous for their fruitiness taste to me the most like a cloudy day at the beach. Their subtle scent of seaweed is simultaneously fresh and pungent. Then there are the thin, fluttery dark-edged Hama Hamas from Washington, not too salty and with a buttery aftertaste. There are the meaty, golden-cast Yaquinas in their broad oval shell-cups, packing a slightly gamy tang. The flavorful, classic Long Island Blue Points are a staple of oyster bars everywhere. There are so many ways to prepare an oyster, but I prefer to eat mine with nothing on them at all, *naked*, as it's called, the better to taste their quintessential oyster-ness.

Eaten live and whole, and tasting strongly of their specific environment, raw oysters are perhaps the most wild of modern foods. To eat
a raw oyster for the first time, one must dare to. What other meat do
we consume while it is still living? Though bloodless, they nevertheless carry the sweet metallic taste of animal life. Famously linked to
opulence and sex, they were also once considered a protein staple of
the seaside-dwelling masses. The working stiff, if you will. Recently
rescued from the realms of aphrodisiac cliché, oysters are simultaneously romantic, adventurous and very *real*. Something about them just
feels authentic, a sometimes elusive quality that more and more people
are endeavoring to pursue. Part of the oyster's considerable mystique
comes from the fact that you can't grow a good oyster artificially. They
need the living tides of the wild world.

Drakes Bay oysters, like the ones I held in my hand, were hearty
and often quite large, with an almost overpowering creaminess. At
least, they have been that way the times that I tasted them. Some chefs
I've talked to say they're better cooked than eaten raw, though others
would disagree with that. These had another eight months or so to go
though, and I handed them back to Oscar to return to the bag.

The forty-horsepower engine wasn't so loud that we couldn't talk
over it, but even so, Oscar stopped it from time to time to let us glide,
pointing out where the farm kept its wooden racks. These racks were
present in a little less than five percent of the estuary. Now, since the
tide was in, all of the racks were hidden under the water unless you
looked directly down on them. Later, with the tide out, they'd be high
enough to walk on without getting your shoes wet.

The sloping land on either side of us was covered in dark green
shrubs, with patches of golden summer grass showing in between.

Even in this protected cove we could still hear the unseen roar of the surf that pounds violently against the northwestern edge of the peninsula, and the wind blowing over the open heath that lies between this finger of the sprawling waterway and the ocean.

The Point is one hundred square miles of gently rolling land covered mostly in grasses and chaparral. Wildflowers—lupine, yarrow, fennel, wild radish and mustard—cling to the roadsides. Further out, in what's referred to as "the pastoral zone," the old farmhouses and barns are battered by salty mists rolling in off the Pacific. In the summer, the air fills with the dart and swoop of barn swallows, flinging their bodies out over the fields and then back again in great, boomeranging arcs. The remaining ranches look like the modest operations they are, the color of rust and weathered wood and greening stucco. There are elk and cattle grazing alongside one another in the same pastures. As you drive out towards the lighthouse, it used to be that the Top 40 radio stations would fade away and all you could pick up was Country. It seems that you could go on forever like this, the land rising and falling, until suddenly you reach it, the continent ceasing in steep cliffs, the curve of the planet visible there on the shining blue horizon.

Across Sir Francis Drake Boulevard from the farm there is a huddle of eucalyptus trees planted as windbreaks in the nineteenth century, separated from a long strip of the same trees that runs nearly down to the sea. Just south is Historic G Ranch, as humble looking as any ranch in the park, where the Lunny family has lived since the 1940s. This, incidentally, is longer than the Johnsons ran the oyster farm.

The water in the estero is relatively shallow, and for most of the distance we traveled that day, thick eelgrass was visible beneath us, the smooth flat leaves bending and swaying just below the surface. We headed out towards the estuary's bright mouth, at Drakes Beach, where the English sea captain Sir Francis Drake is supposed to have made his landing in 1579.

As we talked, I learned that Oscar was from Puerto Vallarta, while Ignacio came from the pine-scented mountains of Michoacán, near where the monarch butterflies gather for their annual summit.

"Do you like living here, in West Marin?" I asked the two. Ignacio looked away, not smiling.

"It's okay," Oscar said while Ignacio busied himself with the ropes and oyster bags. "The people around here are . . . they are . . . they are kind of racist."

Ignacio was nodding.

"Yes," he said, now looking at me with a squint. "Racist."

"Really?" I said. "That's awful!"

"Yes! Awful!" Oscar agreed.

"But what do you mean?" I asked, although I was pretty sure that I knew exactly what he meant. "How are they racist?"

"The white people here, they think that Mexicans are only good for work. Otherwise they don't want to see us."

"Yes, eh," Ignacio ventured, "they . . . if we go to the bars? They don't want us there. I try to go but they say I have to leave."

I was more genuinely surprised than I ought to have been. I didn't really see guys like Ignacio and Oscar out at the local restaurants or pubs, but I hadn't really thought about it. I hadn't thought it might not be by choice.

"Yes!" Oscar insisted. "They don't want us."

"That's terrible," I said, and we were silent for a while.

As we moved closer to the ocean, the eelgrass thinned out and then, suddenly, disappeared entirely to reveal a sandy bottom visible through the clear water. I could feel the skin on my forehead starting to burn. Far off to our left we saw the duo of kayakers from back on the shore, paddling in their brightly colored plastic vessels. I wondered, did they belong on the water more than Ignacio and Oscar did? What was more "natural"? I waved to them, and they waved back.

"So, *bonita*," Oscar said to me. "Do you have a husband? A boyfriend?"

"No," I said.

"No!" he replied. Then, playfully, "No?"

"No," I repeated.

"Well, you mean, no boyfriend besides me," he said, winking.

"Ha, yes," I said. "Not besides you."

I could see Ignacio on the barge, rolling his eyes.

When we got to our planting site, Oscar had me hold the motor steady, steering us in a slow, wide arc while he and Ignacio got to work unloading the oyster bags, tossing them one at a time into the shallow water. A harbor seal, curious about us, swam closer to the boat, about twenty feet away, its dark face inquisitive and friendly as a wet Labrador's.

As we motored back to shore, I got a sinking feeling in my stomach. There was a white woman in jeans and a navy blue sweatshirt gesticulating animatedly to some of the workers. I couldn't hear her, but it looked like was she was yelling. She stormed off.

Back at the dock, I clamored ashore and handed my life vest back to Oscar, shaking his and Ignacio's hands and saying my good-byes. We exchanged email addresses and promised to Facebook one another.

By now everyone on shore was looking at us, and my new friends were no longer smiling.

I wasn't quite sure what to do. Clearly, the tour had not been approved by management, but I was invited out by farm employees so as far as I was concerned I hadn't done anything wrong. I turned on my heels and walked directly into the shop.

A blond college-aged girl, whom I knew to be the Lunnys' daughter Brigid, was on the phone, her eyes wide.

"Um," she said into the receiver, turning away from me, "she just walked in." She hung up. When she looked at me there was flushed embarrassment in her face.

"Hi," I said, trying to sound confident. "How are you? I'll take, um, six of the medium-sized oysters please."

With my oysters in a clear plastic bag, I headed out to my car. Maybe nothing was going to happen after all. But as I went to open the door I could see the woman from the dock again, standing by the Oyster Shack, her body language conveying fury.

*Okay, here goes*, I thought, and walked towards her.


I'D HOPED I'D convinced her not to fire Oscar or Ignacio, but now, a month later, it looked like I was wrong. Standing near the deserted dock, I thought back to the conversation we had. She told me that someone was going to have to lose their jobs over my little tour.

"Please," I had said, "it's my fault. Can I reassure you? Sign a waiver? It wasn't them. The guys I went out there with weren't even who invited me to go."

"Who was it then?" she asked me. "I need to know who."

"I don't remember," I said, quite honestly. "Just one of the guys. But it wasn't Oscar or Ignacio."

"Oscar is the one in charge of that boat today," she said.

"Please," I said again. "It wasn't his fault."

I could understand their nervousness, and told her so. She seemed to soften, and gave the impression that nobody would lose their job and home over this. Then a few weeks later I got a cryptic message from someone in town. "Go check on your oyster friend," this person said, and so there I was.

The fog was fully in now, blanketing everything in wet grayness. I heard laughter, and turned to see three dark-haired children, two little boys and a girl, come running around a bend and disappear between the houses. Behind them, a small group of escaped black beef cows emerged slowly, ambling down the hillside to drink from the farm's drainage pond. There were sunflowers growing in the front yard of the foremost house, which was strewn with children's toys, a prostrate ladder, and an overturned plastic Big Wheel tricycle. A pair of thigh-high plastic wader boots was perched upside down over two fence posts.

As often as I'd been out to the farm, I'd never ventured back through the houses before. I felt like I was trespassing, and worried that this wasn't such a good idea, especially considering what may have happened with Oscar. Then I remembered that I was invited.

*Come visit me any time*, he had said to me when we parted.

I walked past the famous "cannery." It was notable as the only remaining oyster cannery on the West Coast, but the title is slightly misleading. Though impressively put together, it was really no more than a single converted shipping container, and not a factory at all.

There were vehicles parked in front of the trailers and mobile homes, and a cluster of sea-green propane tanks overgrown with blackberry bushes. I heard a rooster, and noticed some chickens huddled together in a plywood coop.

Then I saw the girl again, standing in the road. She was wearing jeans, white sneakers and a pink sweater. She looked to be about ten.

"Hi," I said to her.

"Hi," she said back.

"I'm wondering if you can help me. I'm looking for my friend, Oscar?"

Recognition registered in her face at the name, but she didn't say anything.

"I said I would come by and visit him," I continued, "except that he doesn't know I'm coming today. I don't want to disturb anyone, but I'm just wondering if he still works here."

"Okay," she said, stepping towards me. "I mean, I think he still works here, but I'm not, you know, like, totally sure." Her English was perfect, Californian-American.

"That's okay," I said. "Can we look?"

"Okay, sure!" she said, and smiled, seemingly pleased with the task.

She led me towards the back of the property to a drab-green structure right on the edge of the drainage pond. The windows were dark and dusty, and I couldn't see inside. A few steps led us to a narrow, slanting porch that wrapped around the side of the house, overhanging the pond. It looked to be in danger of falling in. She knocked on the door. Nothing. We waited.

The cows had made their way between the homes now, casually nibbling at patches of green grass, rare in the summer.

The girl knocked again.

"Maybe he's sleeping or something," she said, sounding doubtful.

Just then, a boy about her age came riding up to the house on a BMX bicycle, spewing gravel at the sharp turn of his wheel. He wore jeans, sneakers and a gray hooded sweatshirt, his black hair sticking up in spikes.

"Hey Rosa," he said. "What are you doing?" He glanced from her to me and then back again.

"We're looking for Oscar," she said. "Have you seen him? Or Felipe?"

He looked at me, suspicious.

"Um, Oscar doesn't work here anymore?" he said, in that upturned way that kids have now, though I knew it wasn't a question.

"Is he still around though?" I asked, my hopes falling. There had been so much damage caused by this battle over the wilderness and the oysters. Now, I feared, a man had lost his livelihood and maybe even his home. I knew he'd worked for Drakes Bay for years. There was even a photo of him on display inside the Oyster Shack.

"Is it possible that he still lives here?" I asked, thinking, *Can he?*

The boy shrugged. "I donno," he said. "I just know he doesn't work here anymore."

"Okay," I said, and headed back to the car.

Driving out of the park the summer mists were so thick that I needed both my headlights and my windshield wipers. I couldn't stop thinking about Oscar, and a single phrase kept running through my mind: *One more casualty in the oyster war.*

# 2

# FAULT LINES

O NE COLD SUMMER morning in 1985, a lone young woman came walking through the fog. The imprints of her hiking boots were the only tracks in the smooth, damp sand. Uncommonly tall and slim, her hips narrow as a boy's, she was dressed in khaki pants that were just a little bit too short. She had a bag slung over her shoulder and wore a windbreaker to keep out the moist air, her long brown hair held back from her face with a bandana. She carried a notebook tucked under her arm, and in her slender hands she held a high-frequency radio signal receiver. Her name was Sarah Allen, and she was there to count the harbor seals.

Though she was likely the only person present on more than ten miles of empty shoreline, the soft beeps coming from her receiver told her that she wasn't exactly alone. The fog was so thick that she couldn't see more than ten yards ahead of her. *It's like pea soup out here*, she thought. Still, she knew they were there, even if she couldn't see them; like benevolent ghosts lost in the ether, not far from her, rolling their plump bodies in the surf or stretched languorously on the shore. The seals. Her seals. She'd been observing them in some capacity for nine years now, ever since she was a teenage undergraduate at UC Berkeley studying with Starker Leopold. She was a research associate now for the Point Reyes Bird Observatory where she also worked as an administrative assistant, filing reports and fielding calls from volunteers. She discovered the organization one day while out in the field, when she happened upon their headquarters by chance and went in to ask for a glass of water. Despite the name, the group looked after more than just birds. Marine mammals were Sarah's main interest, and she was learning to observe them under the tutelage of marine biologist David Ainley. Sarah didn't have her PhD or even her master's yet, but was studying towards them at UC Berkeley.

Her colleagues at the observatory described her as serious and exceedingly earnest; as someone who liked to laugh, but for whom levity did not always come easily. At times she seemed to vibrate with the kind of focused intensity only seen in those deeply in love with what they do. Burr Heneman, PRBO's executive director during most of the time that she worked there, later described her as the kind of person who "wouldn't lie even if you put a gun to her head." He would not be alone in expressing that opinion.

As far as workplaces went, Sarah could have done worse than the rugged coastline of the Point Reyes National Seashore. Along the great arch of Drakes Bay, from the lighthouse to its rocky easternmost tip, it is never exactly the same beach. In winter the sand is sucked away from under the high sandstone cliffs and into the water, revealing dramatic rock formations that lie hidden from the summer tourists. When the winter tide is very low and very strong, you can sometimes see what remains of a shipwreck from the 1800s, the doomed *Sarah Louise*. Or maybe it's the *Samoa*. Or maybe something else. Though I made multiple inquiries, the park staff was never completely sure. Somewhere, unseen under the sand, is a lost Spanish galleon called the *San Agustín*, its buried cabin still purportedly packed with silver. It wrecked on a night in November, when the rocks jut higher; a good time for tide pools but a bad time for ships.

Sarah followed the signals on her receiver towards the densest congregation of seals. Although they do head out into the open ocean, the seals need havens, like an estuary, to mate and raise their young. Without it, the pups are more vulnerable to predators, and can drown in the stronger, deeper water.

Despite the peninsula's gentle beauty, the rocks and currents here can be deadly. In the decades after the Gold Rush, these waters were busy with schooners headed to the San Francisco markets, heavily laden with fish and casks of butter. And between their first voyages and the day that train transport replaced them, more than a few of these ships went down. In terms of commercial vessels, you won't see much more than salmon trollers in Drakes Bay now, but even those wreck from time to time. This stretch of beach sees about one wreck per year. Within hours of running aground the hull is usually breached, and in less than a day the sucking sand will have swallowed up half of the vessel, while the surf splinters the rest into mulch. Even close to shore, the ocean is more violent than you'd think.

The beach where Sarah went to count her seals—on Drakes Beach and farther down, near the Limantour estuary—is a good beach for walking. On some days the sand is strewn with seaweed thick with swarming kelp flies, masses of dark brown and purplish tangles eight, ten, fifteen, even forty feet long. They have been ripped from the glooming offshore kelp forests during passing storms. Sometimes the sand will be smooth and firm, or rippled steeply down to the waves like a glassy staircase. Great heaps of foam will gather here, greenish and sickly. Other times a sudden abundance of perfect white sand dollars will be tossed up by the waves, scattered everywhere like an overturned treasure. Some days the sand will be dotted with living ladybugs blown out from the fields, and other times with skittering white feathers that slip out of your grasp as you reach down to try and collect them. The sand is alternately dark and flecked golden and metallic, or light and powdery. Or else a slick of seawater lies over it, especially late in the day when the tide is in, making a mirror for the pale sky. Walking over it on a clear evening, the ground beneath your feet is reflected light blue with swirls of orange and pink, like oil on a puddle. Most afternoons, the light dry sand blows over the dark wet sand like smoke.

Sarah was headed to the mouth of Drakes Estero, where the seals like to congregate. They rest and play and raise their pups there, hauling out on sandbars near where the estuary gives itself over to the Pacific Ocean in a twice daily back and forth of tides. Here the green-capped cliffs slope downwards on either side to reveal a wide expanse of open sand, vaguely lunar and desolate. Still it feels protected. On much of the beach there is a near-constant soft rolling of sea air that meets and envelops; air that has not touched land for thousands of miles.

Gingerly the Western Gulls, their wings outstretched, lift first one rosy foot and then the other from the wet sand, floating gently upward. If you raised your arms out and above you, leaning into that rush of air, it wouldn't feel so very far from possible that you might be lifted in this way, too.

But despite the different kinds of days Sarah had spent on this beach, and there were many, today was a foggy one. The fog is common, especially in the summer, but not constant. Crouching, reaching, soft as mists or wet as rainclouds; ever-present at times, or rolling in suddenly like an ethereal invasion; unobtrusive, a simple graying of an otherwise sunny day, or else so thick as to take on a kind of mystical sentience. Fog, the watcher. Fog, the concealer and keeper of secrets. In fog like this the pale cliffs seem higher, disappearing as they do into the cloud cover.

The seals were emitting radio signals, from transmitters adhered to them by Sarah and a team of colleagues and specially subcontracted experts at the beginning of the summer. In June, she, David Ainley, and fellow researcher Lyman Fancher had captured twenty seals from inside the estuary. They used a long net set over a popular haul-out site, and in this way snagged fifty animals unharmed. They selected twenty, released the rest, and went about affixing radio transmitters to the bodies of the chosen ones. They dotted each animal's back or heads with a splotch of quick-drying epoxy and affixed the disk-like transmitter package. The packs were small, a mere one by one-and-a-half inches, with a thirteen-inch flexible wire antenna. It was no easy feat, and required the help and cooperation of the National Seashore, the National Marine Fisheries Service, the Oregon Department of Fish and Wildlife, the California Department of Fish and Game, Hubbs-SeaWorld Research Institute, and a number of scientists. These included another of Sarah's mentors, Harriet Huber, and a biologist from UC Davis called Roberto Anima; he was studying eelgrass and pollutants in the estero. Now, though, they could finally get real answers about where the seals went, and when. Did they venture out into the Pacific and become more pelagic? Did they stick closer to home? Were they crossing into areas where they would be vulnerable to the gill net fishermen and other hazards? Sarah wanted to know. And, if she could manage it, she wanted to help them. They tracked the seals by hiking or driving along the coast with a yagi antenna to pick up the seals' VHF radio signals. When the seals traveled farther, they'd fly out over the bay and the ocean in a small plane. Sometimes when Sarah and the other researchers would hike out to haul-out sites like Drakes Estero, they would stay there, observing, for twenty-four hours. The stated purpose of research such as this was to inform future management decisions of the park and, when necessary, influence environmental legislation.

The Observatory (now called Point Blue Conservation Science) was formed in 1965, when the details of the Point Reyes National Seashore were still being hashed out. The question of what wilderness meant and how it should be preserved was a notion in flux. For a time in the 1960s, the plan was to dam the neighboring Estero de Limantour to make a freshwater swimming hole with stocked trout to fish for, a snack bar and rental boats. Scientists and local birdwatchers, including PRBO, begged for the area to be preserved in its natural state instead. They proposed a "National Research Area," the plan for which would later become the official wilderness designation it enjoys today. A national park might be able to dam up an estuary, with a snack bar and rental boats in it, but a wilderness area could not; a wilderness area was supposed to remain untouched.

The Observatory started small but grew quickly, bolstered by the burgeoning environmental movement. They were not purely an academic institution, nor strictly a research organization, but a more freewheeling combination of the two. Their goal was to raise awareness of environmental issues, mostly through the kind of long-term research projects that can be difficult to execute in more traditional venues. And, to help guide the growing body of environmental legislation. There was the National Environmental Policy Act of 1969, the Clean

Air Act of 1970, the Marine Mammal Protection Act of 1972, and the Endangered Species Act of 1973, to name a few. A kind of momentum was underway in the country, to protect more and learn from past mistakes. To protect better.

However, when scientists took part in lobbying efforts, their work would often come under scrutiny and be accused of bias. Fair or not, these accusations dissuaded many scientists from acting as advocates when it came to public controversies. Still, one group that managed to finesse that tricky landscape and emerge victorious was the Point Reyes Bird Observatory itself, in its fight to prevent the slaughter of marine mammals and seabirds through an unregulated gill net fishing industry off the coast of California. In his 1989 article in *Conservation Biology* (*"Scientists as Advocates: The Point Reyes Bird Observatory and Gill Netting in Central California"*) James E. Salzman wrote that, when coupled with supportive legislation, the Observatory had shown that focused advocacy—"the presentation of relevant data and insistence that it be interpreted accurately and acted upon"—was an effective method of achieving environmental protection policies that were biologically sound.

By the time Sarah was monitoring her harbor seals via radio signal, the Observatory was going strong. In 1975, the annual budget was around $50,000. By the mid-1980s, it had grown to $860,000, and represented a well-respected voice in policy debates.

The gill net controversy gained momentum in the early 1980s. Dorothy Hunt, a PRBO volunteer living near Monterey, usually counted dead birds while walking along the beach near her home, as part of the Observatory's Beached Bird Project. Sometimes there were no dead birds, and other times as many as five or six—which was a lot. Then one foggy July morning in 1982, she went out for her routine walk and counted 108. Their bodies were tangled up with the flotsam of seaweed, meaning they'd not died on shore, but in the water. Another volunteer, Frances Bidstrup, counted 185 dead birds on one of her walks that same month. According to PRBO director Burr Heneman, more than 1,500 dead birds were counted in a single day. As Salzman wrote: "Gill net fishing had come to Monterey Bay."

The gill nets, brightly colored and innocent seeming, were effective at killing seabirds for the same reason they were good at catching fish. They are very hard to see underwater. The spaces in the mesh netting are big enough for a fish or a bird of the right size to poke a head through, but that's it. When they try to back out, they become stuck. The fish are then hauled flapping onto the fishing boats while the birds, thrown back into the water, have already been drowned. The nets proved effective at entangling and drowning marine mammals like harbor seals too. Media reports at the time said that the gill netting industry had ballooned following an influx of Vietnamese immigrants after the Vietnam War, and noted that many of the gill net boats were manned by refugees from South Vietnam. However, Sarah says this isn't really a fair assessment, since most of the people in charge of the boats were not Vietnamese, and the refugees were likely just taking what work was available to them.

When initial discussions for a legislative solution began, PRBO was able to use data from its Beached Bird Project to show that 90 percent of the spike in bird mortality could be attributed to the gill nets. Plus, the fishermen were moving north. In early June of 1982, two gill netting boats set their nets off Stinson Beach, just south of the Point Reyes National Seashore. The very next day, volunteers counted two hundred dead seabirds, two dead seals, and a dead baby harbor porpoise in the Point Reyes area. While the mammals' deaths could not be conclusively attributed to the gill nets, it seemed like more than a coincidence and the effect was galvanizing.

The Observatory staff sprang into action. Burr traveled to Sacramento to persuade then–State Senator Henry J. Mello to expand the proposed legislative ban on gill nets to include Bay Area waters. He helped draft a bill that would give the California Department of Fish and Game (CDFG) broad authority over the types of equipment used, if that equipment was shown to be extensively injurious to marine life. But the bill was killed by lobbying efforts from the southern California seafood industry. The Observatory scientists, advocates and volunteers did not give up, and by the late 1980s, comprehensive legislation was in place. By working to shift the gill net fishermen into equally profit-able fisheries with alternate, less harmful methods, the CDFG was able to impose wider restrictions to guard the seabirds and marine mam-mals that the PRBO had made it its mission to protect. Much of that was down to Burr.

In Sarah's line of work, it was often hard not to get at least a little attached to the subjects. The observatory scientists, researchers and volunteers also studied elephant seals, and had charted the animals' return to the Farallon Islands and surrounding waters since the begin-ning of the 1970s. On January 20, 1972, the first elephant seal female in a hundred years gave birth on Southeast Farallon Island, marking a return to their former habitat. They'd been driven to local extinction by sealers who hunted them for meat and high-quality oil used for mak-ing paint, lamps, soap, candles and mechanical lubricant. The obser-vatory staff tagged the returning seals and their pups with numbers at first—Cow Four, Cow Five, and so on. Some also had distinctive markings or scars to help personalize them. These animals migrated far and wide, heading all the way into Russian waters before returning home to Northern California. Many had survived shark attacks, and were battle-scarred. Eventually, as the observatory crew became more familiar with the individual seals, they gave them nicknames: Scarface, Redeye, Power, Tarbelly.

"It became an exciting event, similar to greeting an old friend, when a known cow returned to the colony each year," wrote Observatory scientist Steven D. Emslie in 1988. Steve, now a marine biology professor at the University of North Carolina Wilmington, is a tall man with a friendly face and warm smile. He has since devoted his career to the study of seabirds, but was roped into monitoring the elephant seals for PRBO in the 1980s. At the time, the project's longest-lived Farallon-born seal, a female, started life as "Pink 49" but later came to be called Abbey. She was a favorite of Steve and his colleague, Bill Sydeman, and was feisty and strong-willed. She didn't like letting the researchers near her. She bred sporadically and, some years, didn't come home to Point Reyes or the Farallones at all. An elephant seal cow usually lives for between thirteen and twenty-two years, and having fewer babies likely extended Abbey's life. Biologist Harriet Huber, a mentor of Sarah Allen's, wrote about Abbey's behavior as well. But the seals tended to lose their tags over time, and Abbey was without any distinguishing scars to separate her from her peers. By the mid-1980s, her colony had grown substantially, with hundreds of elephant seal cows pupping there each year. Without her tag, it would be impossible to find her.

One winter, when Abbey was thirteen, Steve was standing on the beach, watching the first pregnant cows arriving for the breeding season from their long, pelagic vacations, when he noticed something.

"In the rocks well above the beach, something on the ground caught my eye," he would write. The team sometimes recovered the tags of various seals at the haul-out sites, usually because the tag had simply fallen off somehow, perhaps in the course of a fight or amorous encounter. It was with mixed emotions that Steve saw the tag was pink, with "49" written on it. After thirteen years, they now had no way of knowing what Abbey was up to.

"We'll never know what happened, but in a way I was glad to have found the tag," Emslie wrote in 1988. "Now, instead of having her simply vanish from our records, presumed dead, I can look over the crowded pack of animals on Shell Beach each year and think that perhaps Abbey is still there." Though long gone now, the mystery of her end would dull the edges of their good-bye.

The work of the Point Reyes Bird Observatory researchers was also trying and dangerous at times. Most of the crew, Sarah and Steve included, spent months out of the year on research vessels at sea, or living in spartan conditions on the rocky Farallones themselves. They were a youthful, happy, shaggy-looking bunch, sporting an abundance of long haircuts, beards and moustaches. They wore down vests and bandanas and plaid flannel. The archival group photos, showing people seated together at headquarters or clustered around spotting scopes on the shore, are a study in retro biologist chic. In one group photo, printed in a newsletter, Sarah is seen grinning happily with somebody's floppy-eared puppy in her lap. In all of the photos there is a sense of camaraderie. If you're going to be spending a month in a tiny wind-swept shack with someone, it's a big plus if you get along.

Besides, as Steve Emslie would tell you matter-of-factly, the Farallones were haunted. This was especially true of the old lighthouse

keeper's cottage where the researchers stayed. That was how the stories went, anyway. According to Steve, it was haunted by the ghost of
a woman from the nineteenth century.

"Back in the old sealing days, the sealers stayed out there and they
. . . had a woman with them," he later explained to me, euphemisti-
cally, over the phone. "They didn't treat her very well, and she died."

The ghost did not like men, which, considering her history, seemed
reasonable. There was one room in the old house in particular that
gave researchers the creeps. When male biologists stayed there, they'd
sometimes report waking up with the strange sensation of something
heavy sitting on their chest, unable to move or breathe properly. One
night in the middle of the night, when everyone was in their beds, Steve
swore he heard the front door of the old house creak open, and the
sound of footsteps coming up the stairs. Still, the season for watching
elephant seals was in the wintertime, when the whistling cold winds
and cries of seabirds could easily stand in for the voices and move-
ments of spirits.

The winter of 1983 was particularly bad. Record storms on the
mainland and uncommonly rough seas left the Farallon researchers stranded without supplies. The door to the pumphouse blew
off. Their radio antenna toppled in the wind. One of the elephant
seal blinds washed into the ocean, the lighthouse railing collapsed,
and the fascia of the researchers' house fell off. Maybe the ghost
of the sealers' woman had finally had it with that old place. A rubber raft capsized, dumping a biologist into shark-infested waters.
She survived, though the craft's outboard motor didn't. There were
blackouts, loss of telephone service, and thwarted rescue attempts.
Eventually, though they never completely ran out of food, the

researchers did resort to eating ten pounds of frozen squid originally brought to feed to the seabirds.

Nevertheless, it was exhilarating. Writing about the experience, Harriet marveled at the strength and beauty of the raging ocean, seen at such close range. Burr had been a journalist before turning to ecological work, and managed to convince old colleagues to send the Channel 7 news helicopter out to the island on Christmas Day to bring supplies. Harriet later wrote that she enjoyed these winter storms on the island, with the ground under them stable amidst the chaos of the angry sea.

The Farallon Islands' bedrock is made of granite, as is that of Point Reyes, which, in a geological sense, is just the largest island in the chain. Most of California's deep earth is a carnival swirl of color and minerals called the Franciscan Complex; red cinnabar, green jade, aqueous blueschist and manganese ores ranging from black to shocking pink. Compared to that messy mix, Point Reyes and its attendant islands are austere and pure. Though it connects to the mainland, the peninsula is something of an island itself, perched as it is on the edge of the Pacific Plate. A dab of gold and green, it is scraping against the North American continent at California's San Andreas Fault as it travels north. According to one theory, Point Reyes has been undulant in its trek, sinking beneath the water and then breaching again, like a whale making its incremental way up the coast. The movement isn't gradual. The plates will lock together for many years and then, when the right amount of pressure has built up, lurch forward. In the great earthquake of 1906, fences near Point Reyes were split by a span of sixteen feet and the steam engine parked at Point Reyes Station shook so violently that it toppled over. The place where the ground actually fissured and opened up was directly underneath where the National Park

Service now has its Point Reyes headquarters. Because of all this, there is a popular local notion that friction is therefore in the area's blood.

(I remember the 1989 earthquake well. I was ten years old and sitting on a swing in the yard. Because my feet weren't on the ground, I didn't feel the ground shake. Instead I saw all of the trees on the valley hillside swaying violently, as if in the worst wind I'd ever witnessed. Then the aftershock came, and the trees shook again. The 1906 earthquake was ten times as strong as that.)

Twenty million years ago, the Point Reyes peninsula was down by Mexico. In another fifteen or twenty million years from now, Point Reyes will have traveled all the way up to Alaska, where the Pacific Plate is being sucked under the North American one. The process is called subduction, and a whole other plate, with who knows what continents on it, was already eaten by North America many millions of years ago. Only two little corners, north and south, remain unconsumed. This was the Farallon Plate, related to the Farallon Islands only in name, and its demise is what fueled the upthrusting creation of the Rockies and the Sierras, as one plate slid under another, pushing up the landscape. Its remaining corners are called Juan de Fuca in the north and Cocos in the south, but they are both really just Farallon leftovers. When the Pacific Plate ran up against ravenous America, instead of bowing down it began to slide past, going northward, its motion creating the earthquake-heavy Ring of Fire along the borders of the Pacific. But to the north, at Alaska, the Pacific Plate is subducting. When it reaches that point, Point Reyes will then be pulled down at the Aleutian Trench, into the sea and under the earth's mantle. There it will be melted and turned into the molten fuel for a whole new volcanic mountain range, as yet unimagined.

For now, its fiery demise still a long way off, the peninsula is home to little tremors, shudders and shakes; earthquakes we feel and many we don't, a reminder of this place's particular transience.

Below the surface of Sarah's day out with the seals, another kind of tension was starting to build.

The Point Reyes National Seashore was a relatively sleepy place in the 1980s, but with an unusual mix of uses. Agricultural operations, present since before the creation of the park, continued to function alongside hikers, campers and day-trippers, as well as working researchers like Sarah, Steve, Harriet and Burr. But the surface of that peaceful coexistence was beginning to show some cracks. The estuary where the harbor seals liked to haul out was also home to an oyster farm, run by the Johnson family since 1957. Charlie Johnson had been a wheat farmer in Oklahoma, driven west by the Dust Bowl with his three young sons. His second wife, Makiko, came from Japan, and together they had revolutionized West Coast oystering by importing Japanese oystering techniques using strings and stakes. There had already been a century of challenges in California oystering. However, some locals were starting to get angry about plastic debris from the farm that had started washing up on nearby beaches. Mostly, the litter consisted of plastic coffee can lids in the hundreds, which the Johnsons bought as rejects from a processing plant in Santa Rosa, to use as part of their oyster cultivation method. The lids were used as spacers and to steady the oyster stakes in the estuary's soft bottom, to keep them from tipping over and suffocating the oysters in the mud. The farm did try to keep the lids from dispersing, they told the press, but the lids often escaped their grasp or got stuck, and later washed out to sea with the tide. One man, a surfer who lived nearby, complained to the park that if he walked along the shore he would quickly be able to fill a shopping bag with the oyster farm's debris. It wasn't exactly hundreds of dead birds slain via gill nets, but nevertheless it wasn't a very welcome sight.

Sarah encountered the litter from the oyster farm, too. While she walked along the beaches she saw the lids, but also plastic tubes and mesh bags. She picked them up whenever she could, knowing that such marine debris could be harmful to animals. When she started working out at Point Reyes, she'd been told that the farm was set to leave at some point in the future, and that the area would be converted to protected wilderness. Now, she doesn't recall quite what she thought of that eventuality then. She was engaged in research, and not focused on policy, she told me. Since all this wouldn't happen until 2012, when the farm's forty-year reservation of use permit was set to expire, it still seemed like a very long way off.

# 3

# THE FABLE OF
# THE CALIFORNIA OYSTER

T HE OYSTER PIRATES preferred to ambush the beds by moonlight. Working mostly in pairs, with two men per vessel, they mustered together in ramshackle armadas of thirty or forty small boats. They waited until cloudless nights when the full moon shone brightly on the piles of pale shells on shore, before advancing on the oyster companies' camps en masse, their pistols at the ready. They went by nicknames, like the Porpoise, the Centipede, the Spider or the Shark. One particularly vicious character, known for trying to tear off the faces of his opponents in hand-to-hand combat, was known simply as "Scratch." Their ranks included petty thieves and notorious murderers, fishermen gone crooked and adventuring youths; and, in 1897, among their number was a twenty-year-old undercover Fish Patrol agent by the name of John Griffith Chaney, better known to you and me as Jack London.

The year that London joined the California Fish Patrol, the San Francisco Bay was a Wild West of the waves. Though water-based banditry of all kinds was common, the oyster pirates were among the most insidious. The San Francisco oyster industry had been booming for decades, but some saw the flourishing beds as treasure left out in the open, free for the taking. While still a teenager, or so he tells it, London bought his own sloop, the *Razzle-Dazzle*, from an oyster pirate known as French Frank. London even tried his hand at piracy himself, before switching sides and becoming a freelance deputy for the Patrol, working on commission from the fines that his arrests brought in. But some criminals would not be taken in alive, and many of the most notorious piscine outlaws met bloody ends. In his autobiographical novel *Tales of the Fish Patrol*, London tells of gun battles aboard sinking sloops, and a terrifying Greek fishing kingpin called Big Alec, who bribed senior Patrol members to be granted *carte blanche*. The bay was a veritable fishing cornucopia. There were flounder and rock cod, carp and sturgeon, smelt and salmon year-round. Shad were abundant from October to June, and sardines and mackerel made a strong showing all through the summer. But by as early as 1852, just three years after the start of the Gold Rush, the fishes' numbers were already declining. Laws were put in place, designating seasons and even days of the week for different species. However, fishermen bent the laws at every opportunity, and gangsters like Big Alec simply refused to obey them. The oysters, on the other hand, were a different story altogether. When it came to the oyster market, you were either a company man or a crook. So many men tried their hand at the latter that London and his colleagues at the Fish Patrol tried to make their living arresting them. He writes of infiltrating oyster pirate raids undercover, posing as an oyster pirate himself and actually following through with plundering the beds, hoping to apprehend a few fellow marauders once the job was done.

For decades, the main target of the oyster pirates' raids were the beds of one John Stillwell Morgan, head of the Morgan Oyster Company. By the 1880s his operation had merged with the other major oyster businesses in the area, and he now owned nearly all of the oystering ground in both the north and south bay. To help combat piracy, Morgan kept the workers of his beds on site at all times. They lived in modest houses right there on the docks, or else on houseboats moored out on the water. They were armed, and were instructed to shoot dead anyone who came to rob them. Morgan had artesian wells dug out in the bay, some as far as a mile from shore, and hired cooks to stay on site at each camp. This way, the men never had an excuse to leave the bivalves unattended. It was because of this that the oyster pirates banded together in such large numbers, hoping to appear so threatening in their collective assault that Morgan's guards would not fight back but simply abandon their helpless charges. The guards knew that even if they managed to kill one of the thieves, they'd be shot dead themselves before they could kill another. The pirates would then use the moonlight to guide them to the oysters in the shallower water, gathering up as many as they could to sell on the black market.

Back in 1849, the year that Morgan arrived in California, the peninsular settlement that would become the City by the Bay was not much more than a conglomeration of shantytowns. The nearby ailing Spanish mission, nicknamed Mission Dolores ("Mission of Sorrows," or, if you prefer, "Pain Mission") was full of fed-up priests and dying Indians. But after word spread far and wide that there was gold in California's golden hills, some three hundred thousand people swarmed into the state to seek their fortune. This influx caused the sleepy 200-person village of San Francisco to balloon into a city of 36,000 in a matter of six years.

The forty-niners, as they came to be called, and their immediate successors, were rich and poor, old and young. They were mostly men, but women, too, braved the ocean voyage around the horn of South

America, or else risked the more treacherous overland journey through the unforgiving mountains and dusty plains. They were American, Mexican, Portuguese, Italian, Irish, Chinese, German, French, Filipino, Swiss, Turkish and African. They were cooks from Manhattan and fishermen from Maine and farmers from Virginia. In letters back home they all seemed to agree on one thing at least: In 1849 and the early years of the Gold Rush, everything in San Francisco, from housing to horseshoes, was extremely expensive.

Wrote one San Franciscan in a letter sent back east in 1852, "it costs high to live here and a man without business can soon get rid of his small change." This man, who signed his letters as simply "Orrin," was paying $412 per month for a small house without "any garden or Barn" (sic), which did not include "the price of meat, fuel, servants [or] vegetables." That is the equivalent of close to $12,000 today.

Most of the people pouring in from all over the world were hoping to reinvent themselves in some way, although it didn't always work out as they expected. Rich men became paupers and vice versa. The chance of "making their pile," as it was called—recouping their investments plus enough to make the whole tribulation worthwhile—was a carrot often held just out of reach. For many, the promise of wealth, for anyone willing to dig or pan for it, never proved fruitful. They died from disease or drunkenness or madness, or else simply perished from the dangers of the near-lawless West. But not all. Morgan, a farmer's son from Staten Island, New York, would make a fortune creating the West Coast oyster industry almost single-handedly.

When Morgan arrived in San Francisco in December of 1849, he was a tall, skinny young man of twenty-one. His pale blond hair was already going gray, and by the age of thirty-five it was completely white. This he attributed, rather inexplicably, to his habit of wearing a military officer's cap every day since his late teens, as if the assumed authority of it had literally aged him prematurely. As a child they'd called him Tow Head. At 5'10" he weighed only 135 pounds that first winter in California, but possessed an unbreakable determination far stronger than his slight physique would suggest. He was patient, even-tempered and persuasive. Born in 1828 in the village of Westfield, his father's sixty-acre farm extended down to the water where there were natural oyster beds, and where young John could see the boats going by—coaster ships and fishing vessels and ferries. From a young age he knew that he wanted to spend his life working on the water, and planned to be a sailor. His family disapproved of the choice, but no amount of discouragement could dissuade him.

His childhood was a happy one, though not without the tragedies so common to those times. John was one of ten children born to the family, though only seven lived past infancy. His sisters and other girls in the village would start out summer mornings picking black-berries that grew along the edges of the woods. John's mother and sisters would spin and weave all of the cloth for the family's clothes at home, and then sew them, too. In the winter, the local shoemaker would come and sit by the Morgan family's massive fireplace, cobbling the children's new shoes for the year. John recalled dances in the vil-lage hall, in which rosy-cheeked girls would twirl and skip all night in homemade calico dresses. As an older man he would remember these as some of the happiest times of his life. While he was living through them, however, his thoughts were always of the sea.

He was considered "dull" in school, and didn't manage to learn his multiplication tables until the last year he attended, between the ages of fourteen and fifteen. He would later say he didn't master them until he decided to put his mind to it, as it simply hadn't interested him before. He certainly was determined. As a little boy, he and his brother fell ill with typhoid fever. Though barely able to move from the sickness, he nevertheless got it into his mind that he wanted some cakes, which he knew were hidden in the cupboard of his grandmother's room. This room had been co-opted for his brother and himself as a nursery during their illness. He managed to climb out of the bed, but was then too weak to reach the cupboard or even to climb back under the covers again, and had to be rescued. Still, he had tried.

His mother died when he was eight years old after the birth of his youngest sister, and then less than ten years later his father died too, when John was seventeen, after falling from a hay cart and puncturing a lung. Once orphaned, the older Morgan children looked after their younger siblings. They sold the family house and divided the profits among themselves. For John, this meant it was time to go and seek his fortune.

He crossed over from the island of his childhood to Manhattan, taking up residence on the Lower East Side. Having no experience working on the water, though he'd grown up next to it, he decided to learn shipbuilding. He was also learning staircasing in the process, but it was no doubt the shipbuilding part that interested him most. After a little more than a month he decided he'd had enough of saws and hammering, and wandered along the docks up the East River, looking for work. At the time, New York City was in the grip of an oyster madness that would not subside until the first half of the twentieth century. Walking up or down the river, he passed skiff after skiff covered in the bivalves, and waterfront oyster bars, some doubling as brothels with the excuse of "taking a late ferry to Brooklyn" ready to serve as a cover story for any philandering gentleman. It was a rough area during a rough time, but John managed to avoid all that, and talked his way onto a coaster, a schooner ferrying supplies like wheat and lumber up and down the Atlantic coast.

He told the ship's captain that he knew his way around a kitchen and was hired on as cook. This was a lie. The ship had "a big Negro," as John would (unfortunately) later put it, who used to cook for the crew but had now taken on other duties. (As an aside, a search through the records of John Stillwell Morgan and the archives of the New York Historical Society turned up no evidence as to the identity or name of the man who essentially saved Morgan's bacon.) The man went with John to his room in a poky Lower East Side tenement building and helped retrieve his possessions, which were packed in a large wooden seaman's trunk, and which Morgan had optimistically brought along to the city. Too poor to pay for a lift, the two men hauled the heavy trunk by hand, each carrying one handle, all the way through the city's streets and to the waterfront. As cook, John was to be paid $9 a month.

Once they set sail on his first voyage, John was extremely seasick. Fortunately for him, the man who helped him carry his trunk (whom he also later refers to as "the darky") covered for him once they were at sea and showed him how to cook. In this way, John was able to keep his job. He seemed to have had an earnestness that would serve him throughout his life, his racist language notwithstanding. On one trip back up the coast, carrying a freight of lumber from Virginia, one of the sailors was unable to attend to a matter with the sail. Quick to step in and show his ambition, John volunteered to handle it himself and quickly monkeyed up the mast to fix it. The inept sailor was then demoted to ship's cook and John was given a promotion and a raise of $2 more per month as sailor.

He served as sailor on a few ships, and was eventually promoted to captain. He started trading mostly in oysters, brought up from the Chesapeake Bay for planting in the New York Harbor. He had grown up around them, and besides, it was easy to fall into the oystering business in New York City at that time. The oyster cellars were very prominent, and discovering a new crop of marketable oysters was akin to striking gold; it could be worth millions.

Getting into the bivalve trade was probably one of the most obvious professions for any New Yorker in the 1840s who wanted anything to do with the water. In those days, the lower Hudson had some 350 square miles of oyster beds. They hugged the shorelines of Brooklyn, Manhattan, Queens, Jamaica Bay, and the full length of the East River. They stretched north up the Hudson as far as Ossining, and down along the Jersey Shore to Keyport. They surrounded Staten Island, City Island, Liberty Island and Ellis Island. Oysters graced the tables of the city's elite, but were also a subsistence food for the poorest of the poor—who sometimes lived on nothing all year but oysters and bread. The first oyster cannery opened in New York in 1819, and before long the city's oystermen were shipping their stock—both fresh and canned—upstate and as far away as Europe.

John went to work for a man named Joseph Seguine, one of the richest men on Staten Island, who would eventually offer to furnish Morgan with money and supplies for a voyage west to look for gold and—of course—for possible western iterations of the family *Ostreidae*. Seguine had built an enormous Greek Revival–style mansion on Staten Island in 1838, overlooking Prince's Bay, and by the time he met Morgan, the

Seguines' oyster harvesting business was thriving. Morgan ran freight for the Seguines as ship's captain. But even as early as 1810, some of the oyster grounds in and around New York were showing signs of trouble. "Exhaustion," the oystermen called it. The oysters were traditionally found growing in their natural state in places fed by rivers that ran through limestone—a mineral they use for their shell calcification. It would be a long time before city residents realized the connection between the outpouring of their open sewer systems into the rivers and bays, and the failure to thrive of the oysters that grew there.

When Europeans first arrived on the island of Manahatta and encountered the people living there, known as the Lenape, they found mature oysters as large as eight or ten inches long. There were some oysters described as being significantly larger than this as well. But those first Dutch founders of New Amsterdam also told tales of unicorns appearing in the woods and two-headed tortoises, so some of this may be chalked up to hyperbolic fabulousness.

As the demand for oysters began to outstrip the natural supply, New York oystermen started reseeding the beds with young oysters from other locations. They found that oysters from the Chesapeake Bay matured faster than the New York oysters did in New York waters. Oysters from warmer climates, too, grew fatter faster than the natives in the New York harbor. Thus the shipping of oysters spawned in one place, to be fattened and sold in another, was soon a thriving business. Oyster mariculture was born. And, for a few years, young fair-haired Captain Morgan ran the sloops.

Kitted out with gear and investment funds from Seguine, John booked passage on the bark *Magdella*, sailing around the horn to California. The voyage took an unusually long time. The ship left in

late April of '49, when the lilacs and the dogwoods were blooming in
New York. As was common with such voyages, they stopped along the
way in Central America, but stayed longer than usual because of bad
weather and did not arrive in San Francisco until December. Although
Morgan complained about the captain of the *Magdella*'s caution, calling him "grannyish," many of the ships bound for California met with
ill fates. Besides the danger of wrecking on the deadly rocks near Tierra
del Fuego, diseases often felled travelers, too. Morgan's own brother,
on his way to join him in California in 1851, succumbed to yellow
fever while aboard the ship and died at sea.

John's own voyage around the Americas did not make him sick of
seafaring. Far from it. Many young men spent only a day in the San
Francisco settlement before heading up river to Sacramento and points
east and north, where the gold mining was. But not John. He got right
back out on the water. He saw this strange new place, with its influx
of easterners and Europeans of all stripes and social backgrounds, and
saw a different opportunity: He saw a market for oysters. Many men
came west for gold only to find other fortunes instead; in city business
or in agriculture, such as the "butter barons" on the ranches near Point
Reyes. The first thing Morgan did was prospect the San Francisco Bay
for oysters, but his hopes for instant riches were quickly dashed. As he
would clearly document in interviews and letters, he did not find any
native oysters there at all.

Although this goes against popular conceptions of West Coast oystering history, the evidence here is very clear. There were no native
oysters in the San Francisco Bay when forty-niners like Morgan first
arrived and went looking for them. Seguine had sent him out west
with oyster tongs, which they used in the east, but they quickly proved

unnecessary. The native California oyster, at least as it would have existed in the nineteenth century, is a myth, and one that John Stillwell Morgan would spend the rest of his long and successful life trying to correct. This effort on his part was mostly on account of the extreme personal hardship that came next, making the myth possible in the first place.

Morgan later said he checked surrounding areas as well, including Tomales Bay, though he makes no mention of Drakes Estero. Still, as ships were frequently running up the coast to deal with trappers in Washington Territory, and to supply goods to the settlers there, he certainly would have been aware of it. Drakes Bay and its connected estuary system were known to any sailor on the coast. He did not find it worth mentioning. In none of these places did John find oysters, and there is nothing to indicate that his search was anything less than extremely thorough. He talks about a kind of little whelk, which he nicknamed the "bastard oyster," perhaps in his frustration of not finding his initial quarry, but I must make it clear: This was a joke name only, and the animal was not a real oyster. There were mussels and clams, sure, but these didn't interest him. No other shellfish carries the oyster's particular prestige.

In a way, it was John's own fault that the myth of the California oyster gained such phenomenal traction. His decision to nickname the whelk he found a "bastard oyster" would later create a lot of confusion for the history of West Coast oystering, when people encountered passing mentions of the animal in historical records, without knowing the full story. The "bastard oyster" is described as being small and soft-shelled, a predator that moved and would attach itself to a "real" oyster and then suck the meat out, killing it. They were easy to crush in the hand, shell and all, and were inedible, though not for lack of trying on Morgan's part.

In case this has not been made wholly clear before, oysters are not mobile and certainly not carnivorous. They accept what is given to them and do not predate. They are not like scallops, those cheetahs of the shellfish world, skittering along the ocean floor. If scallops are cheetahs, then oysters are, well, rocks. Their world is entirely internal, their motion constrained solely to the opening and closing of their shells. They have no tongue or foot as a clam does, and spend their lives permanently attached to whatever substrate they happened to land on at their inception, often fused together. If you place a starfish next to a scallop in a tank, the scallop will run away from it. But if you place a starfish next to an oyster, it has no choice but to stay put and weather the onslaught, with naught but the thickness of its shell to protect it. Although M.F.K. Fisher famously wrote that oysters lead "a dreadful but exciting life," full of "stress, passion, and danger," she was taking poetic license. Their lives are dramatic only in the sense that fairy tales of sleeping princesses are dramatic, since all of the action happens around them. Once they are raised from their beds, that's it—the story's over. And for the oysters, at least, it isn't usually a happily-ever-after.

All of an oyster's activity happens in its extreme youth, as shell-less larvae. Once spawned, which happens in open water of the right temperature when floating eggs and sperm encounter one another, sent forth in the millions by their solitary parents, the larvae—called spat—are motile for a few weeks only. Oysters from the genus *Ostrea*, which includes oysters from Europe and Washington State, are hermaphrodites. They can be either male or female, though not at the same time,

and change sex over the course of their lifetime. It is technically possible then for an oyster of this kind to fertilize its own egg, if the change
happens quickly enough. Other oysters, from the genus *Crassostrea*,
such as those from the East Coast or Japan, lack this shamanic ability.
All oysters lack a brain, but they do have a heart, which is three-cham-
bered and pumps blood the color of seawater through their bodies.
The two "valves" referred to are the top and bottom shells which, due
to their sedentary lifestyles, in oysters are rarely symmetrical.

Is an oyster aware? Can a thing think without a brain, or feel without a centralized nervous system? Could an animal with no ability to
flee from pain still have developed the ability to feel it? Can something
that doesn't mate and has no social life experience feelings? I've heard
arguments that vegans should not feel guilty eating oysters, and were it
not for the presence of the oysters' hearts, I would be inclined to agree
with them. I might even agree with them now. I haven't completely
decided. This was not, however, a common concern in the middle of
the nineteenth century. Protein was not always easy to come by, and
protein was protein, and oysters were an excellent source of it.

Once Morgan had finally given up on the idea of there being any
oysters in the San Francisco Bay, or any oysters to be found in the Bay
Area at all, he decided to try his hand at mining. He sailed up the river
to Sacramento and spent six months working in the mines, but with
little result. He became ill, as was common, and his already thin frame
was whittled down even further. He missed the water and hated where
he was, so he went back to San Francisco and pooled his money with
a few other young men to buy a schooner, to start a shipping business
again. The city was growing rapidly. In those early years, most commerce and social life took place right along the water. The docks were

crowded with ships, both active and decommissioned. Many old vessels, past their seafaring days, were converted into restaurants, boarding houses and brothels. It was far rowdier than even New York's
shady waterfront, but Morgan kept his wits about him and stayed out
of trouble. He was happiest, anyway, when out on his ship, with the
virgin California landscape sliding by in the distance on one side and
the unbroken horizon on the other. He liked sailing up and down the
coast, but engaged in river shipping too. He ferried loads of wheat
and other goods to Stockton and back, and after a while he started to
make a little money. Seguine's investment funds were intended to start
an oystering business, and although there weren't any oysters involved
yet, that was what John was doing.

Morgan heard from a trader coming down from Washington
Territory that the Indians had told him there were oysters in Shoalwater
Bay, what's known as Willapa Bay now. He decided he would go and
investigate, putting together a small crew for his schooner the *Ann
Skeer*. But on their very first voyage up, once they reached Shoalwater
Bay the cook accidentally burned the ship down. The fire was started
in the night, and Morgan and the other crew nearly lost their lives.
The next few years were fraught with mishap bordering on farce, and
it's hard to keep track of the names or even the number of vessels that
John purchased and sold or lost. In the end it didn't matter. He had
found oysters on the West Coast, even if they were small and located
all the way up in Washington. He was determined to bring them to
San Francisco and grow them there, the way he'd once brought the
Chesapeake oysters to New York—even if it was the last thing he did.
Had a less tenacious man been at the helm of such an endeavor, it
might never have happened.

The idea was to bring the mollusks to the market. The oysters may have been in Washington, but the market was in San Francisco. On the East Coast, oysters were already being sent as far west as the Ohio River, making their way into the posh hotel restaurants of the burgeoning Midwest. But they couldn't be shipped to California just yet, and were a delicacy that many settlers sorely missed. The oysters in Shoalwater Bay were small, often around the size of a quarter, and had an intense, coppery flavor. Early prospectors were not mistaken this time—they were indeed oysters, although they were not to everyone's taste. Frenchmen and Englishmen liked them. There was something in them reminiscent of the Old-World Belon oyster, or of the oysters once harvested from the Thames. They were in fact from the same genus as European oysters and are called *Ostrea lurida* (Belon oysters are *Ostrea edulis*). Once Morgan finally managed to get a shipment of them down to the Bay Area, he used this association in his branding. They called the oysters "Olympias," and hoped the comparison to European varietals would connote sophistication. It worked. With oysters, branding must never be underestimated.

However, the shipments from Washington down to California were treacherous and prone to failure. When Morgan did succeed in those early years, the oysters commanded an enormous profit. A scant bushel was sold for $23—more than $600 in today's currency, or about $12 per oyster, wholesale. This was compared to the $2 that such a bushel would command in New York, and would later command in San Francisco. Prices were steep, but there were people in rapidly growing San Francisco who were willing to pay them.

For the next handful of years and much of the 1860s, Morgan continued to base his operations up in Shoalwater Bay, taking his oyster crop down to the city when necessary. Orrin, the man who had complained of his expensive house rental in 1852, was in the import/export business and also wrote about the nice young men who tried and tried to get the Olympias to grow in the bay but just couldn't manage it. They were good, moral, hardworking people in his eyes, and Orrin tried to help them out, even though the business had yet to turn profitable. The biggest problem in those first years seemed to be predators—whelks, starfish and stingrays, which Morgan called "stingarees." They stored the Olympia oysters in the San Francisco Bay in increasing numbers, trying out different areas, and built fences around them to keep the stingrays out. They plucked out the other predators like snails from a garden whenever they could. These areas are what would later be referred to as the "native" oyster beds, lining the western shores of the bay's southern half, and running along the eastern shore past Richmond. Still, the early shipments continued to fail. Morgan tried and tried to get what he called the "native" oysters—the West Coast Olympias—to establish in San Francisco Bay. But they simply wouldn't spawn there. If they did, it was in no significant numbers, and certainly not enough for a commercial enterprise. He tried them in the North Bay first, near Tiburon and Sausalito, and then further south near San Mateo, and across the water near Oakland. But it didn't make a difference. He used the bay as wet storage for the Olympias, fattening them there, but that's it.

"$50,000 would not begin to make their loss good," Orrin wrote of one failed crop, which equals nearly $1.5 million today. "Poor fellows."

These were lean years for Morgan, filled with cold, hard work. He was occupied primarily with the transport and marketing, and didn't concern himself so much with growth or cultivation. Because the product grew naturally up north and wouldn't flourish further south, it was more of a foraging operation. While in Washington, Morgan became acquainted with two British brothers living up there, John and Thomas Crellin. The settlement where they lived was called Oysterville, overlooking the bay. The brothers had come to America from the Isle of Man with their father and sisters in 1853. Morgan became business partners with them, and then close friends. By the end of the 1850s he was courting their sister, Sophia, and in April of 1860 he married her, on the same day he turned thirty-two. The wedding took place in Oysterville, but they eventually moved the whole Crellin clan down to San Francisco. Morgan wasn't satisfied with the puny Olympias, and had a much bigger plan in the works.

Although oyster cultivation had begun in New York, it was still largely unpracticed on most of the East Coast. Even if they may have been exaggerating, the oysters that the Dutch settlers first took from the Lenape would indeed grow quite large if left to their natural lifecycle, which can be up to twenty years. Some of the largest oysters in the east were found in the Gowanus River, now a fetid canal and a Superfund site in the heart of Brooklyn, designated by the United States Environmental Protection Agency as "an uncontrolled or abandoned place where hazardous waste is located." (Incidentally, as of this writing, I live next to it.) As the city waters became more fouled with sewage, coal and factory outputs, the oysters around New York needed to be moved around. While the oysters would still spawn in many places, the water was getting too polluted to sustain them to maturity. There were lots of baby oysters that needed a new home, and fast. Many were sent to locations farther out, on Long Island, or up to

Rhode Island or Maine. But Morgan and his New York contacts had a bigger idea, and were just waiting for a certain technological advance to put it into action.

What Morgan wanted was to get eastern oysters out to California. He realized that if he could use the bay to fatten the Washington oysters, then he could do the same with the easterners as well. It was, of course, more than just wet storage. Like wine grapes, oysters take on the flavors of the environment in which they are raised. When it comes to oyster flavor, terroir (or "meroir" as it's been called, from the French *mer* or "sea") is everything, and the meroir in California was good.

The first transcontinental railroad was completed in 1869, and Morgan's oyster business took off almost immediately. He didn't have oysters on the first train ever to go from the Atlantic coast to the Pacific, but this was only an error on the part of his suppliers, and he had them on the second. They were shipped in barrels of seawater. Only about 75 to 80 percent survived the journey, a loss that would prove consistent regardless of age or variety. But with the high freight charge, he found that simply selling those first oysters left him with no profit. He requested that his suppliers send him even younger oysters, so that he could fit far more in each barrel for the same price. He put them in the bay, let them grow and fatten for six to eighteen months, and sold them at an enormous markup. The San Franciscans went wild for them. They still wouldn't spawn in the bay, but that didn't matter. Morgan and his partners the Crellin brothers had barrels of young oysters on nearly every train that came west. Soon they were buying barrels packed with oysters that were little more than spat. They had been buying up oyster bedding land—the land below the waterline— all around the bay in preparation for this for years. Most of the ground was not actually suitable for oysters, but that didn't stop John Stillwell Morgan. He hired workers to cart in shells and dirt and construction waste, anything they could use as landfill, to cover up any grooves or muddy places in order to create hard substrate for the beds. They were also destroying the native tideline habitat, but this did not seem to concern them. Before long the partners of the Morgan Oyster Company were among the richest men in the city.

Morgan was not the only one shipping oysters to the San Francisco Bay from the east, or from up in Washington. Others tried both the eastern and the Washington oysters as well. For a time in the 1870s, there was a man who brought the Olympias down the coast, bedded them down in the bay as Morgan had done, and then tried to pass them off as "California oysters." It was an early instance of trying to cash in on the idea of something being locally grown and region-specific. This aggravated Morgan, who knew that there was no such thing as a California oyster, only those that had been transplanted. His own money, sweat, blood and tears had gone into bringing the industry to San Francisco, and it irked him that another man tried to make it seem as if the oysters simply grew there naturally. He made a point of correcting this again and again, but the story was stubborn.

Never one to rest on his laurels, Morgan kept experimenting. He wanted to find the oysters that did the best in the bay, that were the biggest seller, the best tasting, and that turned the biggest profit. By shipping them out as tiny oysterlings, instead of fitting six hundred to a barrel, he could fit more than ten thousand. Strangely, none of his competitors figured out how to do this, and anyone trying to make their own oyster empire soon found themselves in trouble. Then, more often then not, they were bought out by Morgan until the Morgan Oyster

Company held a true oyster monopoly. The shipping secret was one that he kept close, and even his eventual interviewer for the Bancroft historical collection conducted in 1888 made sure not to publish it.

There is evidence to suggest that the winning oyster, the one that Morgan would rely on for years, actually came not from New York but from the Passaic River in New Jersey. The supply was especially cheap because the Passaic was already too polluted for the oysters to reach maturity. By the turn of the century, not even spat could be grown there.

As Jack London would attest, the waves of the west would remain wild for much of the rest of the nineteenth century. As more and more fishermen cast their nets, the fish stocks continued to dwindle. Most of the species that the fishing outlaws risked their lives to catch were not even native in the first place. Alaska cod were brought down in 1863 to try and bolster the waning numbers. Softshell clams were introduced in 1870, shad in 1871, carp in 1872, and catfish in 1874. In 1876, a greater influx of Italian immigrants brought the use of paranzella nets to the bay, which decimated the fish population. Even the introduced fish species needed governmental protection. The bay had been teeming with shrimp, until waves of Chinese fishermen came and laid waste to them. They caught more shrimp than could ever be consumed by the local population, and their catch went principally for export back to China or to the Hawaiian islands.

Many of the fishing groups on the water functioned almost as gangs, divided by country of origin in their methods and loyalties, even when they weren't breaking the law. The biggest fishing mafia bosses lived on houseboats in the bay, never staying in the same place for too long, and hiding in back rivers among the tule marshes when they needed to disappear for a while.

Morgan's curiosity and need for improvement seemed greater than his interest in merely accumulating wealth. He joked that his partners were far richer than he was, content as they were to simply keep doing what worked and cash the checks. But Morgan kept trying the oysters in different places to see where they would do best. He tried all up the coast and into Oregon. He tried them in Tomales Bay but was unsatisfied—though it should be mentioned that Tomales Bay has changed a lot since then. This is because the bay has filled in considerably. Oysters now do very well, although they didn't do well there in Morgan's time.

By the late 1880s, everything was thriving for Morgan. He saw no reason to think that oystering in the San Francisco Bay would not continue for another hundred years. His second oldest son was following him in the business, and Morgan said that no man besides himself knew more about it.

But there was a new technology that he was excited about too: the steamboats that were coming into use as ferries. He hoped to use these for oystering as well. Little did he know that they would help spell the doom of his empire. The ferries poured coal into the bay and belched out great clouds of black soot, which only compounded the damage being done by the increasing release of city sewage. The fish, already growing scarce, began to decline even further, despite the fishing laws and the presence of young Jack London and the Fish Patrol. Before too long the oysters that Morgan and his compatriots had planted in the bay stopped growing. Then they began to die, both eastern and Olympia.

Thankfully for him, Morgan's company did not go out of business until after he was gone. He never saw the decline, but died at the height of the empire he had built, not understanding the damage to the bay that his enterprise had caused, or that anything would ever be any different.

# 4

# A FRIEND OF THE EARTH

A T TWENTY-FOUR, FRED Smith had never done a tree sit before. His hair was still long then, and he was traveling up and down the coast, through California, Oregon and Washington, living out of his Chevy Blazer, spending time in nature and meeting people. The meeting people part had not always been easy for Fred, but he had some tricks he liked to employ now. He carried a guitar and different types of percussion instruments in his car. He'd drive into Eugene, or Arcata or Santa Barbara, find wherever it was that the hippies were hanging out, and ask if anyone wanted to jam. He also liked to buy fresh produce at the local farmers' markets and give it away to people. In this way, through fruit or through music, he met Jeff, a forest activist living in Ashland. Jeff had agreed to take part in a tree sit in the Siskiyou National Forest. There, a swath of old-growth fir, pine, hemlock and redwood was tagged for salvage logging. It was 1997. The ethereal raven-haired activist Julia Butterfly Hill was about to begin her 783-day vigil in the century-old redwood tree she'd come to call Luna. The tree sits sounded romantic, and fun, and maybe a good way to make a difference while also meeting girls. When Jeff said he needed someone to fill in for him for a few days, Fred said to sign him up.

The tree sit was in Northern California, part of a well-organized campaign. The activists had built platforms between two and twenty stories up amongst the branches. Some were in the shape of stop signs encircling the trunks. Others were simple rectangles about eight feet long by six feet wide. While Fred was there, two people were assigned to each perch. This way, there was always someone up there in case a person needed to get down to go to the bathroom or stretch their legs. They worked in rotations of a few days or a week at a time. Mostly they spent their shifts up in the trees, talking, getting high and eating the food ferried up to them by fellow activists on the ground.

At first, Fred liked living like that, up in the branches. He loved waking up surrounded by those heady-scented boughs and hearing the wildlife of the forest, the woodpeckers, chickadees and nuthatches, singing and calling above and below him. They weren't threatened by loggers while he was there. The forest dome was alive with scurrying animals, with squirrels, chipmunks and wood mice making their way from tree to tree.

"People forget what a big world it is up there," he would later tell me.

Fred's perch partner, another young man, was nice enough. He smiled a lot but didn't like to talk much. One day the young man went down for a quick break and disappeared for four hours. Fred thought he might die from the boredom. Maybe this kind of activism wasn't for him. After a few days, Jeff came back and took over from Fred, so that he could continue on with his travels.

When not traveling, at that time Fred worked for Outward Bound, assisting with their educational programs and doing wilderness instruction. Among his colleagues, the general attitude was that, as outdoor educators, they were doing their part. Other people could be activists. Eventually, though, to Fred that wouldn't seem like enough.

Fred is in his early forties now. He's 6'5" and a dead ringer for a sunburned Dennis Quaid. Because of all his years spent living out of doors, snow camping or hiking in the desert, at all times he has the elements-battered look of someone just returned from an expedition. When I realized who it was he reminded me of, I asked him not if someone had pointed out the resemblance, but how often.

"A lot," he said.

Fred dresses like he's trying to rebel from his own preppy taste. He wears slacks and buttondown shirts from Brooks Brothers, but with the casual disregard of a private school student trying to subvert his uniform. He wears flip-flops or nice loafers with no socks, often kicking them off in order to go barefoot at every conceivable opportunity. He is also partial to funny T-shirts. One of his favorites is black, with green text in the style of the Star Wars opening crawl, which reads WHEN YOU THINK ABOUT IT, ALL GALAXIES ARE FAR, FAR AWAY.

Fred was born in Manhattan, but spent his early childhood in the suburb of Bronxville, an hour north of the city. When his family moved there, the first strip malls were just going in. It was the kind of bucolic American childhood you find in old movies; wide, safe streets full of children of all ages to play with. After school, kids were sent to play outside unsupervised, and then called home for dinner at dark. Beginning when Fred was five years old, the family started spending part of their summers on Fishers Island in Long Island Sound. They rented a modern house built in a young pine forest, a half-hour bike ride into town. When he was younger, he and his siblings would go down to the shore and spend the day picking mussels for their parents. The mussels grew densely on the rocky parts of the island, and seemed inexhaustible. Still, by the time Fred was in high school, nearly all of the mussels were gone.

When Fred was nine years old, the family moved back to Manhattan, purchasing a Park Avenue apartment on the Upper East Side. He hated living in the city, and didn't fit in with the kids at his new private school. He was tall for his age, but not precocious. By eighth grade he was already 6'3"; taller than his parents, his classmates, and all of his teachers. He wasn't very dexterous, either. He was physically awkward and despite his size he "wasn't great" at sports. He felt like the city was too small for him, that it didn't give him enough room to stretch out. When offered the opportunity to go away to boarding school in Rhode Island, he took it. Things were a little better there than they had been in Manhattan, but not a lot. Still, Fred found two seemingly unrelated things that offered escape and solace: the deeply nerdy role-playing game Dungeons & Dragons, and the great outdoors.

Dungeons & Dragons came first. It is, at its core, a fantasy adventure game for people who like rules, but it also helps if you like pretending to be someone else. First launched in the early 1970s, it has historically held a special place in the hearts of young boys for whom being oneself may not be very much fun. Despite the mayhem that the presence of dragons and dungeons would seem to imply, it is very much a game about order. There is a strong sense of moral clarity. The types of character you can choose to inhabit exist on a regimented grid, divided by race, class, abilities, ethical and moral alignment, etc. You can be a dwarf, an elf, a human, or any number of other fantastical non-human and demi-human entities. In addition to this, you can be a cleric, a druid, a magic-user, a thief, a paladin, a bard, and so on. You can be good, neutral or evil, lawful or chaotic.

Almost all of the characters that Fred invented for himself were aligned as "lawful good." He liked the idea of the virtuous knight, or the healer. But while most players, Fred's friends included, preferred the more dashing characters—the heroic paladin or the mysterious elf—Fred's most successful character was a dwarf named Drago.

Drago was a fighter, but also a cleric; able to heal himself and his friends. He was lawful, and good, and as much as is possible for an imaginary being, was well respected among a certain circle of socially-challenged adolescent males of the late-1980s Upper East Side. With Drago, Fred had not only made himself heroic, but being a dwarf, he had also made himself smaller.

The thing was, Fred craved space. In the summers, he convinced his parents to let him attend an outdoor nature camp, where he learned to chop down trees, split firewood, cook with a camp stove and use a compass to navigate. After his freshman year of high school he started taking Outward Bound courses, a practice he would continue through college. Fred was an atheist at this point, prone to writing godless poems, and stories about angry young men whose lives unspooled within a moral vacuum. At Denison University, he wrote his senior thesis on relations between the United States and Cuba. After graduation, instead of moving back to New York and looking for a job, he did what a lot of young people—especially young men—were doing in the 1990s when they were unsure of how to respond to the world: he packed up his car and hit the road.

He set out for the summer in his Chevy Blazer with his father's financial backing and a college friend named Burgh. They were both twenty-two. The young men drove south into Florida, arriving in the Keys on a day when a hurricane was blowing in. They found a bar called the Hog's Breath ("Hog's breath is better than no breath at all" read the T-shirts) and got drunk in the middle of the day with the locals, while the winds raged outside. When the weather cleared, they went fishing at the beach. Fred caught a manta ray. In the Everglades, they were encouraged by a local to antagonize an alligator with a stick.

Fred didn't think of himself as environmentally focused at the time, but it was something that gnawed almost constantly at the back of his mind. During the Outward Bound courses he took, he'd spend weeks in the wilderness, cut off from any sign of civilization.

"We were in the top 1 percent of back-country badasses," he told me of the excursions.

But whenever it came time to come down from the mountains, he was always horrified by what he saw; by what human beings had done to the landscape on the edges of the wildlands.

"As soon as you left the wilderness area, getting back to front country, there were clear-cuts all over the place, cow patties everywhere," he said. "After weeks seeing what a natural system looked like, interacting with the elements, with life and death, and suddenly you see this—I'd think, what the fuck is wrong with these people?"

Driving around the country that summer after college, seeing what he called "the bad development of the '90s"—strip malls and small town centers that were dead now because of big box stores—he was struck by a similar feeling of disgust.

That didn't mean they weren't having fun. He and Burgh found a casino in Mississippi and spent twenty-four straight hours gambling. Fred managed to get his winnings up to $2,000, then $3,000, before

finally losing it all. In New Orleans they found themselves at a bar in
the French Quarter at five in the morning. A woman in a white dress
and dangly bracelets sidled up to Fred and explained that she was a
sorceress, a witch doctor, and had put a hex on her ex-husband, making him physically incapable of entering New Orleans.

"Do you want to come home with me?" she asked.

They continued west, over the green flatlands and red desert of
Texas to Santa Fe, where Fred met an old friend from his summers on
Fishers Island and then went to stay with him in Arizona. They drank
too much coffee and smoked too many cigarettes, and in the afternoons they went rock climbing and bouldering in the desert.

He returned east in the fall to complete a wilderness EMT certification, and started working for Outward Bound. The jobs took him
to North Carolina, Oregon and Colorado. In between those contracts
he hit the road. He started reading more about wilderness and the
philosophy known as Deep Ecology—a belief that the environment as
a whole should possess the inalienable right to flourish, independent
of its usefulness or lack thereof to mankind. This belief system already
had its own literary canon to which Fred would turn, putting aside his
Charles Bukowski and Hunter S. Thompson for the writings of Arne
Naess, Wallace Stegner and Edward Abbey.

Abbey in particular took up the clarion call to exalt nature where
transcendentalists like Emerson, Thoreau and Muir had left off. His
nonfiction book *Desert Solitaire: A Season in the Wilderness*, first published in 1968, became something of a bible to early environmental
activists of the 1960s and 1970s. He was certainly important to Fred.
With his powerfully written prose, Abbey also added to that call a kind
of wild anger and rebellion, a *Walden* for the Beat era. The book tells of

Abbey's time working as a park ranger at Arches National Monument (now a national park) in Arizona in the 1950s. He writes of a sense that the non-wild life, the life of cities and concrete and responsibility, was somehow non-real; that it was a dream from which we could—and should—be woken, and the thing that could wake us was wilderness.

Abbey was passionate, an anarchist, a curmudgeon and likely a true misanthrope—so mad about the state of the world he could spit. He writes:

> My God! I am thinking, what incredible *shit* we put up with most of our lives—the *domestic* routine (same dreams every night), the stupid and useless and degrading *jobs,* the *insufferable* arrogance of elected officials, the crafty *cheating* and the *slimy* advertising of the businessmen, the tedious wars in which we kill our buddies instead of our *real* enemies back in the capital, the foul, diseased and *hideous* cities and towns we live in, the constant *petty* tyranny of automatic washers and automobiles and TV machines and telephones!

When not railing against modernity, Abbey revels again and again in the beauty of the desert, describing it as "the flaming globe, blazing on the pinnacles and minarets and balanced rocks." But the desert was also "a-tonal, cruel, clear, inhuman, neither romantic nor classical, motionless and emotionless, at one and the same time—another paradox—both agonized and deeply still." Wilderness was a place in which one's muddled slate could be wiped clean, where a man could take his place once more in the natural order of things. By acknowledging that vulnerability, there was a power and strength to be found. Mankind was reinstated as predator by his willingness to also be prey.

Abbey's was a path of semi-engagement. More a writer than an activist, he wrote both novels and nonfiction, serving as the Wallace Stegner fellow at Stanford University in 1957. He spent a year in Scotland on a Fulbright. Compared in appearance and comportment as a young man to the actor Gary Cooper, he was known in later years as "Cactus Ed," a weathered man with a prolific beard. When he died at age sixty-two of complications from surgery, he had his friends bury him in the desert in nothing but an old sleeping bag, so that he could more directly return to the earth he loved. He wrote that he wanted to "meet God or Medusa face to face, even if it means risking everything human in myself."

As the twentieth century wore on, more and more young men and women were becoming fed up with consumerist culture, alarmed at the environmental degradation they saw around them. The question was, how to respond to this problem? Many began by walking the same path, reading the same authors and visiting the same places in search of meaning. The question was then, of course, what do you do about it all? Say you've stepped away from what the world expected of you, turned your back on the rat race and absorbed some nature. Now what?

That all depends, in a sense, on what kind of character you choose to play. Will you be a warrior, or a mystic? Chaotic or lawful? For Christopher McCandless, the tragic wilderness wanderer of the early 1990s made famous by Jon Krakauer's book *Into the Wild*, that path was one of disengagement. Less drawn in by the activism of Abbey and more inspired by the contemplation of Tolstoy and Thoreau, he shunned society and its problems entirely, eventually dying alone— through bad luck or folly, it isn't entirely clear—in the Alaskan wilderness in 1992. Many, though, took a far more active approach.

Abbey published a novel in 1975 called *The Monkey Wrench Gang*, which many have cited as the spark that ignited the environmental direct action movement. In it, a small band of vandals set out to stop environmentally damaging activities in the Southwest, particularly the building of the Glen Canyon Dam. The characters are a far cry from the stereotypes of conservationists today. They eat red meat, drive big cars, own firearms and litter the roadside with empty beer cans. Abbey's habits were said to have been similar. Nevertheless, the book served as an adequate, if skeletal, instruction manual for ecological saboteurs to come.

Inspired by *The Monkey Wrench Gang*, in 1977 a Californian anti-pesticide activist named John Hanna founded a group he named the Environmental Life Force—ELF, for short. Rather than declaring war on pesticides, he said that war had already been declared on nature, and he was simply fighting back. Their logo depicted an "elf" holding a cork gun—a confusing message, since their protest *modus operandi* was to set bombs. (More a leprechaun than an elf, the original ELF logo nevertheless would not be out of place in Fred's adolescent world of dark knights and fighting dwarves.)

The original ELF took Abbey's call for anarchy to heart. There was to be no central leadership or chain of command. For Hanna, the spraying of crops near his home in Watsonville, California was both a pressing and a personal matter. He described a crop duster dousing his car with the pesticide parathion as he drove down the highway, while it swooped to spray a neighboring strawberry field. (Parathion was originally developed in Germany as a nerve gas, and EPA scientists have since urged a federal ban.) Not long after the original ELF was formed, the group shot out a window at Senator Dianne Feinstein's empty Monterey vacation home with an air pistol. They then exploded seven crop dusters using homemade napalm bombs while the planes were parked on the tarmac of the tiny Salinas airport. The group also claimed responsibility for the pipe bombing of an Oregon paper company that autumn. Hanna was arrested in 1978 and sentenced to seven years in prison, the only member of the original ELF to serve time. The group disbanded that year.

Two years later, in 1980, Abbey's *Monkey Wrench Gang* served as inspiration for the creation of another environmental direct action group, Earth First! The exclamation point is part of the name, and its members are called Earth First!ers. The founders included the oft-jailed activist Mike Roselle, environmental lobbyist Dave Foreman, and wilderness advocate Howie Wolke. All had read Abbey's work and had ties with the Southwest. The Earth First! logo features a monkey wrench crossed hammer-and-sickle-style with a tomahawk. Bolstered by the environmental ethics of Rachel Carson's *Silent Spring* and the conservation science of Harvard biologist E.O. Wilson, they pledged "no compromise in defense of mother earth," a promise that would become their slogan. Still active today under different leadership, the group has a quarterly magazine with the tagline "media from the frontlines of ecological resistance." Again, this was a group who saw the fight for the environment as a war.

Their approach was biocentric, an expression of the Deep Ecology ideal, but their methods began as more peaceful than that of Hanna's ELF. (Hanna, once out of prison and settled in Santa Cruz, also wrote critically of resorting to such incendiary methods.) They advocated for wilderness proposals that went beyond what mainstream groups seemed willing to ask for, and planned theatrical stunts. In 1981, with

Edward Abbey himself present, the group rolled a plastic image of a "crack" down the face of Glen Canyon Dam. As the black band snaked downwards, it did appear from a distance like a fissure was spreading down the concrete. Activists stood across the way and cheered, holding signs that read TEAR DOWN THE DAM and even NUKE THE DAM.

"I think we're morally justified to resort to whatever means are necessary, in order to defend our land from destruction," Abbey told an Earth First! camera operator before the rally. "Invasion. I see this as an invasion."

Standing on the bed of a pickup truck, Abbey delivered a now famous speech to the small crowd:

The industrialization, urbanization and militarization of the American West continues. [ . . . ] More dams are proposed, more coal burning and nuclear power plants projected, more river diversion projects, more strip mining of our mountains, clear cutting of our forests, the misuse of water, the abuse of the land. All for the sake of short term profit! [ . . . ] How can we create a civilization fit for the dignity of free men and women if the globe itself is ravaged and polluted and defiled and insulted? The domination of nature leads to the domination of human beings. Meanwhile, what to do? Here I can offer nothing but more of the same. Oppose—oppose the destruction of our homeland by these alien forces from Houston, Tokyo, Manhattan, Washington D.C. and the Pentagon. And if opposition is not enough, we must resist! And if resistance is not enough, then subvert! After ten years of modest environmental progress, the powers of industrialism and militarism have become alarmed. The Empire is striking back! But we must continue to strike back at the Empire by whatever means available to us. [ . . . ] We will outlive our enemies. And as my good old grandmother used to say, we will live to piss on their graves!

EARTH FIRST! ORGANIZED their first tree sit in 1985, with just one person sitting in one tree. It lasted only for a single day, and the forest around the tree was all cut down. The tree sitter and activists on the ground, including Roselle, were all arrested. Still, it was deemed a success, and the next time out they built twelve platforms for tree sit activists. Again the sit was short and the activists were all arrested—one directly from his platform by two sheriffs in a crane box.

From the mid-1980s onward, Earth First! was primarily concerned with preventing logging and the building of dams, and other development they saw as detrimental to ecosystems. But by 1987 the tenor of the group had changed, with greater emphasis on anarchist political ideology. That year younger members heckled Abbey while he spoke at an Earth First! gathering, angering the group's founders who were growing increasingly uncomfortable with the change in tone. Abbey died the next year. In 1990, Foreman, Wolke and other members of the original guard severed ties with the organization. Roselle stayed. Thus far their protests had not included firearms or explosives, and though against the law, remained peaceful. Now more of a movement than a specific, centralized group, Earth First! has outposts in a variety of countries on five continents.

Yet despite its increasingly anarchist leanings, Earth First! remained a relatively mainstream organization. This was not enough for some.

After all, even Abbey himself had called on people to defend the land from destruction by "whatever means are necessary." For many, it seemed apparent that the necessary means included more than sitting in a tree. In 1992 the second iteration of ELF, now called the Earth Liberation Front, was formed. More extreme in its tactics than Earth First!, the new ELF specialized in arson. On the attributes and alignments matrix, how good or evil they might be depended on your perspective, but there was no arguing that they were chaotic. Their efforts would be dubbed "ecoterrorism" by the FBI.

Fred Smith's involvement in environmental direct action would remain limited, still more comfortable in a quest he deemed lawful. Though he had friends who would get deeper into forest activism, including blocking logging roads by setting their legs in trenches of concrete, the Siskiyou tree sit would remain his only real act of civil disobedience. In 2001 he enrolled in the graduate program in environmental studies at the University of Montana in Missoula, deciding to fight for the environment by working within the system. He was inspired by those using a legalistic approach to make sure that existing environmental laws were enforced, and to advocate for new ones. The Clinton era, he said, had bred hope for some environmentalists that an aboveground approach would be effective. It was the first time that a president had appointed an ecologist to the head of the Department of the Interior.

"From the perspective of a land-based environmental activist, you couldn't have had a better president," Fred said.

While in graduate school and directly after, Fred worked with a number of groups founded by forest activists, but who nevertheless were taking the aboveground legalistic approach. They would target proposed logging projects and poke holes in Environmental Impact Statements, some of which relied on outdated science from a decade or more prior, when better, updated information was now available. Matt Koehler, Fred's boss at the Native Forest Network (now the WildWest Institute) tutored him in how to "use the law to stop bad shit," as Fred put it.

"We knew the key provisions of every law—the Endangered Species Act, the Environmental Protection Act, the Clean Water Act— they were there to use at our disposal to shut down something that we knew was going to be bad," Fred said. "It was practices like that that essentially shut down logging in the Pacific Northwest with the spotted owl thing. We wanted to save the trees and we used endangered species to do it."

Besides, saving the trees had become fashionable, even if that couldn't have mattered less to Fred. Julia Butterfly Hill, who initially thought she might spend a few weeks at most up in her tree, ended up breaking the world tree sitting record by a long shot, living up in the twenty-story redwood without once coming down for just over two years. Though she was not officially a part of Earth First!, they had organized the tree sit base camp where she started. News crews climbed up to interview the charismatic activist in her perch. Bonnie Raitt paid a visit as well, and performed a benefit concert for her.

In the videos of Hill still living in Luna, her face is luminous as a saint's, her moss-green eyes burning like the eyes in a painting of Joan of Arc. Her purity of conviction was undeniable, not to mention her beauty. She made a compelling poster child for the anti-logging movement. She was featured in magazine, newspaper and television stories all over the world—usually accompanied by an attractive photo. *Good*

*Housekeeping* magazine named her one of its most admired women in 1998, and printed a full-page picture of her looking like an Elven princess out of Tolkien, an Arwen Evenstar of the redwoods. *People magazine* named her one of the World's Most Intriguing People of the Year. Julia came down from her tree at the end of 1999 while Fred was finishing his first semester of grad school. Her efforts had managed to save her tree, as well as a two-hundred-foot buffer zone, which she purchased from the Pacific Lumber Company for $50,000 with money raised by herself and fellow activists. The forest around that buffer zone was cut down. When she finally descended on December 18, thirteen days before the turn of the millennium, she collapsed in the mud at the foot of Luna and wept.

Fred spent the next seven years based in Missoula, working as an aboveground environmental advocate. He still took his long road trips from time to time, and when he got to be in his early thirties he decided he'd like to move to California permanently. When he was thirty-four, he got a job interview for the position of Executive Director of the Environmental Action Committee of West Marin, based in Point Reyes. Before his interview, he decided to take a drive through the local countryside. It was a sunny day in late October and the landscape crackled with the dry beauty of early fall—the shining, fog-free ocean, the flashes of red vines hanging down from evergreen oaks, and the fields of pale grass floating with the fairy-like seeds of thistle fluff. But as he drove through the Point Reyes National Seashore's pastoral zone, he was shocked by what he saw. Farms! Industry! Inside a federally protected natural area! Many of the Seashore ranches seemed to be in poor ecological condition, and in a national park! "Why is the park allowing this?" he thought. If things here were handled the way they were in other national parks, Fred thought, if some of the Point Reyes ranches didn't clean up their act, it was only a matter of time before they would have to go.

# PART II

## HOW TO CURATE THE WILD

Yet perhaps we could do worse
than aspire to be a plump bivalve. Humbly,
the oyster persists in filtering
seawater and fashioning the daily
irritations into lustre.
Dash a dot of Tabasco, pair it
with a dry Martini, not only
will this tender button inspire
an erotic fire in tuxedoed men
and women whose shoulders gleam
in candlelight, this hermit praying
in its rocky cave, this anchorite of iron,
calcium, and protein, is practically
a molluskan saint. Revered and sacrificed,
body and salty liquor of the soul,
the oyster is devoured, surrendering
all—again and again—for love.

—ELLEN BASS, FROM "REINCARNATION"

# 5

## A NEW VENTURE

J OE LUNNY STARED at the five hundred heirloom dry root artichokes that filled the bed of his son's white pickup. It was early summer, 2004, and change was in the air.

"What am I supposed to do with these?" he asked, skeptical. "I'm a cattle rancher."

Joe was in his mid-seventies and had been running cattle his whole life. First he ran dairy cows and then, forty years ago, began transitioning to beef. His father, Joe Lunny Sr., had been the vice president and general manager of the steamship division of Pope and Talbot, Inc., a lumber company with offices in San Francisco. In 1947 he bought a dairy operation out in Point Reyes from a man named Frank Labrucherie, but not the land—that was owned by the Radio Corporation of America. The 1,500 gently rolling acres stretched to the Pacific Ocean on one end, and to the edges of Drakes Estero on the other, effectively cutting the peninsula in half at the tip of the estuary's longest finger. Finding the business too demanding to manage remotely, Joe Sr. moved his family from their comfortable home in the city to a farmhouse on the Point. He experimented with the latest dairying techniques and worked to bring the milk back up to Grade A certification. From the time he was in high school, Joe Jr. worked the farm twice a day, rising in the middle of the night to milk the cows at 3 AM, and then milking them again at 3 PM, after school. When Joe Sr. died in 1959, the business passed to his son. The family remained tenants of the RCA until 1977, when the company sold the land to the federal government. Many of their neighbors—ranchers who had been there since the middle of the last century—had owned their parcels and received government buyouts in the millions, as well as leases to continue operating. For the Lunnys, however, it was merely a change in landlord, with no cash windfall to be had. Now owned by the people of the United States, their pastures were officially added to Point Reyes National Seashore the following year, and the family thus began a series of renewing five-year special use permits with the National Park Service. That year, 2004, Joe was due to sign the next one, though he hadn't done so yet.

The artichokes were the latest brainchild of his son Kevin, a smart and energetic man in his mid-forties. Kevin had been helping run the ranch since reaching maturity. Really, he'd been helping out with the cows since he was old enough to walk. He lived in the ranch house now with his wife Nancy and their adopted triplets, Brigid, Patrick and Sean, now in their teens. His parents, Joe and Joan, lived next door in what had once been the bunkhouse for milkers. His older brother, Joe Lunny III, ran Lunny Grading & Paving out of nearby Nicasio, a speck of a town with a post office, a tiny nineteenth-century church and a restaurant all clustered around a baseball diamond, and not much else. Kevin wanted to find a way to make the family ranch desirable enough so that his own children would want to continue his legacy. Also, he would need to make it profitable.

"I want my kids to feel the same excitement and involvement in being an important, involved part of the ranch that I felt growing up here," Kevin told Steve Quirt, a friend and agricultural advisor for the University of California Cooperative Extension. The two men drove down to Davenport to pick up the artichokes together—an experience Steve wrote about for the Cooperative Extension newsletter.

Steve would write that the quest for the artichokes and the health of the family farm were inseparable, as Kevin embarked on an ambitious diversification plan set to rekindle the enthusiasm for farming he had felt as a child. Like other ranching families in the region, the Lunnys were realizing that organic farming was the logical next step for them, seeing as it was the fastest-growing section of American agriculture. Unable to keep up with the prices of larger cattle operations, they could nevertheless compete by offering a more niche product—beef that was organic, or at the very least grass-fed. In 2004, those efforts were just ramping up for the Lunnys. Being a part of a National Park and subject to special protections already, it was not difficult to get the pasture certified organic. In fact, some 1,400 acres were already certified, making it the largest organic pasture in the county. The next step was to work on the animals, reducing parasite loads through better management and rotational grazing, to wean the operation away from parasiticide and antibiotics.

That weekend, Joe got over what skepticism he may have had about his son's artichokes, and the family all pitched in to plant them together—three generations working side by side as they set them out in eighteen manicured rows.

"We had a fantastic time of it," Kevin said.

They hoped to sell the artichokes from a roadside stand to park visitors, adding berries and winter vegetables if they could get those to work in the soil, too. Kevin also hoped to start a composting business, maybe one that used green waste from the park. Then one day not long after, his closest neighbor paid him a visit with a favor to ask.

Tom Johnson, of Johnson Oyster Company, was in a bit of financial trouble. His family had farmed oysters in the estero that served as eastern border to the Lunnys' property since the 1950s. But the oyster farm was plagued by environmental problems and had been locked in conflict with the county and the National Park Service for years over plastic debris that littered the beaches, and sewage that leaked into the bay. Tom had another eight years left on his lease with the park, but he didn't feel he would make it. He was ready to retire now, and wanted to wash his hands of the farm. At first he only turned to Kevin to ask for help with bringing the facility up to code, to see if they could avail themselves of the service of Lunny Grading & Paving at a reduced, neighborly price. But then another idea occurred to him. He knew the lease was running out, but eight years was still a long time in which to farm oysters. The next day he went back to Kevin—did he maybe want to buy the balance of the lease for the farm?

The history of farming oysters in Drakes Estero began in the 1930s with a man named Pat Quail. A bit of an eccentric, Pat was an artist and biologist who liked to sign his name by drawing a picture of the bird it represented. In 1932 he obtained a lease from the state of California, set up house along the inlet of the estero known as Creamery Bay, and proceeded to try farming oysters. When all of the oyster beds in the San Francisco Bay were killed off at the turn of the century due to pollution, the imported oysters would no longer thrive there, and the Morgan Oyster Company went out of business. But there was still a desire for oysters in California, and so the Department of Fish and Game sent prospectors around the state to try and find sites that were suitable for conversion to mariculture, so they could start issuing leases. Operations were already thriving up in Humboldt Bay, and Tomales Bay was considered a prime location as well, as was Drakes Estero, if only one could get around the problem of the soft mud bottom.

At first, the cattlemen at neighboring F Ranch didn't take too kindly to Pat's presence. When Pat went out to plant his oysters, he was fired upon with a shotgun. Besides that, he contended with some unusual oyster pirates too, namely raccoons who would come and steal the oysters at low tide, as well as an unknown man who would drop down in a light aircraft in the nearby field, gather up as many oysters as he wanted, and fly off. Though Quail soon decided he'd had enough of the local hostility, an oyster company did spring out of his efforts there. He handed off the business to a local, Larry Jensen, who called the operation Drakes Bay Oyster Company. He was helped by a biologist from the Department of Fish and Game named Paul Bonnot, who instructed Larry in the hanging string technique, so that the oysters would not be lost in the mud of the soft-bottomed estero.

They tried farming eastern oysters, brought out via train from New York, just as John Morgan had done, but they didn't do well. Then they planted oysters native to Japan, which came to them via Puget Sound. These oysters were eventually named "Pacific" oysters—perhaps to distance associations from their country of origin, which was about to become politically complicated. The Pacific Ocean was also what linked the two regions—Japan and America's West Coast—and saying that an oyster from California was a Pacific didn't sound too foreign.

The original Drakes Bay Oyster Company did well, selling its Pacific oysters to the San Francisco market until the start of the 1940s, when hostilities with Japan during World War II cut off the oyster supply. The oysters would not reproduce in the California waters of their own accord, and Drakes Bay Oyster Company went out of business once the shipments stopped. Larry had tried and tried to propagate the oysters on his own, but couldn't: the conditions just weren't right.

Charlie Johnson didn't start out in oysters. A wheat farmer from Oklahoma, he was driven west by the Dust Bowl and the Great Depression. Determined to get as far as he could from his failed Midwestern farm, he later said that he used a ruler to determine the farthest away he could get from his former home while still being in the contiguous United States—which landed him in Washington State. He went into the oyster business in 1940, running an oyster company with a partner. He took his three young sons with him. They managed to stay in business despite the war, and he sold out in 1948. He used the profits to briefly try a dairy farm back in Kansas, but when that went broke he returned to Washington oystering again. He worked as a buyer for Coast Oyster Company, making regular trips to Japan. He traveled there so often that he kept a house in Sendai, in Miyagi prefecture. Known as the City of Trees, it was—and still is—notable for its autumn colors and summertime Tanabata celebration, a star festival. The old way of writing *Sendai* meant "a thousand generations," after a temple that once stood there with a thousand Buddha statues. Johnson was likely getting his oysters from the area near Sendai most famous for it, Matsushima Bay, meaning "pine islands," a haven from the Pacific Ocean dotted with some 260 tiny islands, some no larger than a Range Rover and bearing just a single gnarled pine tree. Their pale rocks arch out of the water, forming sculptural shapes and bridges.

It was during one of these trips that Charlie met the woman who would become his second wife, Makiko. He took her back to the States to live with him, and in 1957 they bought the oyster farm in Drakes Estero from Larry Jensen. With the help of Makiko's oyster expertise from Japan, they got the operation on its feet again.

While oystering in Drakes Estero had tapered off due to World War II, oyster mariculture in nearby Tomales Bay was starting to pick up. Larry Jensen also had holdings in Tomales Bay, but the largest operation there at the time was Tomales Bay Oyster Company, to this day the longest continually operating oyster company in the Bay Area. In the 1940s it was run by Oscar Johansson, a Swede who'd been farming oysters in the area since 1925. His partner, an old-timer named Frank Erickson, had worked on the Morgan Oyster Company beds when they still dominated South San Francisco Bay. At Tomales Bay Oyster in the 1950s there were crates stacked high that were stamped OCCUPIED JAPAN, and heaps of gunnysacks with shipping tags from New York. As with Drakes Estero and San Francisco, the oysters wouldn't spawn in Tomales Bay, so they shipped the Pacifics in as seed, or as oyster spat already adhered to scallop shells. The eastern oysters came in fully grown, to be kept in wet storage in the bay for a time before they could be sent to market. They were sent out fully grown from New York and the Chesapeake Bay by the carload. They had not figured out Morgan's secret, that the easterns could be shipped out as young oysters too; larger than newborn spat, but small enough to make the enterprise more profitable. The pre-affixed oyster spats were called "sets." Even then, the kinds of oystering techniques used varied widely even within the same bay. Sometimes it was best to set the oysters on the bay bottom in mesh bags. Other times, the oysters were hung from wires. By 1966, Charlie and Makiko had built a network of redwood platforms in the estuary, each beam sunk ten feet down into the mud, for their new "hanging cultch" method that was practiced in Makiko's home area of Japan.

The Johnson Oyster Company was going strong by the end of the 1960s and the start of the 1970s, when the ranches on all sides of the estero were sold to the National Park Service. Charlie Johnson did not really own Drakes Estero, but possessed leases from the state to farm his oysters there. The 2.6 acres that he did have on land, and what tidelands were his, he sold to the National Park Service in 1972 for $79,200, and received a forty-year Reservation of Use and Occupancy. This was different from the short-term, renewing leases of five or ten years that the cattle ranches were given. Like the cattle leases, however, this 1972 document also had a clause stipulating the possibility of renewal. It wasn't guaranteed, but it was possible.

The Johnson Oyster Company continued to prosper economically into the 1980s, though tensions emerged when locals began complaining that plastic debris from the operation had started washing up on beaches. Still, all of the oyster farms in West Marin were becoming more popular than ever, as people began to see them as tourist destinations: places to go and experience an authentic form of food production. As the environmental movement gained popularity, and more people began to question the compartmentalized way of life that shut them off from the natural world, so too did people long to return to a time when food production was more accessible. The processed foods of mid-century America were going out of vogue, and people wanted an "authentic" connection to what they ate or drank. They wanted to *experience* their food, to pick their own apples or walk through lines of Napa grapevines and see the grapes crushed in vats. The authenticity movement wasn't as prevalent as it would be by the 2010s. Hip young people were still more likely to wear plastic and safety pins than outfits last seen on a lumberjack. Nevertheless, the impulse towards localism and authenticity was growing.

The oyster farms of West Marin were no longer just suppliers, but destinations in and of themselves. In the summer in the 1980s, the Johnson Oyster Company sold 80 percent of their oysters in-shell and on-site to visitors. In the winter, they sold more jars of shucked oysters than those in-shell. A local woman organized tours of the oyster farms in connection with the restaurant at the old Olema Inn, called "Gourmet Wilderness." Guests would go see the oystermen at work on the farms, and then settle in for a fancy dinner.

The farms were not without their problems though. Oyster farms have nearly always occupied a somewhat nebulous space between public and private, at least in parts of the country where they once grew wild. Were oysters a natural resource, like wild blackberries, to be gathered by whomever? Did they fall under fishing rights? Oysters were big business, and taken more seriously than mussels or clams, which were farmed, certainly, but also usually available to any member of the public with a bucket and the will to find them.

At Johnson Oyster Company, the biggest problem so far had been litter, but in the 1990s another headache was added to the mix: leaking sewage. Members of the Johnson family and farm employees were living on the property and the superintendent of the park, John Sansing, had allowed Charlie to keep adding residences in the form of trailers and mobile homes, without acquiring the proper permits. It was more than the property's septic system could handle, and raw sewage ended up leaking into Drakes Estero.

Similarly, there were sewage problems that plagued the oyster farms in Tomales Bay as well. Like many homes in the area, a fair share of the houses built along picturesque Tomales Bay were not up to proper code. Some had septic systems that sat in the water—a practice that was not allowed. There were incidences of contamination at the oyster farms, and one summer all of the farms in the bay were shut down for over a month. It was suspected that the contamination was caused by leaking sewage. Still, the farms managed to stay in business while the county cleaned up the area as best it could.

Unfortunately, Johnson Oyster Company was having greater difficulty. Charlie Johnson died in 1992, leaving the business to his son Tom. Tom's attitude at the time was, as he told local newspaper the *Marin Independent Journal*, "if it ain't broke, don't fix it." Unfortunately, the seams of the business were quickly unraveling. Three years after Charlie's death, in 1995, the county sued Johnson Oyster for not addressing the overloaded septic system that, the suit claimed, posed a significant health and safety risk to the public. The county claimed that Tom promised to replace the septic system, but then did nothing. Tom tried trucking septic waste off of the property, but that cost $4,500 per month and wasn't viable. They were starting to bleed money. Part of the problem was that they needed more room than was currently provided to build a septic system that could accommodate all of the residences on the property—but the park would not (or could not) give up part of the public national park land to the Johnsons so that they could build a new system.

"Defendants have demonstrated absolutely no willingness to reach a solution," the suit alleged. A newspaper article about the suit said that Tom Johnson and his attorney did not return phone calls. He'd agreed to remove mobile homes from the property within six months, but eighteen months later the homes were still there and occupied. In response, the county sought to prohibit anyone from living on the property and to ban on-site retail sales until a new septic system was built—one that accommodated whatever residences remained—and permits obtained for the mobile homes, a well, and the store. The suit noted that Johnson's lease would expire in 2012, and that in the interim he was required to comply with all local zoning, health, safety and building codes.

Still, Johnson managed to hang on through the 1990s and into the early 2000s. In late 2003, aware that the Johnsons might not manage to stay in business until the end of their lease, the new superintendent of the Point Reyes National Seashore, Don Neubacher, a tall man with sandy hair and a graying mustache, sought a government solicitor's opinion regarding the future of the land.

A field solicitor from the National Park Service's San Francisco office named Ralph Mihan surveyed the situation. In his letter of February 26, 2004, to Neubacher, he acknowledged that the opinion could inform treatment of the oyster lease, which "might be terminated sooner for cause or other processes." His opinion was guided by the Wilderness Act of 1964 and the Point Reyes Wilderness Act of 1976 with regards to how, at the national level, the Point Reyes National Seashore was required to implement "wilderness" within its borders.

Because of the 1976 Point Reyes Wilderness Act—which was in fact part of a bundle of wilderness legislature being passed at the time—the majority of Drakes Estero had been designated as "potential wilderness." This is a distinction I will explore later. Mihan referred to language in the House Report (94-1680) accompanying the bill, in which it was said there should be an effort to "steadily continue to remove all obstacles to the eventual conversion of these lands and waters to wilderness status." He also referred to the park service's own management policies on wilderness from 2001, in which it was stated that "in the process of determining suitability [for wilderness], lands will not be excluded solely because of existing rights or privileges (e.g. mineral exploration and development, commercial operations, etc.)."

"The Park Service is to manage potential wilderness as wilderness to the extent that existing non-conforming conditions allow," Mihan wrote to Neubacher. He said that the park service was also required to actively seek to remove from potential wilderness the temporary, non-conforming conditions that preclude wilderness designation. "Hence," he continued, "the Park Service is mandated by the Wilderness Act, the Point Reyes Wilderness Act and its Management Policies to convert potential wilderness, i.e. the Johnson Oyster Company tract and the adjoining Estero, to wilderness status as soon as the non-conforming use can be eliminated."

When Tom Johnson asked Kevin Lunny if he wanted to buy Johnson Oyster Company from him, Lunny wasn't in the dark about the troubles that the farm was in. After all, he'd grown up just next door, and used to cross the fields as a boy to stand at the water's edge and watch the oystermen work. He wanted to help out a friend and neighbor, but there was something more to it than that: He'd heard the call of the sea, of days spent not just next to the water, but on it.

"I fell in love with this oyster farm," Kevin would tell *Marin* magazine a few years later. "It's this unsung hero of sustainable farming."

He knew that Tom had a good heart, but the writing was on the wall, and the walls were caving in on him. Tom's attempts to meet the regulations were driving him to financial ruin.

"Frankly, we knew the oyster farm was Don's biggest headache before we purchased the balance of the RUO," Kevin later said, meaning the Reservation of Use and Occupancy. He told his brothers and his wife Nancy that if Don Neubacher wasn't on board with him buying it, then it would never work and he wouldn't do it. When he spoke to the superintendent, however, he was supportive.

"But he told me he didn't plan to extend the RUO," Kevin told reporter P.J. Bremier in 2008. However, he also said that by then he had "done enough homework to be reasonably sure" that they would be able to get the lease extended anyway, even though Don explicitly told him that the park had no intention of doing so.

"I thought if we proved we could solve all the environmental problems the park would issue a special permit to allow oyster farming beyond 2012," Kevin said.

And with that optimistic intention in mind, he managed to borrow $1 million from the bank, and set out to clean up the farm.

# 6

## THE SAVING OF POINT REYES

CALIFORNIA WAS NAMED after the Isle of California, an imaginary place that appears in a sixteenth-century Spanish fantasy novel, *The Adventures of Esplandián*. In the book, an Amazonian-style warrior queen named Calafia rules over a nation of independent, griffin-riding black women. There were no men on the island at all, and no metal besides gold, which the fierce women fastened into harnesses for their mythical beasts. *California* is just a made-up word, like Rivendell, Narnia or Oz. However the inspiration for both it and the name of its ruler likely came from the Arabic word *caliph*, as in caliphate, the office held by the spiritual successors of the prophet Mohammad. The Isle of California is a treacherous place for the male protagonists in the story, and so the decision of the Spanish conquistadors to give the region that name, which came after Cortez suffered a particularly humbling defeat there, was a little like saying, *This place didn't really work out so well for us*. Perhaps it is a little like naming a place Skull Island or Jurassic Park.

California has always been a little fantastical. As a place it is a generator of legends, whether they spring from the Gold Rush, from Hollywood, from Silicon Valley, or the sun-drenched places in between.

Myth takes hold especially in the accounts of pre-European California: The sky was blackened by a multitude of birds when they took flight; the beaches were blackened by crowds of sea lions. Everywhere, it seemed, life was teeming and abundant. A dark fecundity pervaded, in sea and sky and in the as-yet-untouched cathedrals of the redwood groves. Before the loggers came, when only something as godly as the lightning and wind and time could take those soft-barked giants down. Before an army of Chinese workers was hired and coerced to turn great tracts of the state's marshes into farmland. Before the men and women who had been living on the land for thousands of years were almost all killed off by the diseases that the Spanish monks came bearing, the most virulent having been syphilis. The most prevalent sentiment about these times was of a nature that beguiled the senses, of flocks and congregations that obscured, blocked out, deafened, and overwhelmed.

As beautiful as Point Reyes is and as much as is there, still bountiful and unspoiled, it seems impossible to talk too long about the place without also invoking loss: what was and now is not. Maybe this is true for all of California, and maybe this is true of everywhere, especially to anyone with a long enough memory stretching back more than a few decades. The trouble, of course, comes in parsing out the reality from the myth, the truth from hyperbole. In speaking with old-timers about the time before the establishment of the Point Reyes National Seashore, or in reading the accounts of those who have already passed on and left us, there is something of a rosy glow of the kind usually cast over the beloved past.

I don't think the stories of aboriginal California are false. Or at least, they are not entirely fabricated. There are wide swaths of truth sewn in among the myths, at least. All storytelling is subjective. We remember the past like this, as larger than life, the days somehow brighter than days now. But of course that is not the only thing going on. It's been shown that our forests are growing quieter, with birds fewer and insect orchestras less. Half of the open fields I was driven past when I was a child on the way to school through Marin County's Lucas Valley are housing developments now.

Boyd Stewart passed away some years ago, but in July of 1990 at the age of eighty-seven he was interviewed by a woman named Ann Lage for the archives of the Bancroft Library at UC Berkeley. Boyd had spent his life ranching near Point Reyes. A reluctant interviewee, he was in something of a special position when it came to the establishment of the park. Though a farmer and rancher, his wife had been involved in the Marin Conservation League since the 1930s, and he ended up as something of a spokesperson for the Point Reyes ranchers once negotiations began on the land sale to create the National Seashore. It was in Boyd's kitchen that the ranching patriarchs all gathered one spring night in 1969 and decided, as a group, to sell their land to the government.

For Boyd, no longer a young man even then, the decision came down to wanting to stop the destruction of the land he'd loved his whole life. Farmland along the San Francisco Bay was rapidly disappearing to the point that almost no character of the original landscape remained. Stunning fields were turned into shopping centers and parking lots. Boyd had gone to college at Stanford in the 1920s, in what he called "the fruit basket of California."

"Right on the university grounds, there was close to a hundred-acre field of strawberries," he told his interviewer. He recalled the once-agricultural land between San Jose and San Francisco.

"Well, now it's houses," he said sadly. "All of the orchards were plowed up. It's a long time since the Southern Pacific ran tourist trains into the Santa Clara Valley from the east during blossom time."

Just like autumn leaf-peepers in New England today, Boyd reminisced about the springtime visitors, the petals of flowering peach and cherry and apple trees sailing down on tranquil picnic scenes among the orchard rows.

That was all gone by the time the talk of developing Point Reyes grew serious, and Boyd was having none of it. Some ranchers may have seen it as a windfall: an excuse to take a large cash handout and escape the grueling life of early mornings, mud and fog. But that wasn't what Boyd wanted, and thankfully for those who also love Point Reyes, he was not alone.

But before I go any further or get into the story of the ranchers in Point Reyes and what they have lost and saved, I should start by telling you about Joseph Mendoza Jr.—"Little Joey," for short, though there isn't much about him that's little these days. He is in his seventies and almost perfectly square, with a large black cowboy hat that I've only seen him take off once when he used his bald head to illustrate the barrenness of an overgrazed summer pasture. He and I are friends, or at least I thought of him as my friend while I was living and working as a reporter in Point Reyes. We used to run into each other morning and night, it seemed, at the Pine Cone Diner, or Vladimir's, or the Station House Café, or the Old Western Saloon, where I would be in search of story leads and/or carbohydrates, and where Joey would invariably turn up to talk to people. He's been a rancher for longer than I've been alive, has raised two kids, and at the time that I met him, still lived with his wife on the Point Reyes dairy farm that's been in his family for generations.

When we met over breakfast at the Pine Cone Diner, as we frequently did and sometimes still do when I'm in town, we'd sit at the counter and both order oatmeal. As Joey talked, he carefully covered his oatmeal's smooth surface with a perfectly distributed layer of cinnamon, added an equally perfect upper mantle of crushed walnuts, and then stirred everything in. He takes his coffee black and when, from behind the counter, Gina asked me if I wanted some coffee too, I'd say yes—even though I don't normally drink it. Joey told me stories about agriculture—about drought, his decision to go organic, and about his Portuguese ancestors who sailed over from the Azores on the eve of the twentieth century.

At sixteen, Joseph Vera Mendoza, Joey's grandfather, found himself orphaned on the Azorean island of São Jorge. Interestingly, that island has a rugged coastline topped with green that stretches thinly to a dagger's tip, not entirely unlike Point Reyes. Rock formations stand sentinel in the waves a little apart from the cliffs in much the same way, too. So when the young man arrived in that part of California, quick-witted but illiterate, it must have looked a little like home to him. The rolling hills of São Jorge are still checkered by pasture. Hydrangeas grow wild there, and local delicacies include limpets—fresh, grilled or fried and served breaded, buttered and sizzling in their shallow, starry-edged shells.

Joseph's older brother was already in America when their parents died, and Joseph endeavored to join him in California. He arrived in San Francisco in 1899 and started working in a creamery. People called him "J.V." He was a little man with a big man's aura, a quick thinker despite his lack of schooling. Then in April of 1906 the city was awoken by the largest earthquake in its history. After the quake came the

fires, and San Francisco was all but consumed, losing some twenty-
eight thousand buildings and five hundred city blocks to the blaze.
More than two-hundred thousand people would be left homeless. J.V.
knew he needed to get out of there, and fast. While the fire was still
raging, he managed to talk his way onto a boat with some Portuguese
fisherman, and watched the city burn from across the bay in Tiburon.

If J.V. remarked on the similarities between his ancestral home in
the Azores and the rolling green of Point Reyes, there is no record of
it. He took a job as a butter maker on Pierce Point Ranch on Tomales
Point, the northernmost homestead on the peninsula. It is one of the
foggiest and windiest parts of one of the country's foggiest and windiest areas. The hills slope down gently towards Tomales Bay on the eastern side, and end rather more ruggedly before plunging into the Pacific
to the west. By the time J.V. got there, the non-native wild radish was
already flourishing along the cliffside paths, sown there by the Spanish.
Mixing in with the native yellow lupine, it grows as high as a man and
sometimes higher. It was most certainly higher than J.V., who despite
his larger-than-life demeanor was not a big person—but I've already
mentioned that before. As for the wild radish, it's most commonly purple, but can be white and pink or even blue. In June when it blooms the
most and reaches the highest, the flowers almost form a tunnel over the
trail to Pierce Point, their fragrance subtle, sweet and spicy. The yellow
lupine smells like honey and the combination is intoxicating.

(The last time I was out at Pierce Point in June, I didn't mean to
walk so far down the path. I thought *I'll only go a little ways*, but there
was something about walking down that avenue of flowers that was
like falling, with the wind soft and the reassuring hush of the ocean
below. Before I knew it I'd gone a mile.)

It isn't likely that J.V. had much time for flower-gazing, though. The milkers rose well before dawn, at three or even two in the morning. They had little one-legged stools strapped to their behinds, ready to sit and milk at any time. The butter makers were not required to begin work at quite so ungodly an hour, but no doubt the days were long and began early. Milking took place outdoors for the most part, but as a butter maker J.V. worked in the big barn. There were two ways he could have separated out the cream from the buttermilk, either by letting it rise naturally, the milk sitting in shallow pans on a creamery shelf for a day or two; or else he could use a steam separator, which began to make appearances on the peninsula about twenty years before J.V. arrived. Once he got the cream, whichever way he got it, he put it in an industrial churn powered by a horse on a treadmill. The resulting butter was turned out onto a table, where J.V. worked out the rest of the buttermilk and added salt. The leftover skim was fed to the pigs. The end product was shipped out to San Francisco via schooner, packed in wooden boxes with the trademark Point Reyes star stamped on the lid. This was the famous logo of the Shafter brothers, a pair of lawyers originally from Vermont, who became the area's notorious "butter barons." Their product was considered superior to any around, and was no doubt served in the finest hotels in the city alongside John Morgan's imported eastern oysters, which, by the time J.V. was installed in Point Reyes as a butter maker, had already started to die out.

The Shafters were more landlords than dairymen. They won most of their Point Reyes land as the result of a lawsuit, and at somebody else's misfortune. The Spanish were already running cattle on the open moors out there, and much of the herd belonged to the struggling

Spanish missions nearby. The grasslands were perfect grazing pasture because the Miwok Indians had made them that way, in order to entice the tule elk out so they could hunt them. Or that is how the stories go, anyway. The mission cattle operations were beefed up (if you will) by the Mexican land grantees, faithful soldiers and European supporters of the new Mexican government. Much of the Point went to two Irishmen, who continued to raise longhorns in the Spanish tradition, more for hides and fat than meat. For food they hunted the elk, and did this so successfully that by the 1860s one could find no trace of the once plentiful animals. A man named Andrew Randall bought the majority of the Point Reyes cattle lands in 1852. But he did this on borrowed money, and a mere four years later he was shot in the head and killed in a San Francisco hotel by one of his creditors. The shooter was lynched, but Randall's remaining creditors sought recourse in the courts. After a rather chaotic legal adventure, the lands wound up being owned by the lawyers representing the wealthiest claimant—the law firm of Shafter, Shafter, Park & Heydenfeldt.

It was only after the Shafters took over that dairying came to Point Reyes in earnest. They leased out parcels of land to enterprising farmers, usually men newly arrived from either the East Coast or Europe. Being neither particularly poetic nor sentimental, the Shafter brothers named the parcels, and the subsequent ranches, after the letters of the alphabet: "A" Ranch was closest to the lighthouse, while "Z" Ranch sat atop Mount Wittenberg, above a serrated skirt of bishop pine.

When J.V. was thirty years old, he accepted an arranged marriage with the daughter of the Portuguese cook on the ranch where he worked. The young girl—just sixteen at the time—was sent over from Portugal to begin her new life. Her name was Zena.

Zena was strong willed, and though illiterate as J.V. was upon arrival, she would eventually learn to read and write alongside her children in the one-room schoolhouse financed by her husband. She didn't want to be a tenant farmer, even though by then J.V. was leasing the entire enterprise. She encouraged him to buy them their own ranch further south from Tomales Point. At her urging they bought not just one ranch, but two, and began their own dairy operation on the A and B ranches that lay alongside Drakes Estero. Not long after, she gave birth to their first child, a son they named Joseph—Little Joey's father.

Life on the Point in those days was hard, but in many ways it was also idyllic. The Mendozas' existence was remote, separated from even the nearby villages of Inverness and Point Reyes Station by a series of fourteen cattle gates along a winding stretch of unpaved and often muddy road. There were no public roads to the lighthouse. But the community of ranchers formed bonds with one another, meeting in social halls they built, and throwing lively dances. Barns were gaily decorated with lights, flowers and paper streamers, with music and dancing that went on all night and into the next day. People would nap for a time in the middle of things, maybe in the soft grasses if the weather was fine, and then return to the dance floor again. Men would leave in the middle of the night to do the early milking, with fiddle music pursuing them in the dark as they trudged up and down hillsides or even rowed across the estero, before returning to rejoin the festivities. The landscape was dramatic but dreary when the weather was gray, like the setting of a tragic romance. *Wuthering Heights*, maybe. But the land was also plentiful. Besides the hogs and cattle and chickens they raised, for hunting there were deer and quail and rabbits, and they knew the best spots for gathering clams and abalone. There were no oysters in the soft-bottomed estero then. Far more populous than the area is now, the ranches were lively communities, almost like villages themselves; bright islands of warmth and human effort adrift in the billowing fog.

The Mendoza men are social animals, and as Joey's father Joseph was growing up he was known never to miss a party. He liked "the swish of skirts and the sound of music," as his son would later say in an interview. J.V. was known to ride a horse all the way to Bolinas if that's where the party was, despite it being more than twenty-five miles away. His son Joseph—who would later be called Joe Sr.—was much the same. There was a family with seven daughters living across the estero, and he could frequently be seen in his little rowboat on the calm waters, on his way to visit them.

By the 1930s, things were starting to change fast for the coastal farmlands north of San Francisco. The Shafter family lost their fortune in the stock market crash of 1929, and whatever Point Reyes properties had not already changed hands were then sold. The lands were frequently purchased by their longtime tenants, but absentee landlords snatched up other parcels. Some went to the Radio Corporation of America, while others would eventually fall into the hands of a lumber company. Even before the crash, some of the ranches had fallen on seedier times. U Ranch, near the coast, was used as headquarters for illicit rumrunners throughout Prohibition, though the place was abandoned in 1933 when the laws changed and the rumrunners' income vanished. Other ranches were closing as well. Z Ranch, on Mount Wittenberg, was abandoned in 1930. The rest of California was being developed at a fantastic rate, and Point Reyes was no longer the only place to get good butter. With refrigeration, fresh milk and other dairy could travel further distances, and other parts of the state were proving more successful.

In the wide valley between the Inverness and Bolinas ridges—which is actually the rift between tectonic plates—there had once been a prestigious resort, the Pacific-Union Country Club, for city gentlemen to get away from it all. It was built in the 1880s. Wives were permitted to visit only on certain days of the week. There, club members could enjoy the scenery and go hunting in the surrounding woods and meadows. The club rooms were full of their taxidermied trophies. There was even a racetrack built at one point, but by the end of the 1920s the club's luster had waned and it was soon abandoned.

Though the ranches had always grown their own vegetables to feed their families and workers, during the Depression years many of the ranchers rented out portions of their land to Japanese pea farmers and newly arrived Italians growing artichokes. Aerial photos from the 1930s show artichoke fields covering Drakes Head. During this time, although most ranch children were not educated past high school, and many of the girls did not even attend beyond the eighth grade, Joseph went to study agriculture at the University of California at Davis and one of his sisters went on to Dominican College in Marin.

The 1930s were also when people began talking seriously about conservation in the area. A group of women founded the Marin Conservation League, and their first action was to ban the placement of advertising signs and billboards along the roads out to the beaches. Even then, there was starting to be talk of a park at Point Reyes. But the advancing encroachment of civilization was still slow, and the plight did not yet seem so urgent.

Then came the Second World War. The pea and artichoke farms vanished from the peninsula. The Japanese were sent inland to internment camps and the Italians were banned from the coast. Ranchers were instructed to black out their windows at night so as not to be seen by advancing enemy ships. Military barracks were built on the RCA's property. Closer to San Francisco, the sleepy little towns of Sausalito, Tiburon and Mill Valley experienced a massive influx of labor; men but also many women who had come to work in the new shipbuilding industry. Many of them were African American, coming in from the southern states in search of work. Photos from the time show rows of African-American women in coveralls and welder's helmets, their visors pushed back, laughing in the sunshine. Soldiers, too, poured in from other parts of the country, awaiting deployment in the Pacific theater of war. When the war ended, many of these workers and soldiers didn't want to return to where they'd come from. The Bay Area was gorgeous, temperate, and still largely undeveloped. They wanted to stay.

Thus began the great California suburban boom of the 1950s. Orchards and fields and farmlands were razed and turned into housing development after housing development. Shopping centers and schools and movie theaters and sports tracks. The land prices had not quite skyrocketed yet and the concrete poured freely. Now was when the lovers of Point Reyes's nature and pastoral character began to get worried. As Boyd would later point out, all of the Santa Clara Valley had already been transformed from a paradise of blossoming orchards into suburbia.

Enter Clement Woodnutt Miller—or Clem, as he was called—a Democratic House representative from up the coast. He was elected to Congress in 1959 with a plan already mapped out: He would turn the Point Reyes peninsula into a national park. Clem wrote and introduced a bill to establish it in 1962. Sadly, not long after it was passed he was killed in a small plane crash not far from his childhood home in Eureka. The clock was ticking, since some parcels of land had already been sold to developers. Trees were falling on the ridge and homes were already being erected close to Limantour Beach along Drakes Bay. More than 3,500 homes were set to be built there, along with country clubs and other amenities. Popular sentiment was increasingly in favor of conservation, so it wasn't difficult to rally support. Clem's plan would stop and even undo the developments that had already started, plus preserve the rest of the area.

The trouble was, no one had really consulted the ranchers whose properties fell within the boundaries of the proposed conservation.

"Now, they didn't plan too well," Boyd said of the conservationists. "They wanted the park. Everybody they talked to was in favor of the park. They didn't talk to the ranchers because they didn't have much contact with them, these city people didn't."

Belatedly, the ranchers found out what was going on and immediately tried to stop it.

Here's how this kind of thing usually works: If the government decides to build a highway or a park or something where your house is, your property is "condemned" and you're given a chunk of money for what your property is worth, based on the estimate of an appraiser. Then you move. It isn't really up to you. The ranchers were concerned that a similar fate awaited them. As soon as they got word of the proposed park, they organized, pooled their money and hired a lawyer to send to Washington to advocate on their behalf. Most had been ranching the area for fifty, sixty years or even longer, and were just seeing the next generation take over.

J.V. had died in 1950, but had been involved in earlier efforts to preserve the area. He was good at partnerships, a talent that was passed on to his son Joe. But it would be his widow Zena who perhaps made the strongest impact.

It turned out that the government would not be able to condemn large segments of the pastoral zone within the proposed park boundaries, but a different pressure was mounting. Though the Depression was long over, times were still hard for the Point Reyes ranchers. Milk prices had plummeted, leaving some of them in dire straits and making a buyout from developers look ever more appealing. Nobody wanted to see the Point destroyed in its entirety, but neither could they say who would be allowed to sell to developers and who would not. Besides, without enough land acquisitions, the park could not go forward.

The best option that emerged was for the park to buy the land from the ranchers and then lease it back to them, so that they could continue ranching and the pastoral character of the land could be preserved, free from service stations, parking lots and strip malls. But in order to accomplish that, it needed to be done in bulk. The government needed to set aside enough money to buy up all of the land, and as the plans shifted throughout the 1960s, it looked like maybe what they were allocated would not be enough. Property prices were going up in the area like crazy, and Point Reyes's ranches were no exception. Now it seemed that if Congress abandoned the plan for the park, the ranches would be doomed to fall under the wheel of so-called progress anyway.

The ranchers realized that the park wasn't going anywhere. Dramatic changes were coming to their beloved peninsula whether they liked it or not, and the status quo would not and could not continue. Some realized that even if they declined to sell to either the park or to developers, they'd lose their properties anyway due to inheritance taxes that were so high as to be nearly unpayable. This is a problem for ranchers even now, although many properties outside the seashore have since been saved through the work of the Marin Agricultural Land Trust—or MALT, as it's known locally. However MALT was not established until 1980, and in 1969 the Point Reyes ranchers saw no better alternative than to sell to the government, as it increasingly looked like it would be the park or nothing. They could either enter old age knowing that inheritance taxes would financially cripple their children, or else watch their beloved pastures get paved over. The problem was then whether or not the government would be able to allocate the necessary funds, and as the 1960s wore on this was starting to look less and less likely. As the sales were delayed, the danger grew that ranchers would cave and take the seemingly easy money from developers. If too much of the land went into development, the park would no longer be viable and the whole project would collapse.

The boundaries of Point Reyes National Seashore were drawn in 1962. On September 13, President John F. Kennedy signed the legislation, with a crowd of the park's supporters gathered behind him in the Oval Office. Among them was Clem Miller, who less than a month later would go down in that tiny plane on the California coast. He was buried atop a hillock within the Seashore boundary, near the ocean at the end of Bear Valley Trail, marked with a simple flat stone bearing his name and the years he lived. There were five hundred people in attendance at his burial, despite the remote location and the rainstorm that raged that day. Nowadays, the grave is often decorated with stones, feathers or fallen antlers—signs of respect from passing hikers who are grateful to be enjoying the park that Clem made possible.

The 1962 Point Reyes National Seashore Act states, "The government may not acquire land in the pastoral zone without the consent of the owner so long as it remains in its natural state, or is used exclusively for ranching and dairying purposes." The first land the park acquired was Bear Valley, in the summer of 1963, site of the former Pacific Union Country Club, sold by owners Bruce and Grace Kelham. The National Park Service began construction of their headquarters there, and started drawing up plans for the rest of the area. The ideologies of conservation and land preservation were still somewhat fluid. Of course, they still are, but this was especially true in the 1960s. The common assumption of the time, and one that is still popular today, is that a park is primarily *for people*. This is quite different from the Deep Ecology ideals held by activists like Fred Smith, who would end up working to protect the natural character of Point Reyes too, more focused on wilderness for wilderness's sake, and regardless of its benefits to humans. When the National Seashore was first created however, a park was for people, and its first duty was to provide opportunities to recreate. Hence the proposal to turn an estuary of remarkable biodiversity into a lake with rented paddleboats and stocked trout.

But plans for the park soon stalled. Not long after the first parkland was purchased in 1963, the country was pitched headlong into turmoil. Kennedy was assassinated in November, and by the end of that same month there would be sixteen thousand American military personnel stationed in South Vietnam, up more than 1,700 percent from Eisenhower's nine hundred "advisors." The federal Wilderness Act was passed the following year, on September 3, 1964, declaring over nine million acres of land as wilderness where, according to the act, "the earth and its community of life are untrammeled by man, where man himself is a visitor who does not remain."

In 1965, 3,500 U.S. Marines were dispatched to Southeast Asia, marking the true start to the American ground war in Vietnam. Forty men assembled to burn their draft cards on the UC Berkeley campus before marching a coffin to the Berkeley draft board. The Watts riots shook Los Angeles, two days before Jefferson Airplane debuted at the Matrix club on Fillmore in San Francisco. The following fall in 1966, Lady Bird Johnson traveled to Point Reyes to dedicate the Point Reyes National Seashore. Photos from the day show her wearing a pillbox hat and T-strap shoes, leaning on Interior Secretary Stewart Udall in the surf at Drakes Beach. She said that "the growing needs of an urban America are quickening the tick of the conservation clock." She called Point Reyes "a bright star in the galaxy of conservation achievements of the 1960s."

But as the sixties passed, it looked like Clem's plan was in danger of falling through. Originally, $14 million was appropriated for the purchase of parklands. This was augmented in 1966 with an additional $5 million, bringing the total budget up to $19 million. But land prices were going up, and it looked like what the park was going to be able to offer the ranchers would be laughably low.

"Meanwhile, the speculators were circling," Boyd said. "They were here. They pointed out to us that we could divide this ranch into three pieces. We could get a lot of money for it. They came to us. They came to everybody."

Along with Clem Miller's widow Katy, State Senator Peter Behr created the Save Our Seashore campaign in 1969, with a handy acronym of "SOS." Aware that her late husband's legacy was in jeopardy, Katy became a letter-writing machine, sending missives to anyone who could possibly help get the park back on track. She wrote to environmentalists and journalists and congressmen. She wrote to their wives. There was a momentum building now. California congressman Pete McCloskey became an active advocate for the park as well. He'd been a lawyer working on property condemnation, and wanted to make sure that the land was preserved while also taking care of the resident ranchers. But it didn't look like the pro-park team would be able to raise the money. A Marin County appraiser surveyed the properties and determined that the cost to buy all of the ranches would in fact be $37 million in total. Now it was just a matter of convincing Congress that the purchase was worth it.

Boyd flew to Washington in May of 1969 with a number of large-scale color photographs of the coast, so that the members of Congress could see the beauty of the area they hoped to preserve. It was on the eve of that trip that seventeen or eighteen ranchers had all gathered in his farmhouse kitchen and agreed what to do. Still, Boyd worried that this solidarity might crack and wouldn't last for long. Some ranchers already had doubts, knowing that the longer they held out, the more their property values would rise and the more they'd get. But the government didn't even have enough to purchase the lands at the current price, let alone at an inflated one. So off Boyd went with the photos, hoping to get Congress to strike while the iron was hot.

Fearing that they'd be forced out, Zena Mendoza also flew to Washington to testify before the congressional hearings. It had been fifty years since she first arrived in Point Reyes, as the sixteen-year-old bride of a man she'd never met. But she grew to love both him and the pastures they made their own. Wearing a modest dress and speaking in halting English, she tried to say as much as she could to the packed chamber before emotion got the better of her, and she burst into tears.

"I was not born in this country," she began. "Since I was a child I wanted to come to America, to the land where there was respect for human dignity, the land of the free . . . where the minorities would not be trampled on, where there would be no dictators . . . now I am faced with the possibility of losing everything that I have worked for."

Afterwards, collecting herself in the hallway, she was mortified. She thought that by becoming emotional she had let her family down. Then a lawyer came up to her and said the following:

"Ma'am, I think you just did more for the preservation of those ranches than you can ever know."

Of course, there were a number of factors contributing to the park's eventual success. Pete McCloskey had been classmates at Stanford with John Ehrlichman, then one of Nixon's chief advisors, and was able to call in a favor to his old friend. The two men lived near to each other in D.C., and even shared a car to the Capitol some mornings. He managed to convince Ehrlichman to get Nixon on board, even at the expense of other parks-in-progress. At one point in the White House correspondence, Ehrlichman even says that to afford Point Reyes, the Nixon administration could "cancel a space shot."

In 1969, the *New York Times* called Point Reyes "a patchwork park in trouble."

"I think it absolutely certain that land values in Point Reyes area will continue to escalate at a rate rapid enough to make even the $37,500,000 figure inadequate unless the property is taken by condemnation during the calendar year 1969," McCloskey testified that

May. "There are few areas in the world which compare with the rugged grandeur of California's coastline, and in a world where we spend equivalent sums for a few days' expenditure of ammunition eight thousand miles away in Vietnam, we would be derelict indeed not to recognize the national priority here involved."

Indeed, by June some 4,500 Americans had been killed in Vietnam that year alone. In July, a hush fell over the world as Americans put a man on the moon. In September, McCloskey heard that Nixon's budget director had announced that even if Congress appropriated funds to complete the land acquisition at Point Reyes National Seashore, the funds would not be released by the Nixon administration. He immediately called Ehrlichman.

"The only man who can save the Point Reyes National Seashore is the President," McCloskey told him in a letter dated September 16, 1969. He instructed Ehrlichman on how to get the funds from the Land and Water Conservation Fund, and White House aides began to rapidly correspond about how to make that happen—with one remarking to another that Point Reyes had received a high priority in their thinking, and it was necessary to "do something dramatic."

In October, Congressman Jeffrey Cohelan wrote to McCloskey saying that as far as he knew, the Nixon administration would not release the funds needed to buy Point Reyes.

As Ehrlichman later put it in an interview, Nixon was "not your natural, birds, bees and bunnies man."

However, Cohelan said he intended to introduce a bill designed to release the trust funds for the land acquisition by extending the Land and Water Conservation Act of 1967. It had already been amended to authorize the use of funds derived from oil leases on the outer

continental shelf. The fund had $288.5 million in it, but the Bureau
of the Budget only intended to release $124 million—leaving $164.5
million unexpended "unless we act soon," Cohelan said.

McCloskey wrote to Ehrlichman again, along with White House
staff assistant Tod Hullin, on October 10, urging them to persuade
Nixon to increase funding to Point Reyes. Still he didn't budge, but
there were other priorities. That same day, Nixon ordered a squadron
of eighteen B-52s, packed with nuclear weapons, to race to the edge of
Russian airspace as a show of force against the Soviets. Then in early
November, Katy Miller's Save Our Seashore petitions began arriving
at the White House en masse. I imagine it like the courtroom scene in
*Miracle On 34th Street*. They all began: "Mr. President: Only you can
save Point Reyes . . ."

The trouble was, Point Reyes would have to get funded over other
park projects in Cape Cod and Padre Island. Ehrlichman managed to
convince Nixon that Point Reyes was not only in a uniquely vulnerable
position, but perhaps more importantly as far as the administration
was concerned, saving it would be politically advantageous by appealing to an important California voter base.

Finally, in December, the House voted in favor of the Point Reyes
bill. Only John Saylor of Pennsylvania vowed to fight it, saying his
exception was to saving one park while others remained vulnerable.
Nixon signed the bill to approve the funds in early 1970, and over
the next several years the ranchers of Point Reyes sold their land and
began operating on short-term leases.

In 1972, Charlie Johnson of Johnson Oyster Company sold his
few land-based acres to the federal government, after nearly a decade
of negotiations. He wasn't invited to attend the meeting of ranching

patriarchs in Boyd's kitchen that spring night in 1969. He wasn't much of a player, having so little land to sell. After all, he didn't own Drakes Estero, and had only a lease agreement from the Department of Fish and Game to use parts of it. In all of the testimony, the oyster farm was always spoken of separately from the cattle and dairy ranches. Prior to the Point Reyes Wilderness Act of 1976, there wasn't a clear message of whether an oyster farm could continue operating in a National Park or a wilderness area. For many, what a "wilderness" area was exactly wasn't entirely clear. There were other factors to delay the full wilderness protection of the Point Reyes estuaries, and so the whole area was labeled "potential wilderness" and would be sorted out later. Mariculture wasn't explicitly discussed in the legal proceedings, and the forty years still left on the oyster farm's meter must have seemed like a very long time.

# 7

## ENTER THE BLAST FURNACE

IN A LONDON nightclub in the early 1970s, the man who would become America's foremost advocate for wilderness preservation was a little busy. He had an unfiltered cigarette in one hand, a vodka cocktail in the other, and a prostitute seated on either side. He'd been handsome in his youth, tall, with a passing resemblance to a roguish Jimmy Stewart. But after years of serious hard living he'd gone jowly, and before long would begin to look a little like a debauched Pablo Neruda. He took a drag, squinted through the smoke, and then said something to the effect of, *All right girls, let's get out of here.*

Ladies and gentlemen, may I please introduce to you the man responsible for preserving more American wilderness than anyone else, and for whom the wilderness area at Point Reyes National Seashore is named: Congressman Phillip Burton.

He was in the U.K. for a weeklong NATO Alliance conference, part of his yearly European junket. He'd never let his wife Sala see him like this—he had too much respect for her for that—but to his colleagues, scenes like the above were par for the course. In fact, it might even be considered tame. He once took a junior staffer to the Playboy Club in London where they each picked up three women, took them to a country inn to throw a raucous party, drove back the next day, swapped the women out for new ones, and repeated the experience. When Burton asked the aide, who was twelve years his junior, if he wanted to go out again for a third night—after a Monday of long briefings and hearings—the younger man was forced to admit defeat.

"Phil, I can't do it," he said. "I'm going to bed."

Burton was absolutely infamous. He was a force not just for nature, but of it. Ever since getting his start in local San Francisco politics he was known for tearing through obstacles and red tape with a ferocious intensity that terrified interns and delighted the underdogs he chose to fight for. He was ambitious and abrasive. He had daddy issues. Over the course of his impressive career, and in the years since, he was called many things, including the following: a wild man, an intolerable drunk, uncompromising, incorruptible, an indefatigable worker, a raging alcoholic, a philanderer, controversial, a brilliant tactician and strategist, an SOB, Machiavelli, Mephistopheles, and my personal favorite, "a blast furnace," due to the vast quantities of fuel that he required to keep himself going. For Burton, "fuel" meant cigarettes, booze, food, sex and power.

"I spent thirty-two years in elective office, and I only met one absolute political genius. That was Phil Burton," said the late senator Gaylord Nelson.

Burton was born in Cincinnati in 1926. His father went to medical school while his mother sold ads over the phone for church publications of the Catholic diocese, for twelve hours a day. The family moved to San Francisco in 1941, and Phil served in the Air Force during World War II. After that he became a lawyer, and joined any political cause he could find that aligned with his values. "Whenever a circle of people was hotly debating some issue, Burton was in the middle of it," wrote John Jacobs in his Burton biography, *A Rage for Justice.*

Burton did care about justice, even if he did so especially when it served to elevate his own stature. On election night in November 1952, when the line outside a polling center in a black neighborhood was so long that many didn't get a chance to vote before closing time, Burton wouldn't allow it. "I'll take care of this," he said, and screamed at the (white) precinct workers until they agreed to keep the place open until everyone in line had a chance to cast their ballot, no matter how long it took.

He was elected to the California State Assembly in 1956, and to Congress in 1964. He considered running for Senate in 1969, but then decided against it, opting instead to campaign for House majority leader in 1976. He didn't get it, however, much to his raging chagrin, and wound up as chairman of the House Interior Committee. It seemed like a strange choice for a man deeply interested in welfare, labor and civil liberties, and it isn't clear exactly how the appointment came about. Some have speculated that Burton was pushed onto Interior as a way to neutralize him, to get him out of the way. But others weren't so sure, and insisted he had sought out the "seemingly irrelevant" assignment himself. Said one colleague, "He chose Interior, because he could gain seniority there faster than any place else."

In many ways, there could not have been a more unlikely champion of nature than this carousing, hard-drinking smokestack of a man. Burton liked to joke that the closest he came to be being outdoors was walking fifty yards into a forest by the side of the road to take a leak. He didn't exercise, and colleagues worried about his health. They tried dragging him to the House gym but he just ended up sitting in the steam room, chain-smoking his beloved Chesterfields.

When someone suggested that Burton drive out to visit the Golden Gate National Recreation Area, which he himself had worked to preserve, he replied, "Why the fuck would I want to do that?" before proceeding to stamp his cigarette out on the gravel.

There is a big difference between wilderness and Wilderness with a capital W, and while Burton may not have been very interested in the former, he took a great interest in the latter. With House leadership gone, he realized that environmentalism was his best chance to prove himself, and he turned conservation into an elaborate system of chits.

"I figured out the only thing that really lasts forever is parks," Burton told the director of the Wilderness Society. "That's my accomplishment."

Burton was an ardent liberal, and while he didn't care very much about experiencing nature himself, he understood that it mattered deeply to a lot of people. He was ruthless in trying to preserve it for them.

"We'll pull the environmental community into the late twentieth century," he said when he first took an interest in national parks. "We'll do things no one else has ever thought possible."

And he did—by any means necessary. In at least one instance, when Burton failed to get a piece of land included within a protected area, he instructed the mapmaker to draw it up with the land included anyway. If you've lost, why not just pretend that you've won and hope nobody notices? As independent journalist George Clyde discovered in 2012, at the time, official maps of the Golden Gate National Recreation Area showed Tomales Bay as being included, *even though it wasn't.* Burton had managed to get Congress to pass a bill expanding the boundaries—a bill that refers to a map—before the map was even created. This was a common practice of Burton's in what became known as the "park-barreling" era, and was essentially a way to get Congress to write him a blank check. During the peak of this era, from 1978 to 1980, Burton pushed through legislation for an astonishing number of parks, often without the park service's input and even, in some cases, against its wishes. If there was a problem with including a piece of land, he would get it approved by Congress first and sort out the legality of it later. Bodies of water could be especially problematic, because of the jurisdiction of different agencies, the public's right to fish, and other issues. When Clyde finally got his hands on the original map of the GGNRA, he was amazed to find this note written by the cartographer: "State tidelands suggested by P. Burton to be shown included in authorized boundary on all maps (even though we will most likely never acquire them)."

The park service had managed the bay for more than thirty years even though they weren't supposed to, just because Burton refused to be defeated.

Another way to get around obstacles that stood in the way of preserving an area as official Wilderness, was to designate it as "potential wilderness" instead. This was the case with the wilderness area in Point Reyes, consideration for which had been on the table since the park was first established. Drakes Estero was not included in early maps of the proposed National Research Area, which would later be proposed as wilderness. This is probably due mostly to the fact that Drakes Estero is not as easily accessible by car as its smaller sibling, Estero de Limantour, except for the site of the oyster farm. While it enjoys a higher level of protection than a national park, a wilderness area's stated purpose is still enjoyment by human beings—so long as they do not trammel it, and do not "remain."

Spiritually and practically, what "wilderness" means or entails is somewhat open to interpretation. How wild is wild? There is now no such thing as a place wholly untouched by humankind. There are fields of litter on Mount Everest and plastic bags stuck on thorn bushes in the remote Pakistani desert and rubber ducks trapped in the arctic ice and satellite images of everywhere. Even the landscapes that romantic adventurers like John Muir encountered were not unpeopled, they were just undestroyed. As we lose more species to extinction, through pollution, hunting and fishing, or climate change, how intact does an ecosystem need to be in order to still count? Legally, however, wilderness does have a definition, even if it is rather nebulously poetic. It is: "A wilderness, in contrast with those areas where man and his own works dominate the landscape, is hereby recognized as an area where the earth and its community of life are untrammeled by man, where man himself is a visitor who does not remain." The law says Wilderness with a capital W must be "roadless," but that has been taken to mean roads not maintained by mechanical means. One of the biggest criticisms of the Wilderness Act is how vastly open to interpretation it can be.

The idea of "potential wilderness" was first used by Congress in 1976, the year that the Point Reyes Wilderness Act was passed. It was very much in Burton's style. Doesn't qualify as wilderness? Doesn't matter. All of that could be sorted out. An area could be designated as "potential" wilderness if it was close to wilderness in character, but possessed some marring factor such as a road, a structure, visible pipes or power lines. None of these belonged in true wilderness, it had been decided—except when they do. The thing is, the distinction is somewhat open to interpretation, and the rules can be bent if it is deemed necessary, or if it is considered beneficial to visitors. Obviously, national parks can have all kinds of amenities, even restaurants and hotels. But with a wilderness area the rules are stricter. Wilderness areas do not allow motorized or even "mechanized" vehicles of any kind, including bicycles. However, inside the Sawtooth Wilderness in Sawtooth National Forest in Idaho, for example, there is a river, and motorboats are allowed to ferry tourists upstream. There are also a number of what is known as "wilderness inholdings"—islands of private land parcels within wilderness, which must be allowed motorized access. There are even roads that go "through" the wilderness area of Point Reyes, so that visitors may access trails and beaches.

Looking at the proposed wilderness maps of Drakes Estero created in the 1970s, it is clear that *someone* was thinking about the future of the oyster farm. For one, the land on which the oyster farm sat is not included in the wilderness area in any of the maps, that much is clear. How much of the water directly near to the oyster farm was to be included was a little more confusing. In some maps, the wilderness area is shown to end abruptly in a straight line, leaving out the last portion of the inlet where Johnson Oyster Company launched its boats, like cutting the fingertip off of a glove. In others, made the same year, the boundary extends all the way to the shoreline. This is what the final map of the "potential wilderness" in Drakes Estero looked like. Of course, not all of the oyster farm was on land. Charlie Johnson had put about a million feet of redwood timber into the lagoon on which to hang his oysters, and the farming part of the farm all took place on the water.

All of the bodies of water in Point Reyes National Seashore were designated as potential wilderness in 1976, including Estero de Limantour, Abbotts Lagoon, and the tidelands of the beaches. This was due in part to the need to work out agreements with the Department of Fish and Game, and to remove some other "non-conforming" characteristics, like power lines. In the years that followed, they all were given full wilderness status, except for the majority of the upper part of Drakes Estero where the oyster farm operated.

Now, what was supposed to come next differs depending on who you talk to. Former congressman Pete McCloskey, who is retired from politics and now tends an olive farm in Yolo County with his wife, has come out and said that the intention was always to have the oyster farm stay in operation. He's written letters on the farm's behalf, and I visited him in the summer of 2014 to talk about it. He was very active for an eighty-six-year-old, mucking around the farm in old jeans and a pair of rubber boots, although I had to shout pretty loudly to be heard. He had told other reporters in the past that he was "dismayed" by efforts to remove the oyster farm, although when he talked to me he was a little fuzzy on the details. He started out by telling me that the oyster farm was owned by a nice Mexican family, and kept referring to it as Johnson Oyster. None of this is surprising. McCloskey has done a lot in his life, including coauthoring the Endangered Species Act. He can't be expected to remember everything.

But as I was sitting down with him in his living room to discuss the Drakes Bay Oyster Company, his wife Helen, an attractive blond woman some fifteen years his junior, also dressed in jeans and rubber boots, leaned her head in through the sliding glass door and shouted:

"Don't listen to him! Drakes Bay Oyster is being funded by the Koch brothers!"

He waved his hand towards her as if swatting a fly, and smiled.

"I guess you could say that we have a little disagreement in this house."

McCloskey uses the presence of the ranches in the pastoral zone to support the notion that the oyster farm was intended to stay. Others disagree with him, pointing to the fact that "potential wilderness" was never meant to be a permanent designation. Rather, parks were instructed to "steadily remove" any non-conforming uses, according to House testimony, until the area could qualify as full wilderness.

The funny thing is, it's unlikely that Phil Burton would have cared either way about the oyster farm. In a sense, it is even rather fitting that a man of his appetites would have a wilderness area named after him that included within it an operation to produce aphrodisiac shellfish. Then again, if he saw the "potential wilderness" designation as being weaker or less of a legacy, then maybe not.

In 1983, when he was fifty-six, Burton was in a San Francisco hotel room with his wife when he started having chest pains.

"Jesus, Sala, I don't feel good," he said to her.

A few moments later he collapsed, and was pronounced dead at the hospital, the cause of death later listed as an abdominal aneurysm and severe heart disease. To honor him, in 1985 Congress passed Public Law 99-68, which reads as follows:

"In recognition of Congressman Phillip Burton's dedication to the protection of the Nation's outstanding natural, scenic, and cultural resources and his leadership in establishing units of the National Park System and preserving their integrity against threats to these resources and specifically his tireless efforts which led to the enactment of the California Wilderness Act of 1984, the designated wilderness area of Point Reyes National Seashore, California as established pursuant to law, shall henceforth be known as the 'Phillip Burton Wilderness.'"

# 8

# THE NON-NATIVES ARE RESTLESS

F OR MANY, A trip into nature is a chance to purify and to return. We escape the vibrations of modern life and try to attune our bodies and minds to a deeper and more consistent rhythm. The practice of using nature to help one live deliberately, as Thoreau set out to do, does not always require a sustained separation from our daily routine. One can simply take a dip in the natural world. After we hike a windy trail, or walk through a field and into the waiting shade of a forest, we come back just a little different. We take a wander along a chilly beach and return to civilization a little more wild-eyed and bedraggled, hands numb, hair wayward, skin sticky with salt. It is good to be thus disheveled, to feel the blood pound through limbs made tame by commutes and television; to let the elements lean on us a little.

When I was a teenager growing up near Point Reyes in the 1990s, the practice of slipping out of the world of expectation and into one of wilderness and tides, redwood groves and open hills under moonlight, was an important one. It usually felt as if that land had given you something, like a visitation. It was the same landscape always, but of course it was never really the same. The pageant of seasons and weather and animal life provided constant fodder for reflection. On a lonely beach walk, perhaps a single harbor seal will swim up the shore, following you. This used to happen to me all the time. Maybe you will see an owl in the middle of the day while deep in the woods, or come across a magnificent gleaming snake. Or else an early spring sunset will spread a blush over the land so otherworldly that you'll be giddy with it. Once, while walking near the mouth of Drakes Estero I saw a gray whale breach and let out a plume of spray, impossibly close to land, or so it seemed. The few of us there on the beach whooped and pointed and laughed, with a delight so open it was almost like relief.

I need to be frank about something, and I think anyone who has spent much time out at Point Reyes will have a hard time disagreeing with it. Point Reyes is a little bit magic. I don't just mean that it's lovely, although it is, but that there is some strange power to be felt, which I am not alone in noticing. Spend enough time out there and you will very likely begin to feel as if the trees are talking to you, saying something old and only half-intelligible about water, soil and time. The landscape itself feels sentient. When I was young at least, there was one sight in particular that was considered the pinnacle of magical encounter, for anyone with an even remotely romantic disposition, and that was to have a run-in with the white deer. To encounter them in a meadow blurred with fog felt a little like wandering into a unicorn tapestry.

Once at the age of thirteen I was driving out to the beach with my father on a gray day. We crested a hill and there, standing a hundred feet from the road, was a white stag. We stopped the car, got out, and stayed for a moment in his presence, while he stood there, looking for all the world like a medieval illustration come to life. I'd heard that there were white deer living in the deep forests of Point Reyes, and that they would sometimes come down from the wooded hills and into the open, or even wander onto the beach, but I had never seen one before. It wasn't exactly a unicorn, but for a thirteen-year-old girl well versed in fantasy literature, it was certainly the next best thing. Some locals called them "the ghost deer."

A real animal in its own right, a white deer—and the white stag in particular—nevertheless has mythical abilities attached to it. In legends from the British Isles to the Middle East, a white deer is usually a kind of supernatural being. For the Celts, a white stag meant that the Otherworld was close at hand, and in Arthurian legend, it is the creature that can never be caught, but that draws you ever onward towards transformation. It is what leads queens Susan and Lucy and kings Peter and Edmund out of Narnia and back into their postwar childhoods, as the boughs of the trees that brushed against their arms gradually turned back into the bristled fur of coats in the wardrobe. The white stag is a catalyst, although whether he serves to enchant you or awaken you is unclear.

Fred Smith had only been working as executive director of the Environmental Action Committee of West Marin for a few months when, one calm morning, a distraught older man came barging into the little office. Fred recognized him as one of the organization's members.

"Please, Fred," the man said, with tears in his eyes. "You've got to stop this. They're going to kill the white deer. The park is going to kill all of them. Please, you've got to do something."

This was true, but there wasn't much that Fred could do to change things. He'd arrived in West Marin in December 2006, one month before he was set to start work. Already in love with the area, he felt an extra sense of intimate connection to the place knowing that he had been tasked to protect it.

"I felt like an eco-warrior for this local environment," he would later tell me.

On one of those early nights, he was having a beer at Vlad's in Inverness. This was in the days when Vlad himself was still alive, before he passed the establishment on to his daughter Vladya, and the walls were decorated with pictures of Vlad's true passion: former president Ronald Reagan. (Vlad died in September 2008, and the photos of Reagan are now gone.)

A man and a woman came into the bar, more dressed up than anyone Fred had seen so far in town. Apparently there was a party of some kind at the nearby Inverness Yacht Club. The couple was boisterous and happy, and Vlad introduced them.

"This is Fred Smith," Vlad offered to the couple. "He's taking over the EAC."

The man was warm and jovial.

*I'm Kevin Lunny, the owner of the oyster farm,* Fred remembers him saying, *I don't normally dress like this.*

According to Fred, they talked pleasantly for a few minutes before going about their own business of the evening. He knew there were starting to be some problems between this oyster farm and the park, but it was not yet a prominent issue in the community.

As soon as Kevin and his family bought Johnson Oyster they changed the name to Drakes Bay Oyster Company, as a nod to Larry Jensen's original mariculture effort. In an article in the *Point Reyes Light*, Kevin said he didn't plan to change the name, but apparently thought better of it after the article was published. The problems with the park started right away. As he would later express to *Marin* magazine reporter P.J. Bremier, Kevin had been optimistic that although the park had clearly stipulated that there would be no lease renewal past 2012, he might be able to get an extension if he instituted sufficient improvements and made the farm seem like enough of an asset to the park that the government would decide to keep it around. However at the beginning of 2005 after the sale was final, the park presented him with an agreement to sign. It explicitly stated that there would be no renewal, and that Kevin knew that. He refused to sign it, and the battle for the oyster farm began.

Fred could not have known when he met Kevin that he would soon be spending nearly all of his time trying to put him out of business. During that first year of his tenure as West Marin Eco-Warrior, the biggest and most contentious issue was the proposed slaughter of the white deer.

The "white" deer were not, in fact, all white. There were two species of exotic or "non-native" deer living in Point Reyes National Seashore at the time; the fallow deer (*dama dama*), about 20–40 percent of which were white (they also appeared in brown, red and even black color morphs), and the axis deer (*axis axis*), which were brown. The exact origin of fallow deer in general is unclear. They are usually said to come originally from "the Mediterranean," although whether this means Spain, France, Greece, Lebanon, Algeria, etc. isn't specified. They are now found on every continent except Antarctica, having been brought there by humans. The Romans brought them to the British Isles, and in ensuing centuries, the landed gentry of different eras would often release them onto their private estates. Yet despite their apparent ubiquity, they are still rare, or at the very least shy enough to stay out of the public eye most of the time. To see one still felt like something of a gift. They are sweet-faced, the way a Jersey cow is sweet-faced, with softer features that make their countenance look more like lambs than deer. The axis deer, also called *chital*, which were less showy though no less foreign, hailed from South Asia. When in the Indian epic *The Ramayana*, Sita begs Ram to catch a beautiful deer for her, this is the kind of deer she is likely talking about. Being brown and spotted, at least from a distance it was easy enough to confuse them with the locals. But since even the adult axis deer are speckled with white, as fawns are, they seem to live in a perpetual state of innocence.

The fallow and axis deer were brought to Point Reyes nearly seventy years ago by a San Francisco surgeon named Millard Ottinger. He had a gentleman's ranch on Point Reyes's Mount Vision. The locals all called him "Doc." It was Doc who decided that he wanted the deer, but it was his twenty-six-year-old ranch hand Ambrose Gondola, a small but strong man, with arms like Popeye, who actually drove into the city in a big truck to get them one day in 1949.

The deer came from the San Francisco Zoo, and the zoo had too many of them. Doc was good friends with the zoo's director, Carey Baldwin, who had also curated the animal collection at Hearst Castle. Normally they just fed any excess zoo deer to the lions. This time, however, they permitted Doc to buy between twenty and thirty of them to bring out to his ranch. Of the fallow deer, he wanted only the white variety, though the other colors would spring up over the years due to genetic drift. On Ambrose's way back to the country from the city he was stopped twice by highway patrol.

"What have you got in the truck?" the officer asked him.

"I've got deer!" Ambrose replied.

"You're full of so-and-so," the officer said. But when he looked, sure enough, it was a cartload full of fairytale megafauna.

Ambrose released the deer onto Doc's property, but only a few days later the largest white stag was shot and killed by a poacher. Defiant, the gunman had even strung the animal up outside the Inverness store in the nearby village for all to see. Doc was livid. He cut the carcass down and put it in the back of his Cadillac convertible.

"My property, my deer," Ambrose remembered Doc saying. As far as he was concerned, it was as if someone had shot one of his cows. He had the hide tanned and the magnificent antlered head mounted. If this was a fairytale animal, it was now a grim one, the uncatchable beast having been caught. However, the sheriff at the time retroactively validated a hunting tag for the stag slayer, meaning the trophies legally belonged to him. Doc was then forced to give both hide and head to the poacher.

"That tore him apart," Ambrose later said.

Doc sent out to the San Francisco Zoo again for more white deer.

Ottinger's exotic deer roamed through Point Reyes as quarry for him and his hunting buddies, like fish in a stocked pond, for the next thirteen years or so. Their numbers remained small. But when the park bought the land in 1962 and public hunting stopped, their numbers began to climb.

There aren't many predators in Point Reyes National Seashore anymore that can take down a deer. The bears for whom Bear Valley was named are long gone. There are mountain lions and coyotes, but not many. For the native black-tailed deer, by far the most effective predator is the *currus terribilis,* or car. In the springtime in particular, there is a disturbingly high incidence of roadkill, especially of fawns. But the fallow and axis deer were more skittish. They were almost never seen on the roadsides, and never as roadkill. Cindy Dicke, who in the early 2000s worked at the wildlife rehabilitation center now called WildCare, said the white deer largely managed to stay out of sight and trouble.

"It's strange," she told the *San Francisco Chronicle* in 2006, "but in five years working at the Wildlife Center I don't recall a single incident of a white deer being hit or injured by a car. It just hasn't happened."

In the 1960s, with the park officially created but not yet completed, the herds of fallow and axis deer grew. In the early 1970s when the park began to more actively edit the landscape, it commissioned a study of the exotics by two graduate students. The conclusion of the young biologists was ambivalent. They wrote that "limited degrees of competition may exist" between the native and non-native deer, but that viewing the fallow and axis deer "adds much to the recreational enjoyment" of park visitors. Yet there was talk even then of eliminating the interlopers. The grad students did not see such a plan as necessary or even feasible.

"To attempt to restore a pristine environment will not be possible until the long-term leases of the dairy ranchers expire and the maintenance of the exotic deer population at a prescribed level could satisfy both recreational and local economic interests," they wrote.

The park began an ad hoc culling program, intending to keep each herd of exotic deer under about 350 individuals. Rangers themselves did the culling, setting out with rifles in the early hours of the morning. If the dead deer was easy to collect, then the park donated the meat to one of several local charities. If the animal fell somewhere more rugged, where it would be hard for a vehicle to reach to transport the carcass, then the deer was left to decompose naturally back into the landscape. This was often the case. This program continued from 1976 until 1994, during which time rangers shot around three thousand individuals.

In 1984, the park considered instituting a massive public hunt to eliminate all of the exotics for good. That plan would have entailed closing the park for about six weeks, most likely in the autumn. Burr Heneman, Sarah Allen's colleague at the Point Reyes Bird Observatory, was also a member of a subcommittee of the Golden Gate National Recreation Area, which strongly rejected the proposal.

"Contrary to the impression projected in some newspaper articles, the committee is a long way from making decisions," Burr told the *Coastal Post* in February 1984. "We all agreed an annual supervised deer hunt would not kill enough deer to control the population and would open the door to quail and duck hunting in the park. However, we have a responsibility not to let deer spread all over West Marin. It is a research problem that must be dealt with. We have even discussed the possibility of birth control."

Indeed, they were looking into non-lethal ways to manage the deer population, either through sterilization or experimental wildlife contraceptives that could be administered by dart gun. Barring that, the committee said they preferred a systematic slaughter to an open season, as conservationists were concerned about making the hunt a public affair. According to Fred's predecessor at the EAC, Susanna Jacob, a public hunt would open the park up for "multiple use," which meant deer, quail and duck hunting as Burr mentioned, but also exploration for minerals and logging for timber, she said.

In 1992, an article appeared in the *San Francisco Chronicle* detailing the already existing culling program, and there was a public outcry: people did not want the park to kill the deer, not by any means. Protest continued, and in 1994 when Don Neubacher took over as superintendent, he stopped the culling and announced that the park would do an official Environmental Impact Study in order to see what should be done. Meanwhile, another group of charismatic megafauna in the park was about to take center stage with a controversy of its own.

Tule elk, or valley elk as they are also called, have occupied a 2,600-acre fenced enclosure on Tomales Point since their reintroduction in 1978. In 1998, forty-five elk were individually airlifted by helicopter to a new habitat in the wilderness on the other side of the park where they are allowed to roam free from the Estero de Limantour to Bolinas. But in 2004, elk started turning up in the pastoral zone and mixing with cows on the historic ranches. After a few years, there was an established ranchland herd.

Left to roam freely over the pastures, elk competed with cows for water and forage, and damaged fences and equipment. Antlered males were said to have injured farm animals, and calmer elk were even observed standing in line with cows at cattle feeds. In a 1998 environmental assessment for the elk's management, the seashore posed the elimination of the ranches on the peninsula as one way to handle the burgeoning ungulate population. This option was just one of many, but still that report also mentioned a 1980 public law giving the Secretary of the Interior the right to terminate ranch leases for the sake of preserving "park resources," which would certainly include elk.

In Point Reyes National Seashore, only one of the tule elk's two major natural predators remain: man. For about ten thousand years, it is believed that the native Miwok peoples hunted the elk for meat, tallow, antlers and hide. Living in more than one hundred coastal villages along Point Reyes, they encouraged elk onto the open plains by burning back the grasslands to increase seed production and eliminate shrubs for better grazing. Along with the elk's other major predator, the grizzly bear, the Miwok kept the population in balance. The open expanses of pre-European California provided a wide range for the animals, which swam across bays and rivers to reach better forage. Before the arrival of missionaries and settlers, the elk numbered about five hundred thousand statewide.

But the Spanish, and later other Europeans, nearly wiped them out, shooting the animals in droves for their meat and hides. Market hunters, operating without rules or regulations, and ranchers who were suffering damage to their grains, orchards and fences, winnowed down the population even further. According to historic records, the last tule elk was seen on Point Reyes in the 1860s, swimming across Tomales Bay before "disappearing into the Sonoma wilds." The book *Wild Peninsula* by Laura Nelson Baker tells of a mass elk exodus, when ranchers observed the herds streaming down from the Inverness Ridge towards the bay, the antlers of the males thrust above the gray water as they swam, their harems of females swimming beside them.

By 1870, tule elk teetered dangerously close to extinction, and many thought they were already gone. Then a few were discovered in the San Joaquin Valley, on the land of a wealthy rancher, who took an interest in the animals. The rancher, Henry Miller, was the largest cattle producer in California and among the richest landowners in the country. In 1873 he helped push through legislation to make killing tule elk a felony, punishable by up to two years in prison. Under the protection of Miller's sheltered acres, the elk increased rapidly. But as early as 1904, they were starting to outgrow their home, and Miller soon shipped twenty-one animals to Sequoia National Park. Other small elk groups were foisted on any land that would take them, but in every instance the elk roamed, preferring to find their own ideal pasture. By 1914, there were over four hundred tule elk living in the wild in Kern County, to the south of Sequoia.

"The tule elk are not a containable animal," Wally Macgregor of the Department of Fish and Game wrote in 1973. "Elk in general do not get along well with man."

The problem was that by the turn of the last century, most of the elk's native habitat had already been turned into farm- and ranchland. Tule elk have a taste for green grass and tender vegetation; since they could easily leap over or trample fences, the wild herds began to wreak havoc in the gardens, farms and pastures of newly settled areas. Crop damage became so severe in Kern County that the California Academy of Sciences was asked to supervise a plan to reduce the herd. In 1920, 146 elk were captured and shipped to nineteen different counties. The herds, wherever they were placed, kept growing.

Tule elk advocates were desperate to find them new homes. In 1921, thirteen animals were released in a twenty-eight-acre fenced paddock in Yosemite—well outside their natural range. Advocate M. Hall McAllister had spent years writing to park officials, imploring them to allow "these beautiful animals" to grace the park's meadows. Yosemite superintendent W.B. Lewis said he was in favor of anything that would "increase the variety of attractions to the visitor to the park," but scientists were concerned over the elk's non-native status. Mr. Lewis agreed to keep the elk fenced, as "a small exhibit herd."

The elk quickly destroyed the vegetation in their pasture, and again their numbers ballooned. A female tule elk begins calving at age two, and usually produces one offspring a year for each year of her adult life—which, in cushy environs, can be up to twenty-five years. The herd was increasing by 25 to 50 percent a year.

"A difficult administrative situation is developing in Yosemite," park naturalist Ansel F. Hall wrote in 1928. Prolific and ravenous, the population quickly filled every area it was moved into, decimating the local flora. In 1933, the park gave up trying to manage an animal they could neither control nor legally cull, and moved the entire herd to the Owens Valley.

There was trouble with other transplanted herds, too. In Monterey County in 1922, the entire elk herd from Del Monte Park was captured and moved to a more remote area. But the elk kept coming back. Meanwhile, back in Kern County, the herd of about 140 animals was doing so much damage that in 1934 a large tract of land was purchased by the state, fenced, and named the Kern County Tule Elk Refuge. However the herd soon overgrazed the area and eliminated most of the native vegetation. Malnutrition and disease became rampant, and the sick animals that had not already perished were destroyed to prevent the further spread of illness. The few remaining elk were fed alfalfa pellets. With the native plants eaten, and the original mesquite and willow eliminated by the damming of the Kern River, the area could only support thirty or forty animals. These were maintained primarily as a park attraction, with excess animals regularly sent to the Owens Valley. Today, the Kern County reserve has only around eighteen individuals.

Meanwhile the Owens Valley was rapidly becoming a depository for elk that had outgrown their ranges across the state. Purchased by the City of Los Angeles as a water source, the valley was also home to ranchers and farmers. (In the 1940s it was also the setting of a Japanese internment camp, and it's possible that some of Point Reyes's tenant pea farmers ended up there.) When first transplanted, the elk were content to roam over some three thousand acres. But as their numbers increased in the late 1930s and early 1940s, they spread out. Preferring green forage, they ate local farmers' hay and vegetable crops. They broke through fences to feed on cultivated fields, and competed with livestock for winter browse.

As their numbers grew, a bitter conflict developed between agriculture and wildlife, and some ranchers demanded that the elk be removed from the valley. A compromise was reached when Fish and Game agreed to control the elks' numbers. In 1943, after taking a herd census, the department allowed licensed hunters to cull forty-three bulls, but again the herd increased rapidly. Substantial culls were needed every three to four years.

In 1961, Fish and Game was forced to adopt a formal management plan for the Owens Valley. The elk herds would be maintained "primarily for aesthetic enjoyment," and kept at about one hundred animals per herd. They would not be allowed supplemental feed, and in place of their natural predators, modern hunters would keep the elk in line with the land's natural carrying capacity.

Despite the success elk had in populating new areas, environmental activists were concerned that the animals overall numbers remained low. A concerned Los Angeles resident named Beula Edmiston made the preservation of tule elk her personal crusade. She created an anti-hunting group, and lobbied hard for the elk's protection. Calling them "the monarch of the wild," she believed the elk needed not only to multiply, but to be given unrestricted range. But either unconcerned or unaware of the decades of bitter controversy in the Owens Valley,

Edmiston called the refuge "the only successful transfer of the Tule Elk ever accomplished."

"It is a sobering thought that at least four species of American elk are now extinct," she wrote in 1966. "It should silence those who would 'save the Tule Elk' in a fenced enclosure like feedlot cattle."

(It should be noted however that the tule elk are not a species, but a breed. Scientific tests have shown that they are not even a *sub*species, but have simply developed different characteristics due to environmental factors. While definitely distinct—they are the smallest kind of elk to be found—they could mix with Roosevelt elk, for example, and produce a kind of designer hybrid, like a Yorkie-poo or a Labradoodle. A "tuleroose elk," maybe.)

Edmiston opposed all population control measures. She called Fish and Game's culling efforts "arbitrary," heaped scorn on the local agriculture industry, and accused hunters of being "gunners eager for trophy." She said that the "ghost herd" was seldom seen by local residents and was "few in number and fearful for survival." This came as news to the residents of the Owens Valley, who were desperately trying to find a compromise, as they felt themselves overrun. In 1970, an Interagency Committee on Owens Valley Land and Wildlife was formed, which included the Los Angeles Department of Water and Power, the California Department of Forestry, Inyo National Forest, the United States Bureau of Land Management, Inyo and Mono counties and the University of California.

Elk expert Dale McCullough wrote of the committee: "[Its activities] dramatically illustrate how local city, county, state and federal agencies can work together toward a common goal." Based on McCullough's work, a plan was developed by which elk would be

divided into separate herds throughout the valley. But the very next
year in 1971, thanks to Edmiston's efforts, the California legislature
passed the Behr Bill, prohibiting the hunting of tule elk until the statewide population reached two thousand, or until no further unoccupied
elk habitat could be found. With no predators and plenty of feed, it
was clear that Fish and Game needed to relocate a large number of
animals in order to avoid a catastrophe. But there were not enough
suitable places. So, in 1976, the same year that Point Reyes National
Seashore started culling the fallow and axis deer, Congress enacted
Public Law 94-389, requiring the Department of the Interior to make
land available for the tule elk on military bases and in national parks.
Point Reyes National Seashore was on the list.

Their reserve was to be on Tomales Point, where J.V. Mendoza
once made butter in an open barn. The ranch that sixteen-year-old
Zena, fresh off the boat from Portugal, had refused to stay in as a tenant farmer for the rest of her life, was turned into historic park buildings the same year the elk arrived. The first herd to occupy the fenced
2,600-acre paddock was small, with just two males and eight females.
During their first years in the seashore, the population struggled to
overcome what biologist McCrea Cobb referred to in a study of the
elk as "inbreeding depression," and their numbers were slow to climb.
Then the appearance of incurable Johne's disease, which causes severe
diarrhea in elk, deer and livestock, and can be fatal to animals under
six months of age, made matters worse. The park discussed eliminating
the elk herd entirely. Cobb, who studied the seashore's elk from 2005
to 2008, said that after overcoming their genetic hurdle, and after a
drought in the 1980s, the elk experienced what he described as "irruptive growth."

"None of the existing predators appear capable of regulating an elk population," he wrote in his dissertation at the University of California, Berkeley. "Irruptive population growth patterns, observed at [Point Reyes] and typified by newly established ungulate populations that are free of predation pressure, can lead to adverse habitat and population-level effects." Cobb identified three distinct herds, which he called Tomales Point, Limantour and D Ranch herds. He observed that the herd in the pastoral zone was definitely growing the fastest.

"The herd near the ranches grew 300 percent in five years," he told me in a phone conversation in 2012 from Alaska, where he was then studying wolves. "The Limantour herd is growing much more slowly, and that is due to habitat. The elk far prefer the flat grasslands. Any expansion of that herd is likely to go onto the pastoral zone as well. [ . . . ] I predicted irruptive, rapid growth."

In his dissertation he wrote that future growth was likely to result in conflicts between park management and ranchers, unless proactive actions were taken. However, he said park officials were wary of taking action based on his findings.

"How do I say this? I think they acknowledged that the population would increase and that the results that I found were true," he told me. "At the time they didn't want to take proactive management actions based on my results. Exactly what they would do based on my findings was unclear."

"You don't want to have more animals than the land can support," Jeff Cann of Fish and Game told me in 2012, of the importance of knowing the land's carrying capacity. "There are places where we can only sustain so many elk."

A 1998 seashore brochure described the elk at Tomales Point as living in "a virtual paradise," and said the herd had surpassed 500 animals. By contrast, Monterey County had four hundred to five hundred tule elk in 2012, ranging on 165,000 acres of the Fort Hunter Liggett military base—more than sixty-three times the space given to the Tomales Point population. Even so, local agencies were trying to reduce the herd.

"We don't want [the Monterey] population growing any bigger," Cann said. "We'd actually like to start tapering it off." His response to the size of the Tomales Point herd? "Wow."

There were just sixty elk in Point Reyes in 1986, but by 1992 that number had more than doubled to an estimated 160 animals. Seashore officials in the early 1990s wrote that their numbers were "soaring," and a 1992 Environmental Assessment of the elk considered reintroducing grizzly bears to the seashore, though that option was dismissed as "unfeasible." There was no mention of eliminating the ranches in the more recent study. Ultimately, as had been done with the fallow and axis deer since the 1970s, the seashore concluded that culling the elk was the only viable option. While elk elsewhere in the state were being shipped to other reserves when necessary, it was, and continues to be, forbidden to move elk from Point Reyes due to their exposure to Johne's disease. In 1992, ranger Bill Shook told the *Point Reyes Light* that the disease even made relocating the herd within the seashore impossible, although that would not prove to be the case after additional assessment. Furthermore, the 1992 Environmental Assessment said that if the elk were allowed to roam freely outside of the fenced reserve, "impacts to ranches will include forage competition, fence damage and crop depredation," not to mention the spread of Johne's, for which there is no reliable test.

But again, as was the case with the exotic deer, animal rights groups got wind of the proposed cull and objected. Still, the 2,600-acre preserve had an estimated 140-animal carrying capacity, and something needed to be done.

"I don't want the elk to eventually starve," then-superintendent John Sansing said. The park hired sharpshooters to cull the elk for a time, but stopped due to public outcry. In 1993, the lobby group begun by Beula Edmiston stepped in and began supplying the seashore with information on experimental programs in wildlife contraception, and said their fifty thousand members would pay for birth control. "[The tule elk] are an ideal population for contraception pilot study and future research," the group wrote to Sansing. The contraception program was tried briefly, but ultimately abandoned as expensive and unreliable. In 1993, there were 221 elk in the park. By 1997, there were 465. In 1998, the park decided to establish a second elk colony in the wilderness area.

A 2001 article in the San Francisco Chronicle titled "Running Out of Room to Roam" said that the exploding elk population was pushing the limit statewide. The seashore was similarly pressed, but the next year, park scientists said that the Tomales herd was now holding steady at 450 animals.

Mammals are not the only things that the park must seek to curate. Out past where the sedges and bunchgrass near Abbotts Lagoon give way to rolling dunes, endangered plants have been struggling to survive an onslaught of invasive European beachgrass. Familiar to residents and seashore visitors, the European grass has been making its glacial advance since it was first planted in the late 1800s, and crowding out everything in its path. This includes the Tidestrom's lupine, a plant that is delicate and low to the ground, with small purple flowers and soft, silvery leaves that feel like velvet.

From January to July 2011, the park bulldozed over a hundred acres of beachgrass-covered dunes, as part of a large-scale restoration experiment. All of the vegetation was churned deep under the sand, and the rhizomes, the stubborn root-like tendrils of the grass that can extend more than nine feet below the surface, were either destroyed by the excavators or pulled out. Without the grass's tenacious grasp, the dunes dissipate and blow flat, and the team of biologists then waited to see what native plants, if any, decided to take up residence there. But the process must be "natural," and scientists won't place the plants themselves. When I visited the site in 2012, small fields of the endangered Tidestrom's lupine had taken root and were blooming.

In fact, the majority of Point Reyes's grasses are not native, but were brought from the Mediterranean, both on purpose and accidentally, smuggled in the digestive systems of livestock. When the fallow deer grazed the hillsides, they were Mediterranean deer, eating Mediterranean grass. Many of America's most iconic plants and animals are not native. The ubiquitous tumbleweed of the American Southwest is a monumentally invasive species from Russia, a stowaway in nineteenth-century grain shipments. The apple tree, of course, is also not native to the Americas, even though nothing is more American than apple pie. In every sense we are a country of immigrants.

At the end of the nineteenth century, a group called the American Acclimatization Society took it upon itself to introduce to the United States every bird mentioned in the works of Shakespeare. His plays and sonnets contain some six hundred references to birds. This meant not just rarer birds like Juliet's nightingale or Romeo's lark, but Hamlet's sparrow and Hotspur's starling, two birds that would conquer North America. The starling, although mentioned just once by Hotspur in *Henry IV, Part I* (Act 1, Scene 3), is now one of the most numerous birds in the United States and Canada. A flock of between sixty and one hundred was released by the Society in Central Park in the late 1800s, and just over a century later there were estimated to be more than two hundred million of them, ranging from Florida to Alaska. Small but tough, they are the bruisers of the avian world (and perhaps a fitting bird for the Earl of Northumberland's hotheaded eldest son), and compete with native hole-nesters, including many Red-headed Woodpeckers, Purple Martins and Bluebirds, contributing to those species' decline. Starlings steal grain, wreck crops, and cost the United States $1 billion annually in farm damage. In 2012, the USDA killed nearly 1,500,000 of them via shooting and trapping, still less than 1 percent of the population. They are an otherwise impressive bird, with iridescent feathers and varied calls. Mozart had a pet starling that, when it died, he buried with great ceremony. Such are the perils of romanticism.

Other parks are less squeamish about managing their ungulates. Grand Teton National Park, for example, keeps its elk population in check through an annual public hunt, open to anyone with a valid Wyoming elk hunting license and a permit. But California's Bay Area is not a popular hunting region, and as previously stated, some locals were against killing the animals for any reason at all.

In 2007, Fred quickly found that his constituency was split on the issue. The park had recently announced the results of its more-than-decade-long assessment: It would eliminate all of the exotic deer from the park. NPS spokesperson John Dell'Osso described a fifteen-year phase out that he called "the final plan." By "final" he meant that it was no longer being debated, but that media picked up on and darkly referred to as "the final solution." Now that elk had been transported (individually airlifted, no less) to the wilderness area, there was a chance the exotic deer could also compete with the elk, a protected native animal. The Marin Conservation League and the Sierra Club both supported the exotic deer cull plan. The Audubon Society supported it too, saying that sterilization would be "more stressful" for the animals—although that depends on your definition of "stress," since death is, by and large, considered to be a pretty traumatic event.

The park estimated that there were around 1,500 exotic deer in the park in 2007. The solution, as communicated to the public, would be to capture eighty to one hundred females and inject them with a drug to prevent pregnancy. The rest of the deer would be shot, over a span of years. Still, the end result would be the same: eventually there would be no more fairytale deer in Point Reyes. Many locals were appalled. Point Reyes Station resident Trinka Marris spearheaded a campaign called Save the White Deer, putting pressure on the park to keep the exotic herd but reduce its numbers through non-lethal methods. The Humane Society, In Defense of Animals and WildCare formed a coalition called Friends of the White Deer, and advocated to stop the killing, too. A columnist for the *Marin Independent Journal*, Barry Tompkins, joked that a contraception program was unlikely to be effective, because how were the deer expected to be able to put on condoms? He suggested the park buy the deer televisions, so that they'd start watching *Dancing with the Stars* and stop having sex.

The cull project had a budget of $75,000, and word broke in early summer 2007 that the park would hire an outside contractor to get the job done. One of the companies said to have been up for the assignment was Prohunt Incorporated, a New Zealand–based firm that specialized in the elimination of feral animal populations. It had recently been paid $3.9 million to rid the Channel Islands of feral pigs. In 2006, a similar campaign was carried out on Isabela Island in the Galápagos, where feral goats had decimated local flora and were crowding out the famed tortoises.

There is no way around it: it is a brutal process, the total elimination of a population. Prohunt chief executive Norm Macdonald talked to the *San Francisco Chronicle* in 2007 about the "eradication ethic" and the firm's work with pigs on the Channel Islands.

"It's those little tiny piglets, the ones just big enough to survive on their own, that are the toughest to get," he said.

To root out the stragglers, firms like Prohunt use what is called "the Judas method," whereby a female animal is captured, sterilized, given estrogen boosters, and released with a tracking device.

"Then we drop them all over the range and let them lead us to the stragglers," Macdonald told the *Chronicle*.

The eradication programs were carried out from helicopters, with high-powered rifles, which suddenly made the thought of a park ranger singlehandedly shooting a deer every few weeks in the early morning hours seem like not such a big deal after all. There were roadside signs opposing the cull, and newspaper editorials, and town meetings. Even now, when I bring up the exotic deer extermination, Point Reyes park staff tend to get a little uncomfortable. It was just so unpopular. In July of 2007, California representative Lynn Woolsey got involved. She sent a letter to Superintendent Neubacher, urging him for a reprieve.

"There is no urgency to move forward," she wrote. But she was wrong: her very involvement signaled just how urgent it was. Trinka of Save the White Deer also hoped that time would prove to be on their side.

"It's going to be a fifteen-year project," she told a local newspaper, referring to the announced final plan. "So I think the public has plenty of time to put pressure on the park to use contraception in a larger role than they intend to. We're just beginning."

Unfortunately for advocates of the exotic deer, white or otherwise, the plan did not actually say that it would take them fifteen years to complete the eradication plan; it said that they *had* fifteen years in which to eliminate the deer, *not* that it needed to take them that long to do so. In August of 2007, the park hired a Connecticut-based deer management company called White Buffalo Inc., and things started to move very, very quickly.

The deer were shot from helicopters in droves. They were shot in the meadows, and on hillsides, and near beaches, and at the edge of forests. Unlike the native black-tailed deer, the exotics were more likely to appear in large family groups, and this was to the exterminator's advantage. The public was told that the "sharpshooter," a term that invokes the precision of a sniper, would instantly kill the deer with a shot to the head. But this did not seem to be the case in practice. Fred heard from distraught members of the EAC, many of them avid hikers, that white deer and other exotics were being found injured and dying with wounds to the abdomen. The fairytale deer staggered onto the roadsides, breaking, in their last confusion, the rule they had always kept of keeping out of sight. Being August, that spring's fawns were just old enough to survive on their own, and the sharpshooter had to be certain to kill all of these, too.

While some of the meat was donated to local homeless shelters and a California condor recovery program, much of it was left where it lay. Either the terrain was too rugged, or a mortally wounded animal managed to escape and die alone in some remote place, its body returning to the earth; foreign deer to feed the foreign grasses.

A small herd of female exotic deer remains in the park to this day. Some are sterilized, and still wear their Judas radio transmitters around their necks. They keep to a southern corner of the park, near where a Hindu foundation called Vedanta has maintained a religious retreat center since the 1940s. The center was granted a federal dispensation when the park formed around it, and is open to all faiths. It is also open to all deer, since it refused to allow the killing of any deer on its lands. Now the remaining fallow and axis deer shelter there. There are no fawns now, only the group of remaining females; the ghosts of the ghost deer. While it's possible there are still more white deer hiding elsewhere in the National Seashore, there hasn't been a sighting of a stag in years.

# 9

## REINFORCEMENTS

T HE STRETCH OF road from Point Reyes Station to the little seaside hamlet of Marshall is, I'm convinced, one of the loveliest drives in the world. It follows the eastern shore of Tomales Bay up towards where it meets the Pacific Ocean, at Bodega. In the very early morning, the world as seen from that drive is all blue, in electric shades of cobalt and cerulean, with fog softening the horizon line so that it isn't always clear where the blue of water stops and the blue of sky begins. The trees are sculpted smooth by wind, like topiary, and in the summer the roadsides sing with wild sweet peas, radish and mustard, their blooms lavender, bright pink and yellow. Drive up it on any weekend day from April to October and you'll see that the two biggest oyster operations in Tomales Bay—Hog Island Oyster Co. and Tomales Bay Oyster Company—are clearly booming. The narrow highway near both is usually lined with cars. Visitors often don't seem to realize they are on a major thoroughfare and not a sleepy country lane, as they snap Instagram photos in the middle of the road and park their Zipcars dangerously close to the whirring traffic of speeding local teenagers and trundling milk trucks.

If you continue up past both oyster farms and take a turn at the abandoned Catholic church, you'll eventually reach Barinaga Ranch. It is a sheep's milk cheese operation in the Basque tradition and the home of one Corey Goodman. With close-cropped hair that was once dark but is rapidly graying, Corey has a smallish, spare frame and intense brown eyes so dark they are almost black. If you're even the least bit aware of the Drakes Bay Oyster controversy, you will have heard about Corey Goodman before. The *New York Times* has called him both the "avenging angel" of the oyster farm, as well as the National Park Service's own Inspector Javert. It's unclear if the reporter in question meant the latter nickname to be flattering or not, since, as anyone familiar with *Les Misérables* can tell you, Javert is not the hero of that story.

It all started one Saturday morning in April of 2007, when Corey got a phone call out of the blue, asking him to take a look at a scientific report put out by the Point Reyes National Seashore. It concerned one of the local oyster farms. It was not one of his Marshall neighbors, the oyster farms he was more familiar with, but the one across the bay on the Point: Drakes Bay Oyster Company. Corey had never met the owners before, he says, and didn't know them from Adam. Still he was intrigued.

Corey is a scientist, but not just that. He founded two public biotechnology companies, Exelixis and Renovis, as well as a San Francisco venture capital firm called venBio, of which he is a partner. His stock holdings from Exelixis alone were significant enough that they allowed him to buy his acreage in Marshall and build both Barinaga Ranch and his dream home, not far from where he and his wife had kept a waterfront vacation property since 1993. The ranch is run by his wife,

Marcia Barinaga, who modeled it after the traditions of her Basque ancestors. Her cheeses regularly win awards, and by 2007 she and Corey were already well-liked and well-respected by their neighbors, many of them struggling sixth- or seventh-generation ranchers. If there was a problem in the community, both Corey and Marcia were usually quick to help out.

When I visited the Goodman-Barinaga house in 2012, it was a late afternoon in July, and a battalion of ashen fog was already coming in off the ocean and beginning to roll between the hills. The house is new construction, and though humble and tasteful in design, it neverthe-less glows with an art and sturdiness in the way that only the expertly made houses of the rich can do. If the beautiful wood floors did *not* have radiant heat, it looked like the kind of place that *would* have radi-ant heat floors. Many of the walls were decorated with oil paintings of local landscapes by famous or semi-famous Bay Area artists, and the guest room (the door was open) is appointed in such a way that it looks more like a boutique hotel room than a room in a regular house. It's the kind of house that can easily make you wish that the people living in it would adopt you. Outside the large picture windows, Marcia's sheep grazed in the fields, and a few large, peaceful Great Pyrenees dogs stood stoic and magnificent as Luck Dragons in the encroaching mists, nobly guarding their charges. The day I visited, the sheep were just coming in towards the house from over the pastures. In the distance, Tomales Bay was visible, steely gray but for patches of bright sun falling on the water through gaps in the clouds. Corey's office was clean and tasteful, with lots of exposed wood and a shelf for his scientific awards. His desk sat under another large window that overlooked more rolling golden hills, and more sheep, and more dignified sheepdogs.

The villages of West Marin are all unincorporated areas, not official towns, and thus have no mayor or mayors to speak of. From time
to time, a citizen who is particularly active, beloved or charismatic will
be affectionately dubbed the "mayor" of somewhere. Because of the
alliteration, and because it is particularly small and remote (the road
sign says POPULATION 50, though this is no longer true), Marshall is
a popular place for people to say that they are the mayor. However,
County Supervisor Steve Kinsey is truly the closest thing that the towns
of the region have to a mayor, and he takes the concerns of his constituency seriously. Fred always used to say to me that Kinsey kept
his focus on the three F's: farms, family and fish—by which he meant
watershed and fisheries restoration. He has a BA in architecture from
Arizona State University and bears a passing resemblance to an older
Bill Paxton. In many ways, he *is* local government.

It was Kinsey who reached out to Corey about the oyster farm.
Being a venture capitalist with a background in neuroscience, Corey
had never studied the topics mentioned in the scientific report in
question before. But Kinsey knew that Corey was not only brilliant,
but possessed both influence and an interest in public policy. Indeed,
what Corey may have lacked in marine biology experience, he more
than made up for in clout. His curriculum vitae is nineteen pages
long. With a BS from Stanford and a PhD from UC Berkeley, Corey
was an assistant and then associate professor of neuroscience at
Stanford from 1979 to 1987, and a professor at UC Berkeley from
1988 to 2007. He was elected a member of the National Academy
of Sciences, the American Academy of Arts and Sciences, and the
American Philosophical Society. His CV lists 193 academic papers
of which he is coauthor, with titles like "Analysis of gene expression

during neurite outgrowth and regeneration" and "Heterogeneity in synaptic transmission along a Drosophila larval motor axon." A drosophila is a fruit fly, and for years that is what Corey studied: the neuroscience of fruit flies. There is also considerable ink given to locusts, or rather locust brains, and grasshoppers. Lots of grasshoppers. In fact, the phrase "grasshopper embryos" appears in his publication titles with startling frequency. Sometimes the papers covered both grasshopper embryos *and* fruit flies, as well as a lot about cell signaling pathways and "growth cones" and "ablating axons." In 2007, at the age of fifty-six, Corey had just been hired by Pfizer, the world's largest drug company, to overhaul their global research and development model. They made him president of the Biotherapeutics and Bioinnovation Center (BBC), launched the same year Kinsey invited him to weigh in on the oyster farm. "That's the sort of thing that gets me going," Corey told *Nature Biotechnology* of the Pfizer appointment. "I did it in my academic career. People said 'you can't do a genetic screen for brain wiring and axon guidance.' But we did it."

Unmistakably, there is something of the rebel in Corey. He is an innovator by trade, is used to getting a lot done and by all appearances does not like for things to stand in his way. He speaks with precise diction and a soft voice. He likes to use casual language in a way that can be a little jarring coming from a man who has written regularly in a distinctly erudite academic style about such things as "Slit and Robo proteins in midline commissural axon guidance." For example, he would later refer to adult female harbor seals as "moms" and their pups as "little boys and girls," even in correspondences to high-ranking government scientists. He can come across as deceptively unassuming at first, and I say this is "deceptive" only because Corey is one of the most passionately motivated people I have ever met. Wrangling a succinct narrative out of him can be something of a challenge. His brain is clearly chock-full at all times with information, which he is happy to send your way with machine-gun-like intensity.

The first time I interviewed Corey was over the phone from New York, before heading out to California to work for the *Point Reyes Light*. My travel had been delayed and I was trying to write an article for the paper long distance. Corey called me and proceeded to talk for two and a half hours straight. There was no opportunity to ask questions or interrupt. I had the phone squeezed between my shoulder and my ear the whole time as I typed furiously, a posture that was growing increasingly painful. By the end of the conversation, when I told him I really had to go, I was looking at thirty pages of typed notes on my laptop. The day before we spoke, he'd sent me hundreds of pages of documents via email to read as prep, including elaborate PowerPoint presentations that he himself had made. This was all for an eight-hundred-word article. It would not be the last conversation we had that went that way. From talking to other reporters who have covered the oyster farm controversy, I understand that this is a fairly standard Corey Goodman experience. Said one seasoned reporter from a major national newspaper to me: "I'm afraid of him."

When Kinsey first asked Corey if he would take a look at the park's science, he thought it would be a fun distraction for a week, maybe two. He had no idea his involvement would spool out into a seven-year saga, or that he'd become the oyster farm's fiercest defender, pitting himself against other scientists, the environmental community, and the United States government.

AFTER THE SALE of the Johnson Oyster Company was finalized at the start of 2005, Kevin Lunny and his family got to work on their new farm. As he later told *Marin* magazine, he was excited to invest in cleaning up the operation with the hopes that the park service would see his hard work and extend the lease. But there was a wrinkle to this plan right away. When the park presented him with his new Special Use Permit at the start of their very first year, it was different than the lease for the Johnsons, which he'd seen. The new document contained a provision that he must clear out after 2012. The Johnsons' agreement had contained language that Kevin and his lawyers thought was the key to getting his lease extended. This new lease had no such clause. When he complained, Don Neubacher told Kevin that this was because the Johnsons' permit was drafted in 1972, before the federal wilderness designation in 1976. Don explained that the previous lease had been from before the park "matured," and what the Lunnys were being asked to sign was now completely standard. Also, he'd explicitly told Kevin that they were not going to renew the lease. The park drew Kevin's attention to the solicitor's opinion of 2004, which they'd also shared before the sale was final, stating the estuary must become wilderness after 2012. Kevin didn't sign it. Instead, some squabbles commenced over details on the property; road maintenance, and whether or not an older land survey was more or less accurate than a new one that Lunny himself had commissioned—things that put off the signing of the new Special Use Permit that said the Lunnys would have to leave in 2012.

In June, Kevin emailed Don and asked that they add the following language to the permit:

Permittee and Permitter acknowledge and recognize that [ . . . ]
the Reservation of Use and Occupancy [ . . . ] does allow for
issuance of a special use permit for the continued occupancy of
the property . . . beyond the 2012 term, at the discretion of the
Permitter.

Don told Kevin that this wasn't going to happen. Again, this was
due to the wilderness designation, and the fact that the legislation came
after the initial drafting of the Johnsons' lease. The park sent Kevin a
second draft of the Special Use Permit, containing the following clause
as added by the solicitor's office:

The Permittee acknowledges that they have been informed
about the Congressional designation of the adjacent Drakes
Estero area as potential wilderness. The Permittee also
acknowledges that they have been provided the National Park
Service legal opinion dated February 26, 2004, regarding the
future of the potential wilderness area and legal options after
the expiration of the 1.43 acres of land under the 2012 Use and
Occupancy Permit.

Two days later, Kevin faxed the permit back to the park with that
language deleted.

The Lunnys continued setting up their oyster operations based
on the Johnsons' infrastructure, and were already the largest oyster
farm in the state. But they didn't have a permit. Later that year, Kevin
started meeting regularly with Supervisor Steve Kinsey, to see if he
could help. At the end of December 2005, Kevin received a third draft

of the Special Use Permit from the park, containing a space for the "Permittee's Initials" next to the following text:

> The permittee and permitter acknowledge and recognize that extension of this permit is not currently authorized beyond the expiration of the reservation of use and occupancy referenced in the deed from Johnson Oyster Company to the United States of America. [ . . . ] This Reservation of Use and Occupancy expires on November 9, 2012. The permittee acknowledges that they have been informed about the Congressional designation of Drakes Estero as potential wilderness. The permittee also acknowledges that they have been provided the Office of the Solicitor legal opinion [ . . . ] regarding the future of the potential wilderness area.

Both sides were starting to realize that this wasn't going to be as easy as they had previously thought.

EARLY THE NEXT year, Kevin began a project that he thought would strengthen his claim to the estuary as a worthy steward of water and land: he decided to begin a "native oyster restoration" project. Now, with the research well and truly considered, there is little to no evidence that "native" oysters were ever historically present in Drakes Estero, let alone plentiful, but Kevin didn't know that. There was a popular myth that "native" oysters had been abundant in the San Francisco Bay until the Gold Rush. A small number of prehistoric Olympia oyster shells were found inside shell middens near the estero, i.e. the Olympias, but carbon dating has revealed that those shells varied in age between 1,200 and 2,200 years old—more on that later. These scant shell samples could have come from the estero as living oysters, perhaps during a time when conditions were different, or the shells themselves could have been traded from tribes living further north, where the native oysters were known to be abundant. After all, the Miwoks used seashells as currency, and it isn't impossible that these were simply foreign mint. Because oysters require hard substrate to attach to, the soft-bottomed estuary was a natural habitat for clams, but an unlikely one for oysters. Even John Stillwell Morgan had been obliged to create most if not all of his oyster beds artificially by destroying the existing tideland habitat in San Francisco Bay with landfill, so he could grow them the way he had seen it done in the rocky-bottomed East. Now, some newer Olympia oyster shells *have* been found in the estuary. But both the original Drakes Bay Oyster Company of the 1930s and the Johnson Oyster Company experimented with Olympias at one point or another. There are no shells that have been found that are proven to be from the period after as late as 800 AD and before their introduction by European settlers. None of the commercial oyster operations in Drakes Estero ever harvested native oysters, but rather, as previously mentioned, they failed to get eastern oysters to thrive before landing on the hardier Pacifics, and experimented with the smaller, less lucrative Washington Olympias here and there. The newer Olympia shells could easily have come from these more recent efforts. Besides, John Stillwell Morgan, who was well familiar with the coastal character of the Bay Area, had failed to find any native oysters anywhere near San Francisco or Point Reyes—not in Tomales Bay, and likely not in Drakes Estero, either, though he did not deign to mention it.

It was only due to the aggressive marketing attempts of John Stillwell Morgan's competitors that the idea of an abundant "native California oyster" in the Bay Area had persisted despite its fallacy. Some of this confusion can be blamed on the terminology used at the time on maps of the San Francisco Bay made in the nineteenth century. There are maps that show the beds of the "eastern" oysters versus the "native" oysters. But the "native" oysters were actually the *Olympias*, shipped down from Washington State, being stored in the bay along with the eastern ones from New York and New Jersey. Morgan's records confirm this. However, a quick perusal of these maps would easily lead one to believe that native oysters were once plentiful in the Bay Area, while deeper research proves definitively that this was not the case. All of the oysters in the nineteenth-century San Francisco Bay were imported.

Around the country since the mid-1990s, scientists were beginning to experiment with oyster reef restoration. In many areas where oysters *were* native, the loss of the oyster reef habitat was the harbinger of doom for many a waterway. Since most people who gave a thought to oysters at all were under the (false) impression that oyster reefs had once been a natural part of the San Francisco Bay prior to Morgan's efforts, it made sense to begin "restoring" those reefs, too. Oyster restoration was becoming trendy. After all, some Olympia stragglers have managed to survive both the many decades since Morgan brought their ancestors down the coast, and the bay's less-than-ideal conditions. Beginning in 2006, groups like Save the Bay began working on various oyster restoration projects. The National Oceanic and Atmospheric Administration (NOAA) invested $50,000 in an oyster restoration project for the San Francisco Bay, and hired MACTEC Engineering and Consulting, Inc., to implement the project. When still in the planning stages, one of the MACTEC biologists got in touch with Kevin. If they were going to plant oysters in the bay, they would need to "rebuild" oyster reefs using oyster shells for the new, baby Olympia oysters to attach to. As the largest oyster farm in the state, volume-wise, and one of the few local places that offered oysters out-of-shell, Drakes Bay Oyster Company was a natural choice to approach for shells to use as cultch. Kevin quickly got excited about the idea of putting "native" oysters in Drakes Estero, either to sell or just to have growing there. But this idea, too, quickly ran into a snag.

Meanwhile, Sarah Allen, seal counter and beach walker, had come a long way since her days as a Point Reyes Bird Observatory administrator with a bachelor's degree in conservation. She was less lanky than she had been in the 1980s, but no less earnest. Her thick brown hair had now begun to turn gray and was more likely to be held back in a ponytail than with a bandana. While still working on her research with the observatory, she received her master's from UC Berkeley, writing her thesis on the movement and activity patterns of Point Reyes harbor seals. The dissertation for her PhD, also from UC Berkeley, was on the distribution and abundance of marine birds and mammals in the Gulf of the Farallones and surrounding waters. For eight out of the ten years between 1990 and 2000 she spent the months of May and June on the NOAA research vessel the *David Starr Jordan*, conducting seabird and marine mammal surveys. In 1995 she began work as an ecologist with the Point Reyes National Seashore, and two years later was appointed science advisor for the park. Eventually, the word "senior" was added to that title. Active in local community organizations, she could frequently be found leading educational tours of the now thriving elephant seal colony. She loved talking about the marine life of the region as much as ever, and whether she was needed in supplying technical guidance to local environmental efforts, or if they just needed another pair of hands to pick up trash from along the shore—Sarah was there. She sometimes still conducted research away as well, and from 2000 to 2001 she served as a research assistant studying penguins in Antarctica. She was still passionate about preserving the local environment, too. In a video from one of her lectures, she describes her grief at the ecological degradation she had witnessed in her lifetime alone.

"When I was a child—and I'm not that old!—I remember when I was a child in San Geronimo Creek watching thousands of salmon migrating up a narrow stream, a narrow tributary," she said with emotion. "And to me, it's stunning that there are so few now. It's like death by a thousand cuts. And marine mammals are one of those cuts."

By the time a marine biologist from MACTEC requested permission from the park to use shells from Drakes Bay Oyster Company for oyster "restoration," Sarah had been walking the beaches of Point Reyes and studying its marine animal life in some official capacity for nearly thirty years. But park staff were disturbed by the new oyster farm owner's clear efforts to get them to allow DBOC to stay. Sarah called the MACTEC biologist, Robert Abbott, and told him that not only would a "restoration" of oysters in the estuary be impossible, but that he couldn't even have the oyster farm's shells. He later did obtain permission to take the shells, but in a phone conference with both Sarah and Don Neubacher that April, they explained to him why the Olympia introduction was not something that the park wanted.

Neubacher said that since the Wilderness Act required the estuary to be given full wilderness status (or "revert" to wilderness, as he put it), he did not want to do anything that might encourage the Lunnys to stay past 2012. According to a government report filed later, he also gave Abbott a "heads up" that Kevin was "not good with money" and was late paying his bills. Further details of this "warning" were not supplied.

The previous spring, the park had sponsored a UC Davis study of eelgrass in the estuary, conducted by grad students but overseen by Dr. Deborah Elliott-Fisk, with help from Sarah. In March of 2005, a draft of the report entitled "Drakes Estero Assessment of Oyster Farming Final Completion Report" was released, though not published. Despite being labeled "final," it would undergo revisions. In it, the grad students assert that the oyster company caused "no significant or negative impacts" to sedimentation or water quality in the estuary, and that introduced organisms, aka non-native species, were "not definitively found." It also said that the oyster racks had "no pronounced impacts" on the eelgrass beds, which existed both under and away from the racks and was "an incredibly rich habitat type." That report was soon revised and published two months later, in May, under the same title and with the same comment about the richness of the eelgrass both under and away from the racks.

The new version, however, did mention invasive species, noting that a non-native species of tunicate or "sea squirt" called *Didemnum lahillei* was present as "a fouling community," and had likely been introduced through oyster farming. The report thus concluded that "oyster mariculture has had an impact on the marine fish and invertebrates of Drakes Estero." Elliott-Fisk later told government investigators that the change was made after speaking with experts about non-native species and realizing how "bad" they were. Although researchers could not definitively attribute the invasive species to the oyster farm, the fact that non-natives existed in the estero was significant enough to document in the revised report, she said. This is true. The tunicates were and are present in the estuary, as a kind of orange, underwater slime mold that clings to the oysters and their racks, and over the years their presence only increased. It has been nicknamed "marine vomit" by environmentalists and it plagues bays from British Columbia to Ireland, never without complaint. Like oysters it requires hard substrate of some kind, and so without the presence of mariculture it would have nothing to cling to.

In early 2006, Kevin received a $10,000 grant from the National Marine Fisheries Service to help fund his "native oyster restoration" of Drakes Estero. But the money was withdrawn when the park would not approve the project.

"This is just a real disappointment," Kevin told Peter Jamison, a reporter at the *Point Reyes Light*. He said the proposed research had "no particular financial advantage."

"We're not going to harvest these guys. But to learn about them is big. I'm not sure why that's unacceptable to the park," he griped.

In his grant proposal, Kevin suggested that "restoring" the native oysters could lead to a permit reprieve: "Increased use of the oyster farm for research, education, and restoration activities may facilitate negotiation with the National Park Service to keep the oyster farm operational beyond 2012," he wrote in the proposal. But not only did Don not want to encourage Kevin in that vein, park scientists were rightly unconvinced that introducing Olympia oysters would be any kind of restoration at all. Sarah pointed out to the *Light* that oyster shells were not found in any significant quantity in the park prior to their introduction by European-Americans, and were unlikely to have grown in the estuary.

"Any restoration that we target for Drakes Estero would not have native oysters as a keystone restoration component," she told the paper.

"I thought the park would be thrilled to have this research going on," Kevin said.

Then on May 18 the *Point Reyes Light* published an article claiming that the Drakes Bay Oyster Company had been scientifically proven to have little impact on the estuary. It was based on the unrevised March version of the Elliott-Fisk report, which the paper's energetic new editor had obtained. Sarah was annoyed.

"Check out the article," she wrote in an email to Deborah Elliott-Fisk. "As is usual, I am misquoted and the article is heavily slanted pro oyster. I stated to them that when your study occurred that the oyster farming was at its lowest level in 30 years, talked about other invasive species introduced by oyster farming, and about the major source for sediment being from oyster feces based on a [U.S. Geological Survey] study, but he chose not to include that information." The USGS study she was referring to was the one conducted by Roberto Anima, when he had helped her net harbor seals for tracking in the 1980s while studying pollutants and eelgrass in the estuary.

The park was already starting to have problems with the advocates of the non-native deer, and knew they needed to take corrective public relations action. Thus, Sarah was instructed to begin work on a report to support the government's decision to close the oyster farm down. Kevin, his family and supporters, on the other hand, were already in love with the operation and would continue their efforts to stay. All three Lunny children were involved in oyster farming now. That June they graduated from high school—one step closer to carrying on the agricultural tradition begun by their great-grandfather in 1947 when he quit the timber industry.

In July, Don Neubacher went on the local radio station and announced that Sarah was working on a report to counter the assertions made in the *Point Reyes Light*. He said it would list "long-term, serious impacts" caused by oyster farming, and opined that having a commercial operation inside "pristine" wilderness was "just intuitively negative." Sarah also spoke, focusing on the fact that the invasive tunicate could change fish diversity and abundance. As usual, her attentions were on science, not policy.

. Sarah spent the summer working on the report, and in it there is evidence of her deep love for the place itself. It describes its flora and fauna, the pickleweed, arrowgrass and saltgrass, and the abundance of birds—ten thousand to one hundred thousand of which are present in the estuary at any given time—including Osprey, White and Brown Pelicans, Peregrine Falcons and the Western Snowy Plover. Other species occurring in large numbers, she wrote, were the Caspian Tern, the Ruddy Duck, the Bufflehead, and the Least Sandpiper. It was one of the few places that black Brant geese overwinter. Harbor seals, sea lions and elephant seals were present as well. Although live whales did not venture past the estuary's mouth, several dead ones had washed in and decomposed, including an adult male sperm whale. The report also explained the wilderness designation, the park's version of the situation with the oyster farm, and included two main negative impacts. It said that oyster feces—and yes, oysters do have feces or "pseudofeces" as they are called, since some of the substance is in fact regurgitated and not digested—were a primary source of sedimentation in the estero. The report also stated that the activity of oyster workers scared away seals, and that one sub-colony, on a particular sandbar, had produced 80 percent fewer pups one year, likely due to the activity of oyster workers. The report also pointed out the dire nature of ocean conservation in general, and said that *all* fish species worldwide were expected to collapse within the next fifty years if current trends persisted.

That fall, when seeking input on the report from fellow biologists, Sarah misquoted Roberto Anima's study. According to a government report, a colleague said she had misunderstood or misinterpreted Anima's eelgrass work.

"Oh, I didn't know that," Sarah purportedly told him once he discovered her mistake the following spring, but she did not change the language in the report that autumn. On October 23 2006, a draft of the report was made available in hard copy at park headquarters, and Don gave a copy to the chair of the local Sierra Club group, a man by the name of Gordon Bennett, the founder of a prominent natural foods company, Westbrae Natural. The report was called "Drakes Estero: A Sheltered Wilderness Estuary." It was seven pages long, included photos, and was more like an extended informational brochure than a scientific paper, intended for public consumption. A few days later, Gordon took it upon himself to distribute copies of the text, on site at Drakes Bay Oyster Company, to attendees of an agricultural tour being given by the Main Agricultural Land Trust. Naturally, all hell broke loose in the pro-oyster farm faction.

On December 4, Sarah wrote to an NPS fisheries biologist by the name of John Wullschleger, asking for his advice:

I have been in a dilemma about the Drakes Estero report. We were going to have it revised because there were recommendations in the final draft that we were concerned about but the report was released to the oyster farmer and a few others (in error) before it was completed and peer-reviewed. [ . . . ] We could submit the report as is if you feel alright with that. I also believe that it would be politically difficult to revise it now since it is out already. The oyster operator has been misusing some of the information out of the report to support his position. We have produced a follw [sic] up document summarizing the negative effects of the oyster operation (I attach for your reference). . . .

Wullschleger would later tell government investigators that he was "concerned" about Elliott-Fisk's study, and what Sarah was doing with it. He suggested that perhaps Point Reyes National Seashore was "aiming to find out a little too much in a relatively short period of time with a small amount of money."

IN FEBRUARY OF 2007, NPS uploaded the "Sheltered Wilderness Estuary" report to its website under the section on "Park News," and on April 1st the media battle over the oyster farm began in earnest with an article called "Ollie 'Erster vs. Smokey the Bear."

"I had wanted to interview [Kevin Lunny] for quite a while, ever since I heard he had purchased the place from Johnson's with a warning that the Park Service wanted to close off aquaculture in the Bay by 2012," wrote Jeanette Pontacq in the local *Coastal Post*. She went on to say that the Johnsons had left several hundred thousand dollars' worth of environmental mess to clean up, and that the Lunnys' decision to buy the place was an "early present" for the park. She said that the Lunnys had not signed any statement promising to decamp in 2012, but failed to mention that they had been repeatedly presented with just such a document but refused to sign it.

A few days after the article came out, county supervisor Steve Kinsey met with Neubacher at park headquarters. Lunny later said Kinsey warned him that Neubacher was "crazed" and that he was "going to war" against the oyster farm, wanting it out *even before* 2012. Speaking to government investigators, Kinsey confirmed that he and his aide met with Neubacher but "could not recall" whether he told Lunny that Neubacher was "crazed." (The term most frequently used to describe the place where Don had assembled information on the oyster farm was "the war room.") However, Kinsey did feel it was accurate to say that Neubacher was "very upset" and "seemed obsessed" with proving the oyster farm was harming seals and eelgrass. According to Kinsey, Neubacher made "strong environmental accusations" against Kevin and made reference to "environmental felonies." Again, as oyster farm advocate Corey Goodman likes to stress, that would mean jail time for Kevin. Kinsey's aide, Liza Crosse, on the other hand, recalled that Neubacher was "entirely courteous" during the meeting, but was surprised by his "vehemence" about Kevin's supposed disregard for the environment. Kinsey confirmed that he told Kevin that Neubacher intended to shut DBOC down. Although Kinsey did not specifically remember the exact words spoken, he said the "tenor" of the meeting left no doubt in his mind that Neubacher intended to shut DBOC down prior to 2012. (Neubacher later conceded that he told Kinsey about some criminal violations he believed had occurred related to the family's lease on G Ranch, not the oyster farm.)

A few weeks later, Kinsey called and got Corey Goodman involved. Before that, in mid-April, Sarah and her colleagues began more closely documenting disturbances by the oyster workers in the estero. On April 13 she wrote that she observed an "oyster operator" who was "clearly disturbing and displacing seals." On April 23 she made another entry, noting that oyster bags had been placed on seal haul-out sites, and that oyster farm workers were disturbing seals. She also wrote about the presence of a white boat with two people in it, poling through an eelgrass bed. When the boat went by a group of seals, all but one of the animals flushed into the water. She wrote that the boat landed and two men then "got off the boat, one taller in a green slicker and another in yellow slicker pants." Both reports note the specific start and stop times of each phase of the "disturbances."

A few days prior to the latter trip report, Kevin Lunny wrote to the United States government and requested that the Department of the Interior do an investigation into the actions of Point Reyes National Seashore. He also hired a D.C. lobbyist named Dave Weiman, who ran an operation called Agricultural Resources. (When I asked Dave years later if he was paid to advocate on behalf of the Lunnys, he demurred at first. When pressed, he admitted that yes, he was, but it was "not very much and not very often.")

IN MAY, THE County Board of Supervisors held a hearing on the oyster company issue. Normally Fred would have attended, having started his tenure at EAC that January, but the business with the fallow and axis deer and other local issues kept him away. The purpose of the meeting was to consider the adoption of a draft letter to federally elected representatives from the board, supporting the continued operation of the oyster farm. Essentially, Kinsey sought unanimous support from the board to write a letter to Senator Dianne Feinstein, asking her to step in. Sarah gave a presentation.

"My name is Sarah Allen, and I'm a scientist with the National Park Service," she began. "And, more specifically, I've been studying the ecology of Drakes Estero for almost thirty years. I completed my master's thesis on the harbor seals in Drakes Estero, so I have some familiarity with that population." This was an understatement, as there was likely no one else in the world more familiar with the Point Reyes harbor seals of the last thirty years than Sarah. Later during the presentation, she stated, "The damage of the commercial oyster operations on Drakes Estero is more easily documented, because the park service has over twenty-five years of continuous monitoring data from Drakes Estero." However, Sarah collected the majority of that seal data while at UC Berkeley or with the Point Reyes Bird Observatory, so it was technically not the park's data. It was only the park's "data" in that the data was Sarah's, and she worked for the park.

Then it was Corey Goodman's turn. He immediately began poking holes in the "Sheltered Wilderness Estuary" report, and correctly raised the issue that Sarah had misstated Anima's work. She responded that this was her first realization of this, and when she later reviewed Anima's studies, she realized she had "blundered." She told government investigators later that she "felt like she let Neubacher down by her mistake." Neubacher claimed that this was the first he had heard of any problems with the "Sheltered Wilderness Estuary" report, when Goodman quoted Anima's work. Neubacher later said he "honestly didn't think it was a big deal" that the report indicated that oyster feces was the primary source of sedimentation, but nevertheless agreed to fix it.

Later, Sarah said she was "devastated" by the error.

"It was just an honest mistake on her part," Don said in her defense.

That May, Sarah oversaw the installment of several wildlife observation cameras in the estuary. The projects were run by grad students of UC San Francisco biologist Ellen Hines, and they were trained on areas where oyster workers might disturb harbor seals. The oyster farm and members of the public were not notified about the placement of the cameras.

ON THE 15TH of that month, a week after the humiliating meeting, Sarah finally spoke directly with her old colleague Roberto Anima. She telephoned and asked him to read the two relevant local newspaper articles in which his work was referenced. He was not only "not happy," as he told her at the time, but he later said he was "ticked off" by Sarah's portrayal of his research, and did not feel she offered a good justification for inaccurately referencing his work.

*But hadn't he voiced concern about oysters contributing to sediment in a portion of Drakes Estero?* She wanted to know. According to Anima, on the phone Sarah tried to justify her actions by telling him about the oyster company feud. He said he just wished she'd let him review the work before she published it with his name on it.

"I know, Roberto," she replied. "This is getting ugly."

Anima conceded that Sarah could quote him as saying that the oyster operation played an "important" role in sedimentation, but not a "major" one. He also sent her an email.

Hi Sarah. After reading the Kinsey-Goodman Testimony and the statements made in the Pt. Reyes Light, and the Coastal

Post, I really can't support the statements made that: 'Research has identified oyster feces as the primary source of sediment in the Estero, and this sediment smother [sic] native species.' or 'Furthermore oyster feces add sediment to the eelgrass beds of the Estero. Researchers from the U.S. Geological Survey identified the feces of oysters—as much as a metric ton per 60 meter square oyster raft—as the primary source of sedimentation, which degrades eelgrass habitat and its ability to support abundant marine life.' After re-reading my thesis I do suggest that the quiet water environment of the upper parts of the estero could allow for the deposition of silt-sized material in the form of feces and pseudofeces produced by oysters. And that once deposited the material is resistant to erosion. I end by stating that more research is needed to ascertain what amount of silt-sized material is being produced by oysters in the lagoon. I did not directly study the amounts or the areal extent of the deposition of feces in the estero. The statements made in the thesis were based on observations and literature sited to support the observations. No hard evidence of the effects of oysters on fine sediment accumulation were made. I wish I could have been more help. —Roberto

At some point in the next two months, this email was deleted from Sarah's computer. Her response, which began "many thanks for your quick reply," was not deleted, however, and would later be referred to by Corey as "the smoking gun."

This was the summer right before the exotic deer extermination, and park staff were busy. Still, they had even more work on their hands when Corey Goodman submitted his first Freedom of Information Act request, asking for all of the seal data that Sarah had mentioned at the hearing, and a number of other documents. He requested harbor seal monitoring data pertaining to Drakes Estero from 1973 through the "day you provide the data" in 2007. It was clear already that Corey wanted to get to the bottom of all this. He was hooked.

In May the park uploaded a revised version of the "Sheltered Wilderness Estuary" report, with Anima's requested corrections. But then Senator Dianne Feinstein got involved. After being contacted by the Marin County Board of Supervisors, she called a private meeting at the Olema Inn with Corey, senior park staff (but not Sarah), and the Lunnys. Afterwards, and at her request, the "Sheltered Wilderness Estuary" report was removed from the park website altogether and replaced with a notice saying "acknowledgment of errors." In August, with the whirr of White Buffalo Inc.'s extermination helicopters in the air, the investigation set in motion by Kevin back in April began.

Sarah's office was searched by federal investigators from the Inspector General's office. In a file marked "communications" they found the deleted email from Anima, which the park had failed to give to Corey in his FOIA earlier that summer. Investigators then began interviewing some seventy individuals from the park service, scientists and members of the community. They interviewed Fred. It seemed like they were interviewing everybody. Things were starting to get ugly, indeed. This continued through the fall. It wasn't the first time that Feinstein had gotten involved in agricultural issues in Point Reyes. One rancher, who was a proud Republican and active in politics as pertained to his family business, told me that he got on so well with Feinstein, Senator Barbara Boxer and Representative Lynn Woolsey that he jokingly referred to them as his "Democratic girlfriends." But Senator Feinstein not only got involved with the Drakes Bay Oyster issue, she even went to meet with the Lunnys in person at their home. Still, even with her guidance, the Lunnys and the park could not reach an agreement on the oyster farm permit. The park wouldn't allow a permit that didn't explicitly mention the solicitor's decision to return the acreage to wilderness after 2012, and Kevin wouldn't sign anything that included it.

In January of 2008, Kevin wrote a letter to Jonathan Jarvis, then-director of NPS's Pacific West Region.

"Something is terribly wrong," he wrote. "Instead of resolving our differences, you are working overtime to make them worse. For that, our hearts are heavy. We are being treated unjustly. Our family is intimidated and fearful for our future and our financial survival."

"Kevin," Jarvis replied. "You have stated many times that you would like to go back to a former time, when the relations with the NPS were cordial. I agree. Unfortunately, this issue now involves attorneys, reporters, DC lobbyists, environmental and agricultural constituency groups, elected officials, scientists, investigators, state regulators and now the highest scientific body in the United States."

He urged Kevin that the best way to bring the relationship back around would be to negotiate in good faith.

"We have attached a permit that meets all the points we discussed with the Senator and it is my hope you will sign it," Jarvis wrote. "With your signature, we can move this back to an on-going operation and collaborative relationship."

With advice from Senator Dianne Feinstein, Kevin Lunny decided to sign.

# 10

# THE WORST-CASE SCENARIO

T HE SIGNING OF a Special Use Permit for the Drakes Bay Oyster
Company did not, after all, bring the conflict to a close or diffuse
the air of hostility that was rapidly seeping into the community. If anything, things were only getting started. The permit contained a number
of specific stipulations regarding how the oyster farm was to operate so
as not to disturb seals or harm eelgrass.

"A couple of these conditions are a little overdone and a little over-
protective," Kevin told the *Point Reyes Light* just two days after signing. "We just want the option for those to be adjusted once the actual
situation is studied."

At least the oyster farm was no longer operating illegally in a
national park.

"Knowing all along that this permit would be signed, things were
taken in good faith and the operation was allowed to continue," said
John Dell'Osso, the park's spokesperson. "The good news is that we
have a signed permit from Drakes Bay Oyster Company and that's
positive news for everyone concerned."

The first line of the new permit read as follows:

[Drakes Bay Oyster Company] is hereby authorized for a period ("Term") commencing on _____ April, 2008 ("Commencement Date") and terminating on November 30, 2012 ("Expiration Date") to use the following described land, improvements and waters . . .

The commencement date was left blank, but the permit was signed by both Kevin Lunny and the park's deputy regional director George Turnbull, on April 22, 2008.

Meanwhile, as part of the negotiations she brokered, Senator Feinstein and the National Park Service had jointly requested that the National Academy of Sciences review the science in Sarah's "Sheltered Wilderness Estuary" report. The task was twofold; the special committee appointed by the academy would evaluate the existing park science on the estuary, as presented, as well as come up with a new set of best management practices. The review would be carried out by the academy's operational wing, the National Research Council, established in 1916 with the purpose of "furthering knowledge and advising the federal government." The committee, dubbed the Committee on Best Practices for Shellfish Mariculture and the Effects of Commercial Activities in Drakes Estero, Pt. Reyes National Seashore, California, included scientists from academic institutions in Oregon, Washington, Rhode Island, Virginia, Massachusetts, Connecticut, Southern California, Ireland and Scotland. The committee was to be overseen by a number of professionals, including scientists from the Monterey Bay Aquarium Research Institute and the Woods Hole Oceanographic Institution, but also representatives from Boeing and Exxon Mobil. At the park's request, the Marine Mammal Commission, a government agency created under Title II of the Marine Mammal Protection Act of 1972, also began separate investigations.

In the sleepy seaside towns around Point Reyes, the debate surrounding the oysters and the wilderness was starting to heat up. The conflict was splashed across the pages of the local paper every week. In early April, Corey published an opinion piece in the *Light* calling the park's actions a "shock and awe" campaign against the Lunny family, and invoked the language of war.

"[Neubacher's] reason to take those actions—his overwhelming data—like Bush's weapons of mass destruction, did not exist," Corey wrote. After a lengthy account of his own ongoing investigations, he called the National Park Service a sinking ship with a broken moral compass. It wasn't enough that the park had removed the offending report and requested an outside inquiry by the National Academy of Sciences. Corey didn't believe that Sarah had made a mistake. To him, this was a clear case of scientific misconduct—criminal actions—and he wanted Sarah and her superiors to be held accountable.

"In the end, this story is really not about oysters, and it is not about harbor seals," Corey wrote.

> Rather it is about the arrogant misuse of false science to support a political agenda. And with that political agenda comes collateral damage—a relentless government assault on a family—an attack condoned by some locals who appear to believe that the ends justify the means. At the core is the viability of agriculture in Point Reyes National Seashore and West Marin. This is not about oysters and harbor seals, it is about the future and integrity of our community.

Others, however, weren't having it.

"The closure of this business has nothing to do with whether its methods of raising oysters are 'sustainable' or environmentally sensitive," wrote local resident John Sutherland in a letter to the editor of the *Light* a week later.

> Their lease isn't contingent on the Seashore's Master Plan, scientific reports, or attitudes towards agriculture. The company's blizzard of claims against Point Reyes National Seashore is simply a shell game: a private business enlisting Supervisor Steve Kinsey and lobbying Senator Dianne Feinstein to initiate an act of Congress to extend Drakes Bay Oyster Company's lease. This precedent would set at risk all lands protected by the Wilderness Act.

Fred Smith, now spending an increasing amount of time trying to battle claims made by the oyster farm and its supporters, was similarly frustrated, if not surprised. After all, he was used to encountering pushback from locals about a conservation project, especially if it meant shutting down a business and the loss of jobs. That was the case when it came to logging and timber companies, so why should this be any different? The only difference here was that, as far as Fred was concerned, this battle had already been won back in 1976. It was just a matter of getting people to accept it.

"It is unfortunate that Dr. Goodman chose to label most of the well-respected scientists who disagree with his dissenting opinion regarding the effects of the oyster farm on Drakes Estero as 'collaborators' with the Seashore, as if there is a grand scientific conspiracy against him," Fred wrote in his own letter to the editor. His tone was pointed, if jaunty. "I hope that Dr. Goodman and other oyster farm supporters will hold their claims to the same high standards that they accuse the Seashore of violating."

Fred stressed that the owners of the oyster company took over the operation with prior knowledge that Drakes Estero was slated for full wilderness protection in 2012. Through his eyes, Drakes Bay Oyster and its supporters were campaigning to reverse that wilderness designation, with perilous repercussions.

"Such a result would set a dangerous precedent, emboldening efforts by private industry to increase and expand commercial activity in wilderness areas throughout the country," he wrote.

Wilderness comprises less than 2.5% of the lands in the United States, while close to half of its land base is managed for agriculture. We should be able to ensure sustainable food production for Marin without overturning legislation for acres that have already been designated for wilderness protection.

Corey responded by challenging Fred to a public duel of sorts, suggesting that the two of them duke it out intellectually. Still, Corey's focus was on science, not policy:

"To help the community reconcile this issue, I make a proposal to the EAC," Corey wrote in the paper, addressing Fred directly. "Let's have a discussion of the harbor seal data, and an analysis of Neubacher's claims in front of the community. Let's look at the data together and try to reconcile this issue."

But Fred wasn't all that interested in the data. He wasn't a scientist; he just knew the law. The trouble was that an increasing number of people in the community either didn't understand the estero's wilderness designation, or else they thought it was downright wrong. So what if the Solicitor General's office had decided that the farm didn't belong inside a wilderness area? Maybe they didn't *want* a wilderness area in their backyard, thank you very much. Or at least, they didn't feel they needed a bigger one: the connected Estero de Limantour was a marine wilderness already, having been converted from potential wilderness to full wilderness status in 1998 with the removal of some adjacent power lines. Its waters were just a small part of the 33,373-acre Phillip Burton Wilderness Area, which included forests, grasslands, ridges, and stretches of spectacular beach along the rugged coastline. A third of the park was a working landscape, and many didn't see why Drakes Estero couldn't just be lumped in with that. Wasn't a national park's protection good enough? To some, it didn't make sense that the surrounding fields could be kept as pasture for cattle and dairy ranches, but that the oyster farm must cease. Besides, after the debacle with the exotic deer—the failed contraception attempts, and the rapidly deployed extermination—local trust in the Seashore administration was at an all-time low. People developed passionate opinions on both sides, and shouting matches broke out in front of the post office or bakery. On the little streets of West Marin's villages, the social climate had grown decidedly chilly.

Fred, Gordon Bennett and others in the environmentalists' camp made attempts to appeal to politicians as well. In June, they drafted a letter to California's other senator, Barbara Boxer.

"Recently, there has been a flurry of ill-advised proposals assaulting America's public lands, such as plans to sell and commercialize 15 national park units," they wrote. "But thanks to the voices of Americans from sea to sea, these reckless ideas were rejected."

The letter was cc'ed to Feinstein, Lynn Woolsey and Nancy Pelosi, among others. However, their pleas for strong public support were not gaining traction. Gordon veered a little away from the accepted agenda and tactics of the environmentalists when, at a Board of Supervisors meeting, he threatened to block another environmental issue until the oyster farm controversy was settled.

"If we're going to lose wilderness out in Point Reyes, then we are going to work against open space measures here in Marin," he told Steve Kinsey and the rest of the board during discussion on a quarter-cent tax increase initiative. He was speaking as a private citizen, but said he planned to ask the Sierra Club to back him. However, the move would backfire, and the Sierra Club would eventually ask Gordon to stop representing them.

"This is a hold-hostage effort but it's misplaced," Kinsey said of the move.

More and more, people were questioning the wilderness designation of Drakes Estero. After all, there'd been an oyster farm there for longer than most people could remember. What was so wild about it? Besides, as far as food went, what was wilder than an oyster?

"We are farming in farmland," Kevin Lunny would tell the *New York Times*. "Drakes Estero is surrounded by commercial livestock production. These also are cultural resources that the Park Service is mandated to protect."

By comparing the estuary to the pastoral zone, it was a way of denying the existence of the wilderness designation altogether. However, Phillip Burton hadn't been concerned with what made a wilderness area a wilderness area; only that he had the power to make it so. Roads and other signs of man could be removed, and if the proposed

wilderness had already been trammeled a little, well, then his subordi-
nates had better get moving and un-trammel it. One can almost hear
him, after taking a long drag from his unfiltered Chesterfield, saying,
*It's wilderness if I say it is, son.*

The Inspector General's report came out in July 2008, finding
that Sarah and her colleagues had misrepresented data, but not necessarily deliberately. Mistakes were made, but misconduct required
intent, which there was no proof of, and no charges would be filed.
While it raised questions about the quality of the science, it did not
validate Kevin's claims that he was being treated unfairly, or that the
park was trying to force him out before 2012. Rather than putting
to rest questions that the community had, it only served to inflame
things further.

A man named Samuel Thoron, one of Sarah's relatives, wrote a
local letter to the editor as well.

> It is now time to put the controversy between the Point Reyes
> National Seashore and the Drakes Bay Oyster Company into
> proper perspective. The report of the Inspector General shows
> us that neither side is completely clean. However, the full report
> makes it clear that the Superintendent and his staff are not the
> villains they have been made out to be [ . . . ] The repeated
> personal attacks on Mr. Neubacher and Dr. Allen, orchestrated
> on behalf of Mr. Lunny by professional publicists, lobbyists
> and other apologists, have been shown to be unwarranted and
> without merit. They must cease. It is now time for Mr. Lunny
> to stop behaving like a schoolyard bully, trying to change the
> rules when the game is not going as he wants. It is time for him

to stand up, be a man, and honor and live by the terms of the agreement he knowingly entered when he acquired the business that is now Drakes Bay Oyster Company. Most important, the core issue is the preservation of the integrity of the Wilderness Act for the benefit of all. It is unthinkable that this hard won protection of our national treasure should be compromised for the commercial interests of one family, or any business, whether here in West Marin or elsewhere in the country.

THAT SEPTEMBER, THE National Academy of Sciences began their review of Sarah's science in earnest, as well as their own assessment of oyster farming in the estero, based on studies already done by others. A two-day kick off included a boat tour of the oyster operation, and a daylong panel discussion at a hotel in Mill Valley, a posh San Francisco suburb. Fifty members of the public crowded into the small conference room to hear presentations from ten scientists and other stakeholders from 10 AM to 6 PM. Jonathan Jarvis spoke, stressing that the issue had larger implications than just this one farm in this area. A young scientist from Point Reyes National Seashore, Ben Becker, presented his report-in-progress on the estuary's harbor seals. Corey gave a PowerPoint presentation and complained that other panelists had misquoted every single study. Becker countered that no, it was Corey who was confused, to which Corey replied that even that rebuttal was "yet another example of scientific misconduct." The next month, the academy added two members to the panel. In November, they brought in a seal expert from the University of Aberdeen in Scotland.

Tensions continued through the fall. The *Point Reyes Light* had a new editor now, a young woman not yet thirty with no prior journalism experience before being promoted from advertising sales when the current editor and new owner didn't want to edit anymore. Although she herself had only been living in the community a few years, she wrote in an editorial that park visitors, as opposed to farmers, were like "voyeurs," and that wanting a landscape purely to protect and recreate in was "the misanthropy of the elite."

As the oyster farm controversy moved further into the limelight, the ranchers on the surrounding seashore properties were starting to worry about their own permits with the park. After all, their own leases were short-term arrangements that could be terminated at any time, if doing so was necessary to "protect park resources," according to the NPS management plan.

"The ranchers are nervous," Laura Watt, a professor of cultural resources management at Sonoma State University, told *Marin* magazine in November 2008. "Is the oyster farm the first domino? If it goes, will ranchers be next?"

While the seashore ranchers preferred to keep their dealings with the park quiet, some in the agricultural community who were not in the park were more outspoken.

"I see the park as against 'everyone else,'" said Henry Grossi, former president of the Marin County Farm Bureau, and a rancher in Marshall. "The signs have been there all along. Their intention is to eventually take over the ranches."

The conflict reached a boiling point over New Year's. Throughout the autumn, Feinstein had been trying to broker a deal between Kevin and the American Land Conservancy. The proposal was to give

Kevin a cash payout, somewhere in the neighborhood of $300,000 to $500,000, and move his oyster farm to one "equal in scope" in nearby Tomales Bay, which was neither a park nor a wilderness area, and which had a handful of oyster farms operating in it already. Feinstein advised Kevin to take the deal, which seemed generous to many given the fact that the Lunnys had only been farming oysters for three years at that point. The offer was coming from the park service, with the ALC merely acting as a go-between. The ALC president visited the oyster farm that December, and handed Kevin a proposal that included a dollar amount, but not details on the relocation.

"It wasn't a proposal, it was a guaranteed bankruptcy proposal," Kevin told the *New York Times*. "This doesn't include keeping a food source for our community, keeping the last oyster cannery in the state."

Even though Kevin had already told media that he knew the park did not plan to renew the permit past 2012, he wrote to the executive director of the Ocean Studies Board at the National Academy of Sciences, Susan Roberts, in February of 2009. He said his decision to buy the farm was based at least partly on the wording of the Johnsons' lease and the assumption—or at least the hope—that he'd get an extension. Also, he says it influenced how much he was willing to pay for it: "The value of the leasehold interest was based on the conditions of the reservation of Use and Occupancy and [Special Use Permits] that were in place at that time," he wrote her.

IN THE MEDIA, other details of the farm were starting to warp and change a little. For example, the farm's age. In 2009, oysters had been farmed in the estero for as long as seventy-seven years. That had not been continuous, either, since supply of the Pacific oysters was cut off for much of the 1940s due to the war. Still, it was reported that the oyster farm had been in operation for "more than eighty" or even "more than ninety" years. (And by 2014, it would be regularly bandied about that the oyster farm was one hundred years old). The number of oysters produced by the farm seemed to vary widely as well, with anywhere from 30 to 60 percent of all oysters grown in California being cited. There were other problems, too. Kevin insisted that his workers knew to stay away from seals, and that if his records indicated a boat wasn't out on the water, then it wasn't out on the water. However, the park's wildlife cameras would show that (what appeared to be) one of the DBOC boats was indeed present in the estuary when the company's records indicated that it wasn't. The workers did not always follow the rules.

Meanwhile, oyster culturing was growing increasingly popular in the United States, and an aquaculture lease was something to hold on to. The oyster renaissance begun in the mid-1990s was only growing. In the waters around Long Island, home of the famous Blue Points, oyster harvests doubled from 2000 to 2008, and New York state aquaculture leases increased from thirty-eight to fifty-one during that time. There are oyster farms in Maine and Texas, Alaska and Alabama—every coastal U.S. state except Delaware. There are even oyster operations in Puerto Rico, farming *Crassostrea rhizophorae*, or mangrove oyster.

In spring of 2009, an anonymous source leaked an early draft of the National Academy of Sciences' report to the *Point Reyes Light*, in a move that would be called "deep oyster," fomenting further local tensions. In May, the NAS report came out in earnest. It found that Sarah's "Sheltered Wilderness Estuary" report had "in some instances selectively presented, over interpreted, or misrepresented available

scientific information on DBOC operations by exaggerating the negative and overlooking potentially beneficial effects." However, other
than the fact that Sarah had misreported Roberto Anima's findings, the
main argument made by the NAS was itself fatally flawed. The report
worked from the assumption that "native" Olympia oysters had been
prevalent in the estuary, and that the Pacific oysters were replacing their
ecological function after the prehistoric Olympias were overharvested.
However, this was not the case. There is no scientific or historical evidence that *Ostrea lurida* was ever either part of the baseline ecosystem
of Drakes Estero, or a food staple of the native Miwok. The most recent
archeological study of the area also assessed previous archeological
research and found that it was possible that the surveyors were mistaken, having taken Pacific oyster shells, *Crassostrea gigas*—of which
there were thousands—to belong to *Ostrea lurida*, because no distinction was made between the two. The more recent and more thorough
study found just nine Olympia oyster shells. The area was a mixed site,
a former dump of the Johnsons' that had trash such as mattress springs,
broken glass and roofing materials mixed in. The site was overgrown on
the boundaries with non-native thistle. In the 1990s, a human skeleton
was found there during excavation with a tractor, deemed to be Native
American in origin, and was reburied. They believed they did find nine
*Ostrea lurida* shells, which could mean nine oysters but could also mean
as few as five, given that each oyster has two shells. Other studies did
not carbon-date the shells they found but only took a visual notice. The
shells that were carbon dated had a wide range. The oldest was from as
long ago as 220 BC, while the youngest was from as recently as 800 AD.
However, the shells were found in a site deemed likely to be a trade site,
because of the presence of other materials not found near the estuary,

including abalone and mussel shells (which did not grow there), and obsidian, which likely came from Napa. Cooking sites around the estero showed clam shells that had been charred through cooking, but no oysters. Furthermore, ethnographic accounts supplied through interviews with remaining Miwok people did not indicate that oysters were a common food, or even a known food at all.

One Miwok elder, Tom Smith, said that oysters were found in Tomales Bay, but then described how they were dug with a stick out of the mud. This is not how oysters grow, and it is likely that he was confusing oysters with clams or another shellfish. He also had not come of age by the time that Morgan's oyster efforts began. All in all, between five and nine oysters, stretched out over a span of nearly a thousand years, and all of them more than 1,200 years ago, does not a thriving native population make.

Many *Ostrea lurida* shells have been found in San Francisco Bay as well, but this is only natural considering John Stillwell Morgan shipped down thousands of them. A few have been carbon-dated and proven to be prehistoric—again, more than 1,500 years old, but none of interim age. Those archeologists hypothesized that perhaps native oysters gave way to mussels in San Francisco Bay around 430 AD, and that mussels gave way to clams around 800 AD. But the untested Olympia-like shells were all located near where Morgan farmed them, and it is not impossible that even the prehistoric shells were brought down from Washington along with the massive shipments of oysters dredged from Willapa Bay, as part of the oyster reefs there.

MEANWHILE, THE MEDIA was still struggling to understand what was going on. For example, the *New York Times*, in an otherwise sound article, referred to Drakes Bay Oyster Company "extracting wild-life," as if the oysters were naturally growing there. The oyster feud was a strange political dispute in that both sides seemed to be liberal Democrats—liberal Democrats who supported organic, "sustainable" farming on the one side, and liberal Democrats who supported wilder-ness on the other. Many said that they supported both, but had come down on a particular side for one reason or other. One reason might have been that the Lunnys were already running what the *Los Angeles Times* called a "potent" campaign.

What was clear was that it wasn't up to the staff at Point Reyes National Seashore to extend the oyster farm's lease. It would take an act of Congress to let it stay past 2012. Fortunately for the Lunnys, they had a senator very interested in helping them out.

In July 2009, Dianne Feinstein authored a rider on the 2010 spend-ing bill that gave Secretary of the Interior Ken Salazar the option to renew Drakes Bay Oyster Company's lease for another ten years, although she included language saying that the move should *not* be used as a precedent and that nothing in it should be cited for the man-agement of lands outside the Seashore.

"Just because someone decides to write that in there," Fred told a local reporter, "it doesn't mean wilderness protections won't be chal-lenged in similar situations in other parts of the country."

"This exception is not just about the slippery slope," Jerry Meral, a respected conservationist, former deputy secretary of California's Natural Resources Agency, and vice chairman of the EAC, told the *New York Times*. "It's the beginning of the end of wilderness."

In July of 2009, Jonathan Jarvis was made director of the National Park Service. In their letters and quotes, supporters of the oyster farm

failed to make a distinction between the pastoral zone, which did not
have any kind of wilderness designation, and the estuary, which did.
Either you respected the wilderness designation of Drakes Estero, or
you didn't.

"The 10-year extension of the Drakes Bay Oyster Company's lease
will preserve 30 jobs at the last remaining oyster farm cannery on the
West Coast while making sure that the ecology of the estuary is protected," Feinstein wrote in her support of the rider. "This is an area
with 15 historic dairy farms and cattle ranches, along with many roads
running through it. It is not a remote wilderness." Even Feinstein was
denying Burton's wilderness win.

Nobody was saying that the dairy farms, cattle ranches and their
roads were wilderness: they were saying Drakes Estero was. What
had made Point Reyes's wilderness so appealing in the 1960s—its
proximity to civilization—was damning it now. Meanwhile, Drakes
Bay Oyster Company was violating the Coastal Act by refusing to
sign necessary permits, racking up fines in the tens of thousands of
dollars.

In October of 2009, Feinstein's legislation went through, meaning
that in three years, Salazar would be able to extend the oyster farm's
lease if he saw fit to. She also managed to get the park to offer longer,
ten-year leases to the Seashore ranchers. Unfortunately for one rancher
at least, that good news had come too late.

Little Joey Mendoza, third-generation Point Reyes dairyman, had
just gone out of business. Milk prices had plummeted that spring to
their lowest point in fifty-four years—since Joey was just eleven years
old. That, combined with high feed costs and the tanking economy,
meant that some dairy farmers were losing as much as $100 per day

per cow. They were bleeding money. In California, several dairy farmers committed suicide. Under a National Milk Producers Federation program to remove cows from milk production, more than one hundred thousand dairy cows were sent to slaughter.

Joe Sr. had died the previous autumn, and at sixty-five, Little Joey was the Mendoza patriarch now. He ambled from their weather-beaten house, built nearly a hundred years before by his grandfather J.V., towards the empty milking barn. Light filtered down into the empty space. It was a bright day, unusually sunny for late June, and the yellow lupine was in riotous bloom all over the property. But the familiar sight of his Holsteins silhouetted against the gleaming ocean was missing. He tried but failed to keep from breaking down in tears in front of reporters.

"To have to let them go . . . that was very difficult," he told Santa Rosa's *Press Democrat* of the more than four hundred cows he'd recently sold to slaughter. "And part of the reason is, it's been my life! And it has been for forty-five years so that . . . is not an easy thing to do."

One of his workers, Valerio Salgado, had raised every single cow in the herd from the time they were calves, and he cried, too, when they were sent away. "I cry, because I am seeing how these cows are going to be . . . how you say? Slaughter?" Valerio said. "Because I saw them day after day, day after day, seeing them. Living here."

Despite his tears, Joey would try to be resilient.

"When you get knocked down, you dust yourself and you get back on your game," he said. "I'm gonna try that. If you made a mistake, learn from it and go from there."

"It's sad, but it's something you economically have to do," he told a reporter from NPR. "You also have the guilt pangs because of your heritage. Everybody works so hard to build this thing, and you're the one that has to terminate it and let it go. It's humiliating. You're not very proud of yourself when you've got to do something like this."

It wasn't only his children and the memory of his parents and grandparents that he felt he was letting down, but the eight families, all Mexican, who depended on his dairy for their livelihood.

"I was raised to be an honorable and fair guy," Joey said, his voice breaking. "So when your decision indirectly affects families like that and their kids—wow, that leaves a bitter taste in your mouth."

# PART III

## THE GEOGRAPHY OF HOPE

A scientist is never certain.

—RICHARD FEYNMAN

When the facts are on your side,
pound the facts. When the law is
on your side, pound the law. When
neither is on your side, pound
the table.

—LAW SCHOOL ADAGE,
  ORIGIN UNKNOWN

# 11

# CASINO

O N A SATURDAY night in November, the multilevel parking garage of the Graton Resort & Casino stands conspicuously empty. This is in contrast to the adjacent parking *lot* that, albeit, is both vast and marginally closer to the casino's entrance, but that is also packed full with parked cars. Still more vehicles circle and circle through the lanes, looking for vacant spaces, despite the virtually empty structure just next door. There is no signage for the casino from the highway. The building however, in a minimal, modern design, proudly displays the backlit word CASINO above a waterfall wall at one entrance, and another glowing CASINO sign hangs from an asymmetrical, wave-like arch at the other. Once duly de-automobiled, visitors are greeted by a petite, be-suited man who welcomes them and wishes them luck.

Florence and the Machine's "You've Got the Love" is playing on this particular Saturday, and the plushly carpeted interior smells of artificial fragrance and cigarette smoke. Once inside, any music that might be playing is all but drowned out by the buzz of bar revelers, card dealers, pinging slot machines and the frantic, shout-y ocean sounds of various sports (football, ring fighting) coming from the casino's many, many televisions. The card games are up front, and the machines are in back—some three thousand of them. Scattered throughout are a variety of bar spaces to fit different purposes or moods. G Bar, a sports bar, boasts the highest number of TVs in an already TV-heavy space. I count more than forty. Sky Bar is lit fluorescent purple with white couches and wine-dark drapes, giving off an air of exclusivity, or at least the attempt of it. Another bar, called "8," has beaded curtains, red velvet armchairs and cigars to smoke. According to the casino's website it also offers "high limits and luscious libations," and unlike the other bars is open twenty-four hours a day. There are four "casual dining" restaurants (steakhouse, fancy North Beach–style pizza, dim sum, grill) and a food court with a sign that says MARKETPLACE. Each vendor is a local chain—Three Twins Ice Cream, Habit Burger, Beach Hut Deli—but the feel is still more mall than local market; it is defi- nitely a food court, and the presence of a Starbucks and a gift shop selling cigarettes and cheap dresses only adds to this impression. The Starbucks, like "8," also never closes.

On the gaming floor, the brown carpet is patterned with enormous blue, pink and lime-green flowers—which looks more contemporary than it sounds, but which nevertheless will likely seem very dated in just another ten years. Some of the light fixtures look like giant abstracted pine cones, while others, a cascade of scarlet glass, resemble flurries of red butterflies tumbling down in a cone-shaped swarm. The clientele, although ethnically diverse, is skewed above age forty, with a generous salting of white-haired senior citizens thrown in. The ATMs all have $4.50 surcharges and display prominent signs for a gambling addiction hotline. There are surprisingly few college students, given the casino's proximity to Sonoma State University, but I guess gambling takes money to burn, which college kids are not known to have a lot of. Besides, there are more solitary customers than parties. A man in a brown leather jacket with a washed-out brown mustache slouches lazily at a slot machine, feeding it quarters and giving off the impression that he has been sitting there, doing just that, since sometime in the 1970s. This is despite the fact that this particular casino has only been open for one year.

Nearly every detail of the place is down to the vision of one man, Greg Sarris: novelist, screenwriter, university professor, Indian chief—his term, at least sometimes—and now, casino owner. He is also the great-great-grandson of the last Miwok medicine man, Tom Smith. Officially, he's the tribal chairman of the Federated Indians of Graton Rancheria, the only remaining American Indian nation in the Bay Area. Tall and European-looking, Greg wears pressed jeans and crisp button-down shirts in colors like pink, light blue and lavender. He has teeth like a movie star and it's clear he works out, making him look decades younger than his more than sixty years.

As a tribe, the Graton Rancheria Indians are something of a hodge-podge, made up of the Coast Miwok, the Southern Pomo and the Wappo to the east, as well as a few others. The U.S. Bureau of Indian Affairs recognizes over five hundred tribes in America. The California nations are mostly divided up into "Rancherias"—which is what the Spanish called both the indigenous workers' quarters on mission ranches, and also the villages later set up for homeless Indians in the beginning of the twentieth century, once the missions had long faded. Because indigenous men and women were traded and transported from all over the state, many of the Rancherias were home to a mix of language groups and origins. Unlike the Navajo or the Apache, the California Indians became known less by their nation or tribal names and more for the places that collected them, sometimes less than a hundred years ago. For many Rancherias now, what matters is not that you can trace your lineage back to an indigenous ancestor, but that your ancestor was living on your particular Rancheria at the time of its official establishment.

In recent years, some California tribal members have been disenrolled, meaning their Indian citizenship is revoked and they no longer receive the monthly payments from the casinos that most of the California Rancherias operate. If a California tribe doesn't have a casino, they are still eligible to receive funds from a designated pool of the other tribes' profits. The disenrollment practice is something that has climbed in a number of states over the years, but has gained particular momentum in California since 2000, when Las Vegas–style gambling was made legal on Indian land. Some call the practice an important act of due diligence, while others have cried corruption, saying it is used to unseat political rivals or increase the casino payments by winnowing down the number of beneficiaries. Some disputes have involved gunfights, militia raids and standoffs at barricaded tribal headquarters. Disenrollment is serious business and has affected thousands of people across America. Some have called it a new wave of Native American genocide, including in the July 2014 issue of *Native Max* magazine, which publishes under the tagline *Stay connected to your culture*. Not only does disenrollment strip a person of her or his Native identity, but it can deny them access to health care, tribal schools, housing, and federal education grants, not forgetting the aforementioned monthly checks.

The entire Graton Rancheria tribe was stripped of their official tribal identity by the Bureau of Indian Affairs under the Eisenhower

administration in 1958. The movement, starting from the 1940s, reasoned that Native peoples would be better off if they assimilated into
mainstream American society, and thus some of the smaller tribes
were no longer recognized as such. This was accomplished by revoking
their protections and terminating their land agreements. The Graton
Rancheria land was only fifteen acres to begin with, a mere three acres
of which was viably inhabitable. After termination, just a single acre
remained, the private property of one member—this for a people who
once roamed over all of Marin and Sonoma. The tribe began petition-
ing to be reinstated in 1997, and in 2000 Congress passed the Graton
Rancheria Restoration Act (coauthored by Greg Sarris). Eight years
later, having saved up their payments from other California casinos,
the Federated Indians of the Graton Rancheria (or FIGR for short),
bought 254 acres of land and started lobbying for permits to build a
casino of their own. To complete the project, the tribe took out loans
for nearly a billion dollars.

As is to be expected, Greg is a busy man. In 2003, FIGR donated
$1.5 million to Sonoma State University to create an endowed chair of
Native American studies. Greg was given the position, and has held it
ever since. It therefore isn't a surprise that between teaching, writing,
and running a billion-dollar casino, Greg doesn't really have time to
talk to me. Or if he does, he doesn't want me to know that. Just getting a phone interview with him takes the kind of finagling usually
reserved for Wall Street fat cats—with secretaries emailing to set up a
specific ten or fifteen minutes here or there with "Mr. Sarris" between
his other, more important engagements.

When we finally do talk, he wants to make sure I'm not writing
fiction. He writes fiction about his people himself, but as far as he's

concerned, I shouldn't; I am an outsider. He's cagey about a lot, and talking to him for any period of time it is also clear that he is angry. Or if it isn't anger, it is at least a passionate dislike. I'll call it anger, for ease's sake. He's angry about how his people are often written about or discussed, and angry, too, about how Native Americans in general are so often erased from the conventional wilderness history of Muir and Thoreau. In the decade-long battle over Drakes Estero, and the arguments over whether or not to return it to its "original," wild state, he says I am the only person to have contacted the man whose people lived on its shores for thousands of years, before there were oyster farmers there, or cattlemen, or missionaries. It is the Miwok who lived on Point Reyes, in the Olema Valley and along the eastern shores of Tomales Bay, and the stories Greg tells me about them are strange and fantastical.

The Miwok people believed that the dead walked into the afterlife along the path of light thrown by the moon onto water. It was their belief that the land of the dead lay somewhere out past where that path dwindled on the horizon, under the waves. So when the English pirate Francis Drake arrived in his galleon the *Golden Hind* in June of 1579, gliding on the sea's shining passage at nightfall, the Miwok were beside themselves. Who was this man, pale as the dead, and traveling from such a long distance on death's road? He came into Drakes Bay from the direction of the Farallones, which the natives called the Islands of the Dead, or the Islands of Spirits. (You see, biologist Steve Emslie was not alone in thinking the Farallones were haunted, and perhaps the ghost of the sealers' woman had company.) But the Miwok did not only see pale faces aboard the *Golden Hind*. Drake had a beautiful young African woman with him named Maria, a concubine he stole

from a Spanish conquistador some months prior during a water battle near Central America. There were also two "rescued" male indigenous slaves from Panama, named Guatulco and Paita. The Miwok
were dark-skinned themselves, with broad faces. Maybe the African
woman and Panamanian men read more as "living" to the native
Californians, and the interaction between the seemingly-dead and the
apparently-alive provoked a dramatic response. Longing to see their
departed family and friends, the Miwok went down to the beach to
greet Drake, weeping, their bodies smeared with pale ash, asking (or so
the Englishmen thought) for Drake to take them as living passengers to
that land of lost loves below the water.

This misunderstanding was remedied soon enough, however, and
Maria, Drake and his men spent a month with the Miwok while they
repaired their vessel. At that point in their voyage, the *Golden Hind*
was already sitting low in the water from the weight of purloined
Spanish silver, the former hoard of Maria's previous master. It is said
Drake buried some of the booty in the hills near Drakes Beach, and no
one has ever found it. Originally part of a fleet of three galleons sent
forth by Queen Elizabeth I, the other ships were lost in a storm near
Tierra del Fuego, and the *Golden Hind* continued up the West Coast
of the Americas alone. Aside from Drake, Maria and the Panamanians,
the *Golden Hind* was also the temporary home to Drake's twenty-
two-year-old brother Thomas, a fifteen-year-old cousin or nephew
named John who served as ship's artist and head page, and the ship's
captain under Drake, a man named John Chester. There were also
forty-five seamen, five "boys," and nine officers, including the ship's
master, William Hawkins. Hawkins would later make his fortune pioneering the British slave trade, adopting as his crest the image of an

African man bound at the chest and neck with rope. A tenth officer, by the name of Thomas Doughty, was tried for mutiny and beheaded by Drake while the *Golden Hind* was still in the Atlantic. Doughty's brother John, also on board, was kept locked up for the rest of the voyage, and upon returning to England attempted to have Drake tried for murder. It didn't work.

Many, many people came from the surrounding areas to see the foreigners and their giant wooden boat, bringing gifts and performing long orations. In his detailed diaries of their Northern California sojourn, the ship's chaplain goes to great pains to describe just how virtuous the crew were with the local women and girls, despite their shocking lack of modesty. They tried and tried to get the women to cover up their bare breasts, he said, but they just wouldn't do it.

Beautiful Maria was the only woman these sixty-four foreign men had seen in many months, but even so I hope that the chaplain's story is true. It's likely, though, that some English blood found its way into the Miwok lineage as early as then. If so, there is no mention of upset, and I hope it was consensual. The crew were outnumbered by many hundreds of natives. Besides, Greg tells me that rape was unheard of for the Miwok and Pomo peoples, out of respect or, at the very least, fear of women's superior spiritual abilities. Drake later claimed that the Miwoks crowned him as their "king," but who knows. Their power structure wasn't that simple.

Greg doesn't tell me where he gets his own stories from, but he has lots of them. He tells me about the cult of the Human Bear, and sends me a story he's written about it. It began, the legend goes, when grizzly bears kidnapped a boy while the boy was out picking black-berries. They took him and raised him, schooling him in their secrets and giving him powers beyond that of a normal human being. Later, initiates into the cult of the Human Bear were also kidnapped. Some might be warned beforehand that they had been selected, but the actual induction came as a surprise: you were pulled out of your daily routine and into the world of the supernatural.

The Human Bears were frequently women, and they worked to broker treaties with the grizzlies—treaties that the bears seem to have honored. The bears were given free rein of the vast redwood forests, while the people would stick to the open plains, hillsides and lighter pine and oak woods. There was overlap, of course. The grizzlies had to come out into the open to hunt the tule elk.

There were other cults as well—hummingbird cults and bobcat cults, cults for animals and cults for places. Greg says the Miwok and Pomo believed that sorcerers could actually shape-shift, turning into a bird, if need be, to avoid capture. The magic they practiced was intrinsically linked to the land, to specific groves, valleys or beaches. Some places were good for healing, others for poisoning and curses, and each had its own song that could be sung to invoke its particular power. When I asked Greg to give me some examples, he said he couldn't; too much had happened and it was all changed now. He does say that he laughs when he hears about people going up Mount Tamalpais to get married, because that was where the poisoners went to learn dark spells.

"I see that and think, well, that's not going to last!" he joked.

Greg especially rejected the idea of a pristine and humanless landscape, of a place only being "pure" if it remained untouched by human hands. Not so, he says. The land was populous, the most populous part of the Americas outside of the Aztec cities, he tells me, and the landscape was heavily managed. Knowing that the elk wanted open plains to graze on, the Miwok cleared wide spaces for them using controlled fires, to make for better hunting.

Greg's own great-great-grandfather, the medicine man Tom Smith, was known to be especially powerful, but was also prone to exaggeration. "He was a trickster," Greg tells me. He is the one, Greg says, who made up stories for the ethnographers because they paid him for each story, and he wanted to be able to afford a nice suit to be buried in. When asked about oysters near Point Reyes, he said, *Sure, they're over by Valley Ford. We dig them up with a stick*, even though oysters do not grow that way. He also took responsibility for the 1906 earthquake, claiming it was his own show of strength in a contest with another medicine man. Clearly, he considered the other medicine man to have lost.

Myth and reality meet each other in Greg's stories, and I wonder if, in telling them, he is at any point taking after his great-great-grandfather Tom. I don't mean this disrespectfully. He has written a story about a native man named Fidel, who, to avoid capture by ranchers, ran not to the cover of the woods but to the open meadows of what the natives called the Hummingbird Coast, on Tomales Point. Fidel was a member of the Hummingbird Cult, Greg reasoned, and was perhaps seeking that magic ground to turn himself into a hummingbird to fly away. He also tells of a mysterious green light that can be seen on that coast from Marshall, on the opposite shores of Tomales Bay. It seems to signify something—some source of magic—although what, I'm not exactly sure. I've never seen it myself, although I spent some weeks living on the water just across from that location. It sounds Gatsbyesque.

"I saw the green light," Greg writes in one of the stories he sent me, and then, two sentences later amends it: "Maybe I didn't see it, and only know it in my imagination."

Greg and his tribe have had some problems with the casino, in that a vocal contingent of locals did not want it to be built. It is in Rohnert Park, about an hour's drive from Point Reyes. When I was a kid, my family would go to Rohnert Park to go bowling or to the roller rink. There is a mall nearby on an expanse of former wetland. The residents there argued that a casino would bring unsavory elements into the community and take money away from local businesses. But Greg is quick to chalk up his opposition to prejudice. He says white Americans want their Indians to be penniless and selling beads quaintly from the roadside, content with their poverty. Anything else and they are "wagon burners," he says with detectable vehemence. Greg says his goal is to use success with the casino to once again make his tribe stewards of the land. They already have organic and sustainable farming projects underway, and he tells me—with rather staggering ambition—that he eventually wants to "buy back all of Marin and Sonoma," some of the most expensive land in the country.

Greg is interested in the idea of managed landscapes. After all, his people knew and managed the land around Point Reyes intimately. Aside from the land's magical properties, the Miwok knew all of the ways to access its bounty. Along with burning brush to create better habitat for the elk, they also knew where the quail laid their eggs, they pruned food-bearing trees and generally sculpted the landscape to fit their purpose. This was a tamed landscape, he said, not a wilderness. There were wild lands out where no people lived, sure. But the native peoples of Northern California were not living in the wild. This was their garden.

Greg talks about writing as a path, as navigation, and about the land as literature, as a book or text. However while he hopes to read the histories of his people in their original geography, he knows there is no going "back." In much the same fashion, the fantasy of "returning" the land to some "original" condition that is humanless is just that—a fantasy. If humans have been living around Drakes Estero—far fewer of them in the last 150 years than the thousands that came before—what does it mean to return it to the wild? This is what is all too often missing from the familiar wilderness scriptures of Muir and Thoreau: that the land was not empty when they found it. The first peoples of North America had already been laid waste by diseases before the settlers with their covered wagons ever started to move west. Diseases came to kill the Indians with the original settlers, with the Russian fur traders who settled near Bodega and wiped out the local sea otters, and the Spanish monks who were not so chaste, so that by the time of the Gold Rush 90 percent of the native population had already died out. The wild lands of America were a ghost town, not an Eden. Or if it was an Eden, it was a rather recently vacated one. In California, the Spanish missions spread diseases accidentally, but also treated the natives as second-class citizens, if not outright slaves. They were not allowed to leave the missions. Their lives were worth less. When a native woman was struggling in childbirth, it was not uncommon for a priest to perform a crude caesarean section, knowing full well that both woman and baby would die, but cutting into her living flesh anyway so the doomed infant could be baptized before death.

When conservationists talk of returning Drakes Estero to its "original" wild state, to what state are they referring? By the 1860s and 1870s, the homescape of the Miwok and Pomo was almost unreadable.

Even something as simple as the grass had changed—the native perennial bunchgrasses having been overtaken by European annuals like
wild oat, rattlesnake grass and foxtail barley. These are the golden
grasses we usually think of when we think of California's golden summer hills. They do not belong, and yet are so triumphant, and have
replaced what was natural so thoroughly that they could never be
removed. Their seeds came from the dung of Spanish cattle and horses,
during the height of the Spanish missions between 1769 and 1824, so
that by the time of the Gold Rush, the very ground beneath the natives'
feet was unrecognizable. The plains and grasslands and prairies were
important to Northern California's first people. They believed there
was safety in openness. It was in the open that the bears could not
harm them, where their food was abundant, where the spirit could
fly. Good magic was practiced there. The Miwok believed that karma
worked: that to wound a person or an animal, or even a tree, would
invite swift retribution. But the Europeans seemed to be above the laws
of the natural world; they killed people and cleared forests and emp-
tied the coastal plains of pronghorn and elk. They betrayed not only
the Indians, but each other. Francis Drake returned to Plymouth in
September of 1580, the year a young William Shakespeare, not more
than twenty years old, left Stratford-upon-Avon to begin his career on
the London stage. But before returning home to fame, fortune and a
knighthood, Drake stopped on a small island devoid of people, where
he left Maria, his mistress, pregnant with his bastard child.

The truth is harsh sometimes. Or not even sometimes: often. This
is why we need myths. Both to understand and escape from this harsh-
ness. Most of the time we live in the casino-world—all sounds and
distraction (all sound and fury, signifying nothing)—not the world of

the Human Bear. When we turn now to nature, what are we looking to remember, and what are we hoping to forget?

# 12

## DAVID V. GOLIATH

I CAME BACK TO Point Reyes in the first week of May 2012, to start work as a reporter for the *Light*. All of the fields were still overgrown and flecked with wildflowers, a few weeks away from being cut. Some seemed to be nothing *but* wildflowers, or at the very least, the grasses and the wildflowers were thoroughly tangled up. By June they'd mostly be mown down for silage or in preparation for the drier and more incendiary months. For now though there were Red-winged Blackbirds perched in the tall weeds of the roadsides, and on tree branches and power lines, their plaintive cries like the creak of rusty swing sets, saying *oooPREEEEEEoom, oooPREEEEEEoom*. From the edges of little woods you could hear the Hermit Thrushes singing from somewhere in the deep green, like something played on a pan flute. *Zheeeee freediila fridla-fridla*, they trilled. I'd forgotten that they sounded like the month of May to me, it had been so long since I heard them.

I say I was starting work as *a* reporter for the *Light* but really I was to be *the* reporter; the only one, save an intern who would also write stories, though not every week—not while I was there. And I say Point Reyes, but I really mean West Marin, the constellation of rural villages tucked into the hills and along the water, where I grew up.

The *Point Reyes Light* was not actually *in* Point Reyes anymore, but rather in the even tinier village of Inverness just across skinny Tomales Bay, a ten- or fifteen-minute drive away. The residential population is actually larger there, but there are fewer amenities; just a country store and, across the way from that, a post office, café and restaurant, which used to be the store where Doc Ottinger's poached white stag was once strung up. Vladimir's Czechoslovakian pub is on this block, too. (And yes, the place where Vlad came from isn't called Czechoslovakia anymore, but it was when he left it.) Tucked behind these was the one-room newspaper office. The rent was cheaper, and, well, you know how it is with newspapers now.

The bay was just across the road, and I'd often go stand at the edge of it while talking to sources on my cell phone, near where the wreck of an old fishing boat called the *Point Reyes* has spent the last several decades of its afterlife picturesquely stuck in the mud. Between Vladimir's and the post office there is an enormous overgrown bush of tiny, pale pink climbing roses. If I wasn't getting cell reception by the water, I'd sometimes stand by this rosebush and pick off a little bud absentmindedly, slowly peeling back the petals to reveal the powdery yellow-green stamen cluster while I listened or talked.

The town of Point Reyes is really called Point Reyes Station, named during the railroad days, but people don't usually say the Station part. There's a proper main street there with a grocery store, a bakery, a post office, a bank, a lumberyard, a hardware store, a barber, a bookstore, a bar, a tack and feed that also sells clothing and some toys, and a few restaurants. There are also several gift shops, a few art galleries, a doctor's office, and a vet. On a perpendicular street you'll find the gas station, the pharmacy, two kayak companies, the diner, and Tomales

Bay Foods, where you can buy gourmet picnic supplies and watch arti-
sanal cheese being made behind a glass divider. This is famous cheese,
from Cowgirl Creamery, which incidentally you can get at nearly any
gourmet grocer in Brooklyn worth its salt. In 2012 there was still a
stationery store that also sold goofy knickknacks, which had been
there since I was little. It's gone now, but I remember going in and
being allowed to buy tiny plastic farm animals or little rubber monster
finger puppets with googly eyes and jiggly arms. Tucked into other
crannies of the town you'll find a yoga studio, an herbalist, the radio
station, a thrift shop, the small library (where my stepfather is one of
the librarians), an elementary school, the fire station, Fred's little office
of the Environmental Action Committee, and a few other things—you
get the idea. It's pretty idyllic, and in recent years that fact has not
gone unnoticed. Real estate and rental prices have skyrocketed, and on
weekends the streets are busy with tourists. There is a farmers' market
on Saturdays with a booth where you can buy a grilled cheese sand-
wich for $8. Great big groups of cyclists clad in spandex will all ride
out together from the city or more suburban towns, and congregate
at the bakery to buy coffee and bear claws or sticky morning buns,
their special bike shoes clacking on the tiled floor. My sister calls them
"locusts."

When I arrived at the paper I was feeling pretty optimistic. I'd read
up a little on the Drakes Bay Oyster Company controversy, but felt
that in the *Light*'s coverage at least, the story seemed to be fairly one-
sided. To get acquainted with the history of the thing, I'd been told to
listen to what Corey Goodman had to say about it, and to read the
hundreds of pages of analysis and PowerPoint presentations that he
sent to me. He told me that he was sending them to the White House,

too, and could tell when they'd been opened because they did so by accessing an online file-sharing platform. In terms of articles I'd only read coverage from the past few months, and there didn't seem to be very much coming from the pro-wilderness camp. I was surprised by this, and thought that I would remedy it, a plan I communicated to the newspaper editor. She said that was just fine, and gave me the contact information for the people I'd want to talk to. Right away I rang one of them up.

"Go back to New York!" this person yelled at me over the phone. "We don't want you here. That goddamn paper! Why don't you get a real job?" And they hung up.

"I'm sorry that your career has taken such a downward turn," another told me nastily when I explained who I was, also over the phone.

"I'm sorry you've had bad experiences with other reporters," I tried to soothe, completely taken aback. "But I'm really just trying to do a good job. If you have concerns, I'm happy to listen."

"Your boss is the devil," this person said to me. And that was that.

I hadn't realized it, but I was walking into the Oyster War at the height of its ugliness. I also did not realize that Corey Goodman was arguably the de facto publisher of the paper where I worked. Or maybe not. It was hard to tell. The paper as I knew it growing up had been sold to a youngish Columbia journalism grad named Robert Plotkin some years prior. He was brash and liked to ruffle feathers, and the *San Francisco Chronicle* described him as being like "Jerry Seinfeld with a *Granta* subscription." I kind of see what they mean, although I like Robert. The first time I met him we were debating Middle East gender politics less than three minutes after introducing ourselves. The second time I met him he made a joke about how I should enter into a polygamous marriage with him and his wife. The third time I met him he made the same joke. His tenure in the community was somewhat fraught, and after a few years he decided to sell the paper at a substantial loss. By then he'd ruffled *so* many feathers that a whole other newspaper had sprung up to challenge his journalistic hegemony, called the *West Marin Citizen*. In 2010, members of the West Marin community pooled their money and formed the Marin Media Institute (MMI) with the intention of buying the historic *Point Reyes Light*, its Pulitzer legacy and the famous lighthouse masthead, thus combining the two papers to heal the rift.

By far the largest donor was Corey. The idea was to make the newspaper itself a 501(c)3 nonprofit, or at least what's known as a "low-profit liability company"—an L3C. However the *Light*'s application for nonprofit or low-profit status was never approved, and so it remained the property of the MMI and failed to merge with the *Citizen*. It has been argued that the paper was really legally owned by the eighty-six individuals who donated the money to buy it, with a majority share belonging to Corey—but I don't know the definitive answer on that. He was then chair of the MMI's board. I fielded calls from other reporters around the country while I worked at the *Light*, asking if Corey was the owner. Did he technically own it? I don't think so, but the relationship was certainly enmeshed. He had already set himself up as the oyster farm's most powerful local ally, that much I knew. But I was surprised to find that so many people were so angry at the paper. I thought I was coming home, to a place that would recognize that I belonged there, and where I could get something of a break, but right away I was regarded as an outsider and one worthy of suspicion at that. When I was hired I was told that it probably wouldn't even be a full-time gig, and I'd surely have time to pitch other freelance projects to supplement my income, which was not enough to live on. After taxes I was getting paid about $1,500 per month. Monthly rent for a one-bedroom apartment in town was about $1,500. Based on how much I actually ended up working, my salary amounted to around $5 an hour. Minimum wage in California at the time was $8. I also spent around $100–$150 per week on gas while driving around for stories, and was never reimbursed. Luckily I was able to find a cheap room to rent, and my sister gave me a car she wasn't using—a tan 1991 Pontiac minivan with a weird pointy front like the starship *Enterprise* and a mysterious blue blinking light on the driver's side windshield that I couldn't turn off. It was pretty much the ugliest thing you've ever seen. The gas mileage was good though.

To get better acquainted with the oyster farm story, I was also introduced to Dave Weiman, the lobbyist hired by the Lunnys. I wasn't really supposed to refer to him as a "lobbyist," though, and if I did I was corrected. Or not corrected—*adjusted*. Yes, he *was* a lobbyist, but it would "be more accurate" to describe him as "an attorney who has been advising the Lunnys." Being a lobbyist made it sound bad. We were connected by email, and spoke frequently on the phone, although we only met in person once because he was based in Washington, D.C., most of the time. He was personable, and funny, and often spoke in riddles and folksy analogies that sometimes made sense and sometimes did not.

"Imagine you and I are at the malt shop," one of his analogies might begin. Or, "Just imagine that you're gonna sell me a prize hog." He sent me emails that had more questions in them than statements.

"Who is Brigid Lunny and why does she figure in the story of Corey being a LIAR?" he wrote to me. "This is the tip of the iceberg."

He meant that Corey was *not* a liar, of course, and we all knew who Brigid Lunny was. She was Kevin and Nancy's daughter. I guess Dave was trying to foster a sense of drama, or maybe that was just how he talked, but I was quickly becoming extremely busy with my duties at the paper, and the mystery routine could get a little old. Between Corey's written sagas and Dave's analogies and questions, it was a lot. Every week it was not uncommon for me to spend at least two hours or more on the phone with one if not both of them. They were very interested in telling me what the "story-of-the-story" was. During these conversations I was rarely able to ask questions or say anything at all.

From what I gathered, the "story-of-the-story" according to the *Light* was that the National Park Service had swindled the Lunnys, and that the Lunnys were shocked when they found out their permit would not be renewed. More than that, I was given the distinct impression that the Lunnys were told their permit *would* be renewed, and that they had purchased the farm and paid to have it cleaned up based on this information. Then, they'd been framed for environmental crimes they did not commit, spied on and harassed. I was told the park had once planned to rebuild the ramshackle oyster farm into a shiny new visitor's center to showcase the mariculture operation, and had even hired the same architectural firm that designed the park's headquarters. I was shown drawings. It looked pretty convincing. Dave implied that the reason the park had changed its mind and decided to make the estuary a wilderness area was that being a "National Seashore" wasn't impressive enough. "It isn't even really a *park*," Dave said to me, with flourish. "I mean come on, what's a *seashore* anyway? But a *park*, now a *park*. That's something." The idea was that the wilderness designation would bring them more power and clout. The *Light* was determined to uncover this upsetting case of government fraud, and in doing so, might even win the paper another impressive national award. This was suggested to me by newspaper staff, as well as individuals associated with the DBOC story. Never mind that the scandal the *Point Reyes Light* had uncovered in 1979 had to do with a local cult stockpiling firearms—and that it happened less than a year after the Jonestown massacre, giving the discovery even more national significance. Nevertheless, when I arrived the newspaper's Wi-Fi password was "Pulitzer."

But the thing was, it took a while for me to start digging into the oyster farm story in earnest. With in-depth community obituaries that required me to spend hours interviewing the very recently bereaved, and school board meetings, and fishing competitions, and local elections, and people who wanted me to investigate "chemtrails," and a small but dramatic shipwreck I had to hike two miles along the shore to reach, I didn't have very much extra time for research. Most of the time I loved it, don't get me wrong, but during my stint as a West Marin reporter I was not able to take even a single day off. The files on DBOC as I found them were an unorganized mess anyway. Besides, the local oyster farms had other things to worry about besides the feud with the park.

In July of 2010, Kevin Lunny walked out to his concrete cultivation tanks on the edge of Drakes Estero to check on his latest batch of oyster larvae, and was met with a nasty surprise. The baby oysters were dead, all six million of them—a loss of about $10,000. Unfortunately, this kind of complete crop failure was getting more and more common, and Kevin was pretty sure he knew the culprit all too well: ocean acidification. It is a part of climate change that you don't hear as much about but is readily measurable and observable. Excess carbon dioxide from the atmosphere is settling into the world's oceans and lowering the pH. Ocean waters are also made more acidic when excess nitrogen from sewage and agricultural runoff causes algae blooms that overwhelm native ecosystems and result in carbon-emitting decay. The oysters and other shellfish take calcium carbonate from seawater to form their shells, but that process can only take place within a specific pH range. When the pH drops a little more than normal, some of them die. If it drops too much, they all do. This is a very big deal.

"I wondered, did we just fill our tanks with corrosive seawater and kill our larvae?" Kevin mused to the *Light*. He told the paper that this was just another reason why he wanted to try farming "native" oysters, i.e. the Olympias, because he speculated that they might be more resilient to acidic water. Unfortunately, that hypothesis isn't true, and all of the oysters are vulnerable.

This kind of thing was already happening up and down the West Coast. In Willapa Bay, where the Olympia oysters once came from courtesy of John Stillwell Morgan, fuel emissions had turned the seawater there so lethal that the little oysters would sometimes no longer grow at all. When oyster larvae grow ill, they turn pink and stop feeding as they struggle to build the exoskeletons that will become their shells. Then they die. Most oyster farms in California, Oregon and Washington grow the Japanese Pacific oysters. But the water is too cold for them to spawn, so baby oysters are produced in hatcheries that *use* the local seawater but are able to force the reproduction with cultivation techniques, and then sell the results. Some farms, like Drakes Bay Oyster, hatch their own.

Ocean acidification is not uniform, but collects in different regions and then spreads in currents and upswells. The corrosive seawater from Willapa managed to make its way down the coast to Oregon, killing off entire oyster hatcheries there, too. It can come from anywhere, and oyster farmers have had to get creative. In 2009, Dave Nisbet of the Goose Point Oyster Company in Willapa Bay was forced to move his entire hatchery all the way to Hilo on the Big Island of Hawaii—three thousand miles away. The Nisbets employed seventy people in Washington and felt responsible for their seventy families. If they went out of business, it wasn't just they who would suffer. The little oysters grown in Hawaii were then shipped back to the Pacific Northwest—where the water was not too polluted to sustain them, just too acidic for the little ones to get started. Other hatcheries have managed to coax their oysters to maturity by adjusting the pH in controlled tanks, like you would an aquarium. But this doesn't solve the problem for the wild shellfish living in Pacific waters, and besides, by 2014 Willapa Bay oyster farms were starting to encounter problems with the grown-up oysters, too. Many oyster farms countrywide are losing up to 40 percent of their crop every year. In Tomales Bay, the owners of Hog Island Oyster Co. have teamed up with biologists at the Bodega Marine Laboratory of the University of California, Davis, to track rising temperatures and acidity. Drakes Bay Oyster Company wanted to do their part to support ocean research too, but for them things were a little more complicated.

Not too long after I started investigating the feud between DBOC and the National Park Service, a *New York Times* reporter would remark that the conflict had grown increasingly convoluted. Other journalists complained of the "dizzying" procession of reports that had sprung up around the issue. I will tell you that there are in fact nine scientific and investigative reports that are key to this story, and the next two chapters of this book deal with four of them—what insiders called "Becker," "MMC," "Frost" and "the DEIS." All of those four were released between the time that Dianne Feinstein managed to put the possibility of a lease extension for DBOC on the rider of a spending bill, and the time that Secretary of the Interior Ken Salazar arrived in Point Reyes to make that call.

A person could go crazy sifting through the mountainous minutiae of scientific data and analysis produced between 2004 and 2014 with regard to the oyster farm, and to be honest with you, I think I very nearly did. This was before realizing that most of it didn't ultimately matter. There are hundreds of thousands of photographs that mostly show an expanse of blue water; hundreds of pages of dense debate about whether or not a group of seals had stopped hanging out in a particular part of the estuary for a few years because of an elephant seal, or maybe it was because of the oyster workers, or maybe it was something else. The bottom line is that it is impossible to know for sure. Again and again the conclusion of the reports—most of which extrapolated data found elsewhere in an attempt to apply it to Drakes Estero—was that "more research was needed." More research needed. Data was insufficient. More data was needed. *Better* data was needed. Was the oyster farm causing harm? Maybe. Was it very severe? Probably not but we didn't know yet. Could it be mitigated through an adaptive management approach? Most likely.

A top government scientist in Washington, D.C., spent several hours on several occasions speaking with me off the record about the case, his voice calm and measured. I won't name him here due to his request for anonymity, but I think what he had to say was important. The gist of it was this: if the park wanted the oyster farm to stay— *assuming there was no wilderness designation to get in the way of that*—then it seemed perfectly reasonable that the park and the oyster farm could find a way to coexist more or less peacefully. This would only happen if the park service was reasonable about setting up rules, and the oyster farm impeccable about following them. But the question of whether or not the farm was harming the flora and/or fauna of the estuary was not the central issue—even if nearly everything written about the controversy made it seem that way. The scientific and investigative reports can also get confusing because they are nestive to a degree, seeking to evaluate, expand upon, prove or disprove one another. The IG report of 2008 was made in part to investigate the "Sheltered Wilderness Estuary" report of 2006 and 2007. The report of the Marine Mammal Commission, the MMC, released in 2011, evaluated the science found in that report as well as in what's called "the Becker report," which itself was created to expand on, investigate and examine assertions made in the "Sheltered Wilderness Estuary" document, which was also dissected in the "Frost report," an investigation by a government solicitor to see if park scientists had committed scientific misconduct. For those not intimately familiar with the whole thing, it can get quite confusing.

As soon as the bill with Feinstein's rider was passed, the National Park Service was tasked with producing an Environmental Impact Statement with which to help Ken Salazar make his verdict. While that report would assert, rightly, that the Secretary's decision was one of policy and not science, it acknowledged that science could however potentially *influence* that policy decision. If the oyster farm was not causing any harm, Salazar was still entitled to say no to the proposed issuance of a ten-year Special Use Permit. If it *was* causing harm, it would probably make the issuance of such a permit, to continue operating in a potential wilderness area, a lot less likely.

That statement, first released as the Draft Environmental Impact Statement, or DEIS, set out to examine four potential outcomes. In "Alternative A," no action would be taken, the permit would expire in November 2012, and the oyster farm would be removed. In "Alternative B," a ten-year extension would be issued that would expire on November 30, 2022, with onshore and offshore facilities as they existed in the fall of 2010. "Alternative C" would allow the same extension, but with scaled-back operations as they existed in spring 2008 when Kevin Lunny signed the current lease, plus the option to renew again when those ten years were up. "Alternative D" would also allow for a ten-year extension, plus the ability to expand and improve the farm's infrastructure—i.e., build a new onshore facility. These options reminded me of the debates between the Israelis and Palestinians that I heard at the United Nations, about whether East Jerusalem could be made Palestine's capital or not, and which settlements if any would be dismantled, and if the borders would be based on those drawn before the Six-Day War of 1967, or thereafter.

The Becker report was really titled "Modeling the effects of El Niño, density-dependence, and disturbance on harbor seal (*Phoca vitulina*) counts in Drakes Estero, California: 1997–2007," by Ben Becker, Sarah Allen and Dave Press, for the National Park Service. It was previewed in 2008, published in 2009, and then republished in 2011, with corrections. Whereas Sarah's initial claims of harm on the part of the oyster farm were based largely on individual disturbances observed by park scientists and volunteers, the Becker report shifted the focus to compare overall seal numbers with annual oyster harvest yields, the latter serving as a proxy for mariculture operation levels. Those stats came from the Department of Fish and Game. Ultimately, the report concluded that both El Niño weather events *and* oyster farm activity "best explained" the seals' haul-out patterns, i.e., where in the estuary the seals chose to spend time. The seals' numbers were highest in 2004, a year with very little oyster yield, since Tom Johnson was floundering and his family's farm was winding down. Based on this report, it would seem that more oyster farm activity meant fewer seals.

When I spoke to Kevin Lunny about it, he found the whole thing extremely frustrating. According to him, the use of annual production—shucked oysters, at that—was "fundamentally flawed" and didn't reflect the true activity of his family and employees.

"We set out hundreds of millions of oyster larvae per year," he told me when I was working for the *Light*. Per that line of thinking, he explained, even a 1 percent change in the survival rate of that seed could indicate an "increase in production," even though it would not change the number of boat trips that the workers took. It was the boat trips that allegedly disturbed the seals, although just three or four of some forty oyster bedding areas were located near seal haul-outs. A drop in larvae survival could be chalked up to a number of factors, most of them environmental, and would just mean that the oyster bags or bars, once hauled up, would have fewer oysters in or on them. Kevin said of the farm activity:

The park service didn't make any effort to ask us. We would have been very happy to share how the farm works, but none of the authors of the Becker Report have even been with us in a boat, or even talked with us about how we do what we do. It's all speculation. . . .We're getting lost in the weeds of statistics when there is something really easy to understand here. The high-low harvest does not have a linear relationship with our efforts in the bay that could translate into additional concerns for seals. There is nothing true in that high-low means more boat trips, or more disturbances or more anything. It's something they guessed might be true, and they guessed wrong.

If you'll recall, the National Park Service first approached the Marine Mammal Commission about Drakes Estero in spring 2007, just before the Marin County Board of Supervisors meeting when supervisor Steve Kinsey proposed getting Dianne Feinstein involved. In 2009, the MMC agreed to review the available science on marine mammals in the estero; their findings were published in November 2011. The goal was also to help Salazar make his decision, and noted that the ultimate judgment would be one of policy, not science. Still, like the DEIS, the report said that science could *inform* policy. The MMC said there were two separate issues on the table. One, was DBOC harming seals? And two, should the permit be renewed? The commission would not concern itself with the latter, but offered guidance and expertise with regard to whatever was decided.

If the central question of the MMC report was whether or not Drakes Bay Oyster Company was in some way "disturbing" harbor seals, it more or less takes seventy pages to say "maybe." The panel members did not agree on everything. There was debate about what constituted a "disturbance," and how that disturbance could be measured. The commission set out to evaluate the statistical data of the Becker report by three different parties. One was selected by the National Park Conservation Association (NPCA) and Save Our Seashore (SOS), one was selected by DBOC and Corey (and was, in fact, Corey himself), and a third was selected by the commission. Then the MMC would report and comment on the findings of all three. The scientist chosen by the NPCA and the SOS, a man named Dominique Richard, found the Becker report of 2011 to have used "appropriate statistical methods" that supported the conclusion that oyster harvest and seal haul-out use were related. The statistician hired by the MMC found the Becker methods to be "generally appropriate" but also made recommendations for improving them. Corey, on the other hand, with the help of a few others, completed a set of analyses that he believed countered the Becker results.

This was based on the following: Apparently, there was an especially aggressive elephant seal that showed up in the Point Reyes National Seashore in 2004, at a place called Double Point, some miles south of the estuary. Corey hypothesized that the reason the Drakes Estero harbor seal population was so high in 2004 was not that the oyster farm was winding down, but that *other* harbor seals from elsewhere in the seashore were driven into the estuary to escape what he called the "marauding elephant seal." Therefore, he posited dismissing that year's number as an outlier, thus producing a completely different analysis of oyster yields versus seal numbers that countered the Becker report's findings. However, the MMC made a note that it found

Corey's analysis to be "difficult to evaluate because his statistical models are confounded by built-in dependencies that are inconsistent with the statistical procedures he used." Corey was not at all happy with this public dismissal of his work. He'd completed it with the help of other scientists, including someone from Stanford. He wrote to the executive director of the Marine Mammal Commission, Tim Ragen, to appeal.

Whenever I spoke to Tim he seemed laid-back, with the demeanor of a man resigned to finding himself embroiled in a big controversy less than a year before retirement. He would eventually respond to Corey's lengthy protestations through a twenty-page letter of his own, in which he wrote that there were "fundamental errors" in some of Corey's interpretations of the data, which he said rendered them "incorrect," "invalid" and "unreliable." He also argued that Corey did not apply the same level of scrutiny to the oyster company's records as he did to those of the National Park Service.

"My view of this case has not changed," Tim concluded in the letter. "I continue to believe the Commission's report summarized the situation accurately. The park service has provided 'some support for the conclusion that harbor seal habitat-use patterns and mariculture activities in Drakes Estero are at least correlated.' The evidence is not overwhelming, but also cannot be dismissed."

On the phone to me Tim intimated that while Corey may have been an expert in other scientific fields, when it came to this he was out of his depth. There were other unanswered questions with regard to the marine mammals in the estuary as well, such as the mystery of the dead baby seals.

In 2008, a volunteer reported seeing a number of fresh seal pup carcasses located near the mouth of Drakes Estero. During that year's breeding season, the park staff counted thirty-five dead pups in a span of just thirteen days. Sixteen of the dead pups were taken in to a lab to be examined, but no obvious cause of death could be found. Most of the babies all had a normal, healthy amount of blubber on their little bodies, and one even still had milk in its stomach. No one could figure it out. Denise Greig of the Marine Mammal Center in Sausalito prepared a poster on the mysterious event for a scientific conference held in San Francisco. There are photographs of the infant carcasses as they were found on the sand, looking like once-loved children's stuffed animals left out in the rain. There are also photos of the dissections, which are fascinating but grisly, the ribcage cut away to reveal gleaming organs and flesh in various rosy hues. She concluded that there were no signs of bodily trauma to the babies, and while the two thinner ones may have perished due to malnutrition, most if not all likely died simply because they were separated from their mothers. This usually happens due to environmental disturbances, for example, when a large group of seals is startled into the water and a baby gets lost in the shuffle. Greig wrote, "These data suggest behavioral disruption rather than disease predisposed these neonatal seals to trauma. Sources of disturbance for seals previously reported for Drakes Estero include primarily humans and occasionally birds, planes, kayaks, and motorboats."

(Note to humans in Point Reyes National Seashore: Do not go near the seals!)

One thing that is important to remember with regard to Drakes Bay Oyster Company's operations is that this wasn't a murder trial. It wasn't necessary to prove guilt beyond the shadow of a doubt. The MMC was choosing to adopt the "precautionary principle," which means that in the event of uncertainty, one should err on the side of resource protection. After all, it was still unknown what made seals choose or abandon particular areas, and how deeply or not they could be affected by a "disturbance." It could be benign, a mere inconvenience, but it could be quite severe, as shown in Greig's report. This was a sensitive natural area under federal protection after all, whether there was an official wilderness designation or not.

Lots of people didn't like or didn't agree with the Marine Mammal Commission's report. For one, it also found that oyster boats were not even the most disruptive presence to seals in the estuary, in terms of what made the seals flush into the water. By far the biggest source of observed disturbances to harbor seals were "other humans," i.e., park visitors. Frankly, these are people like me who walked blissfully down the beach and then either stumbled upon a group of seals on the other side of a dune, or else intentionally approached them in order to snap a photo or have some kind of "authentic wilderness experience" only to spook the seals in question. I am certainly guilty of all of these. After "other humans" (seventy-nine observed instances in nine years), the next most disturbing thing was "unknown" (fifty-three instances), birds (thirty-eight), aircraft (twenty-six), clammers (thirteen) and then oyster boats—just ten instances in nine years. After that came coyotes and researchers, a tie, then non-motorized boats, then fishermen.

Critics of the MMC report also noted that the individual responses of the panel members, which informed the final conclusions, were included in unedited form in the report's Appendix F. I heard some in the pro-oyster camp allege that the responses were "hidden" there, and a joke circulated that one should not let the other side marginalize you, i.e. "Don't let them Appendix F you." There certainly is some confusing and conflicting information in there. One panel member didn't seem to think that there "should" be any problem with harbor seals and oyster boats coexisting in the same bay. After all, seals and oyster farms could be found together elsewhere in the country. Furthermore, a panel member provided a link to a YouTube video of seals on a San Diego beach, barely moving as visitors walked within a few inches of them. The message seemed to be that harbor seals were not disturbed by humans whom they no longer feared. As Kevin would point out to journalists, "They're called *harbor* seals." However, as Tim pointed out to me, it didn't ultimately matter what populations of seals in other parts of the country did or did not find disturbing; what mattered was whether these particular activities disturbed the seals that lived *here*. And what the MMC had found was that the data on disturbances to harbor seals in Drakes Estero was "scant" and already stretched to the limit.

# 13

# SHELL GAMES

WHEN YOU GROW up next to a national park, as I did, it is easy to feel like you own it, and in a very real sense you do. National parks are the property of the American people as a whole. However that doesn't mean you can do as you like with them, as I have personally been reminded on a few occasions.

I am an inveterate flower picker. I can manage to find flowers to pick in even the most unlikely of places, not unlike the way our family's daffy but determined golden retriever Ropher could find water to jump into pretty much anywhere that we let him out of the car. I have picked flowers on five continents, in wild places and in cities; legally, unknowingly illegally, and on occasion with a willful disregard for the law (I'm looking at you, flowering Brooklyn magnolia trees with low-hanging branches: sorry). When I'm in New York I live in one of Brooklyn's more industrial neighborhoods, but still I have picked flowers there, too. I have picked flowering weeds poking out through the chain-link fences of vacant lots, and on one very late and slightly tipsy spring night, I plucked a sprig of lilac from a sidewalk garden near the Gowanus Canal. Again, my sincere apologies. When I was younger and living in bucolic Northern California, it was a rare hike that I went

on that did not result in some wild bouquet—yellow acacia or plum
blossoms in February, daffodils and narcissus in March, forget-me-
nots and roses and foxgloves and honeysuckle and nearly everything
else from April through June. There was flowering coyote bush in July,
Pink Lady lilies in August, colorful leaves in the fall, and evergreen
and red berry branches in winter. I didn't know it at the time, but even
in the county-protected open spaces near my childhood home, this is
actually illegal. In Point Reyes National Seashore just a short drive
away, it definitely is, too.

　I was once walking back to my car from a trail hike through the
wilderness area near Limantour Beach. I had begun by heading down
through a wet little wood of young trees with a small musical brook
running alongside. I then came out into a wide open field of tall dry
grass with a view of the ocean. I could have continued on that path to
avoid the sand, but instead I scampered down a dune to the beach and
pulled off my shoes, opting to walk in the surf for about a mile. I then
turned back towards the hills and away from the sea, trying my best
to brush the sand from my salty-wet feet with my socks before putting my shoes back on, and rejoined the trail where it climbed upward
again. The way was overhanging with fragrant purple ceanothus, a
native shrub in the buckthorn family that's also called California lilac,
its fuzzy flower-clusters busy with fat and wriggling bees. There is
a meadow at the top of the ridge, next to a pine forest, which has
grown back now with incredible fecundity and denseness following
the Mount Vision fire of 1995, but at the time was still a little charred.
Then the trail slopes down again to meet the place where I started, near
a daffodil field. Naturally, by the time that I was walking back to my

car I had collected a modest but diverse little illicit bouquet. A park ranger drove up alongside me.

"You can't take that," he said, rather guiltily, gesturing towards my flowers as his engine idled. I was around nineteen years old then, my long hair wild and curly from the coastal breeze. I was wearing hiking boots but also a dress, and with my flowers in hand was generally doing my best impression of Marianne from *Sense and Sensibility*. It was apparent that the ranger did not want to be telling me this thing about the flowers. Similarly, I did not really want to hear it. There was so much abundant nature around my family's house that appeared to be free for the taking, and this just felt like more of the same. Even though of course I knew it was a park, I wasn't consciously poaching federal property. I just didn't think about it. I was told I had to leave the flowers there by the side of the road. Yes, even though they would just wilt in the sun. Yes, even though I had already picked them.

Another time, a few years before, it was a fellow park visitor who verbally slapped my hand away from picking flowers. It was March of 1996 or 1997, I can't remember which. There is a kind of native iris that grows all over Point Reyes in the springtime—Douglas iris—which is mostly purple but occasionally also white or pale pink. There were already lots of them before the fire, but in the years afterwards there have been even more. Anyway, on this spring afternoon I was driving back from the beach with my boyfriend when I demanded that he pull over so I could collect some wild irises—they were just so beautiful. But as I was leaning down to pick some from among the tender green grasses by the side of the road, another car drove by and an older woman leaned her head out of the passenger-side window.

"No! No! No!" she screamed angrily as they whooshed past, as if she'd just witnessed me savagely beating a child or abusing a baby animal. Or maybe not quite that severe, since whoever was driving the car did not find it necessary to slow down.

In my defense, I was in high school and there are worse transgressions I could have been committing, and I have since reformed my ways. Nevertheless, when it comes to protecting the nature of Point Reyes, people can get very passionate indeed.

In 2009 Sim Van der Ryn, a local architect famous for pioneering environmentally friendly construction models, completed a concept design for a possible new farm-meets-store-meets-hatchery-meets-visitor-center at Drakes Bay Oyster Company. The introduction began:

> Drakes Bay Family Farms asked the EcoDesign Collaborative to re:invision [sic] their existing oyster processing facility so that it may better meet the needs of their operations and mission in the 21st century. Our scope of work for this stage was to formalize the building program, understand the best uses for the site and to derive a conceptual design and master plan that reflected the values, priorities and future aspirations of Drakes Bay Family Farms. This project has many variables to contend with; our hope is that this initial vision can add inspiration to the overall goal of creating a world-class processing building and visitor's center that enhances the natural ecosystems and cultural resources of our Point Reyes National Seashore.

I'm going to be honest with you: looking at Sim's design made me sad that it will never exist. Thinking of the creativity and care that went into it is a little heartbreaking. It made me want very badly to go there, although admittedly I'm a sucker for pretty much anywhere with an aquarium. Add oysters into the mix, and I'm sold. If this were an alternate universe without the controversy, with no issues of wilderness or mud-slinging or seals, and this facility had actually been built, it likely would have become one of my favorite places in the seashore. What they came up with is not only lovely but rather ingenious. It is beautiful. As the proposal states, even the design is a teaching tool. It has a living green roof and is raised off of the ground to accommodate tides and also a possible sea-level rise due to climate change. The proposal calls it "future-proof." The roof extends outward from the neighboring cliff, so that when seen from above it looks like a natural formation with vegetation growing on top, that just happens to have a jetty coming out of it. Instead of the cluttered sheds and vats on the shore, everything would be streamlined, orderly and logical.

Based around the life cycle of an oyster, visitors could observe the oyster farm employees working in the lab and the hatchery, sorting the oysters harvested from the bay, shucking and packing. There is space for an exhibit, a kitchen, a shop, and an oyster bar. Everything is visible through glass that shows all the way through to the estuary on the other side, so that the pristine view is not obstructed. In place of the village of rundown homes, there would be a visitor parking lot. Where the oyster farm currently had picnic tables and piles of shells, there would be a visitor observation deck. Surely there would also be nerdy little science exhibits, and in the retail store the computer rendering depicted large tanks of tropical fish and coral that take up two whole walls. Other than the worker housing, the only thing missing is the mountains of oyster shells, for which no clear space has been designated (although an area marked "storage yard—6' fence" might be a likely candidate). Perhaps the assumption would be that the shells would all go back into the estero to create reefs for the "native" oysters to use as cultch, which Kevin was so keen on importing. If done right and well-maintained, Sim's design could have been amazing. It was submitted by DBOC to the National Park Service to be included in the DEIS. This was meant to inspire Secretary Salazar to go with "Alternative D": that the farm not only be allowed to stay, but to overhaul its entire system.

This wasn't the first professional redesign of the oyster farm I had seen. When I started working at the *Light*, the editor showed me a Xerox copy of some architectural plans for a new visitor's center at the oyster farm. I was told the plans had been commissioned by the park. There wasn't a name on them, but I'm pretty sure the editor told me that the designs had been made by the same architect who did the Bear Valley Visitor Center at park headquarters. Or maybe Dave Weiman told me this. I'm not exactly sure. The information came from somewhere. Later, when Ginny Lunny showed me around the oyster farm, she also invited me into their office, located inside a single-wide trailer onsite. There was an obviously Photoshopped picture tacked to the wall of Kevin riding a Jet Ski through the waters of Drakes Estero.

"What's that?" I asked, pointing to it. Ginny laughed and said it was a long story. Then she showed me the architectural plans. They did look very much like the park headquarters in their aesthetic. Like the ones I'd seen in the *Light* office, these too were copies and the edges were cut off, so that no identifying information could be found. I don't remember Ginny telling me either way if the park had commissioned or approved the designs, just that she was rather mysterious and twinkly about it, as if to say *Can you believe this?* The implication was that this was strong evidence that the National Park Service once intended to allow the oyster farm to stay. I have heard this cited by other oyster farm supporters as well. The only problem with this is that it isn't true. I eventually saw the original designs in the park archives, which had both the name and contact information of the architect who made them. His name is Charles Dresler. I called him up.

"No, the park did not commission or approve those," he told me. He explained that Tom Johnson paid for the designs when he was in the middle of his legal problems with the county, when sewage from the worker housing was leaking into the estuary. Even at the time, Charles said he knew the design was unlikely to be implemented, but Tom wanted to use it to illustrate how the Johnson Oyster Company might clean up its act. Otherwise, they were going to be shut down more than a decade before the end of their lease. In applying for a loan from the Bank of Oakland to cover the cost of bringing the oyster farm up to code, Don Neubacher wrote a letter of support on Tom's behalf, but pointed out that the lease was set to end, and when.

"The NPS purchased the land and facilities from the Johnson Oyster Company in 1972," Neubacher wrote to the bank on November 22, 1996. "A condition of the sale was that the Johnson family would have a forty-year reservation of possession (ROP) of the site that will expire in 2012." He goes on to say that NPS couldn't terminate the lease before 2012 without offering financial compensation, and added that the park was "genuinely excited" about the planned changes. As Kevin Lunny later pointed out, the oyster farm and its environmental problems were Don's "biggest headache."

Two years later in 1998, NPS completed an Environmental Assessment (EA), as required by law, to ascertain if the renovations to

Johnson's Oyster Company could be made without harming the flora and fauna of the protected area. Making reference to the Johnsons' legal troubles with the county board of health, the stated reason for the EA was put thusly:

> The purpose and need for this proposed project is to bring the JOC into compliance with federal, state and Marin County regulations. Existing facilities do not currently meet federal, state, and county health and safety codes. *Failure to perform the necessary improvement would result in Marin County and the NPS issuing cease and desist orders for operation of the facility* [italics added].

The proposed renovations were not part of a grand, park-generated plan to build a gleaming new oyster-based visitor center. Rather, they were an attempt to keep the Johnson Oyster Company in business. The talk of shutting the farm down due to health hazards began a good twenty years before the lease was set to expire. The architectural drawings were just an example, a "what if" of Tom's. What if they had the money. What if the park wanted them to stay. (What if, what if.)

On June 6, 2008, Sarah Allen received an email from a graduate student about what would come to be called the "hidden cameras." In the documents I was able to examine via a Freedom of Information Act request, the student's name was redacted in nearly every instance save one, by mistake. Nevertheless I will not be including it.

"Hi Sarah," REDACTED wrote. "Here are the images from the stationary cameras that might be of interest."

She included the following information, connecting time-stamp ID tags for the images with observational notes.

*2008-4-03, 2:08 Boat leaves [oyster bar] channel and there is possibly one seal that flushes into the water*

*2008-5-15, 2:07 Boat leaves [oyster bar] and seals flush into water*

*2008-3-23, 5:23 Boat leaving Home Bay*

*2008-3-25, 5:01 Boat leaving Home Bay (might be a boat, its blurry) [sic]*

*2008-4-14, 6:21 and 6:25 Boat going into Home Bay and then leaving (possibly a boat, hard to tell)*

*2008-4-15, 5:05 Boat leaving Home Bay*
[etc.]

These were instances of oyster boat movement during pupping season, some of them near harbor seals, which lasts from March 1 to June 30. REDACTED was working with biologist Ellen Hines at UC San Francisco to study the harbor seals at Drakes Estero. In her project proposal she states that the research sought to examine seal behavior in relation to the presence of oyster mariculture. She liked the work, but her ability to tend to the camera and monitor the photos was intermittent, and all in all the whole enterprise seemed disaster-prone.

"I have attached a word document which contains the activity at Drakes Estero captured by the camera," REDACTED wrote in an email to Sarah Allen on November 5, 2009. "I apologize that I am sending it to you two months after I took the camera down, I'm hope

[sic] [harbor seal monitoring coordinator] told you that I lost the original word document when my computer crashed and thus had to look through the photos a second time. Not bad photos to look at though!"

It took her another two months to mail the CD containing the photos, and she had other problems besides an unreliable computer. She didn't have a car of her own, and often had a hard time getting out to the site where a Reconyx stationary wildlife camera was trained on Drakes Estero, allegedly taking one photo per minute, all day every day, although plenty of things went wrong. Sometimes the camera got knocked over and took pictures of the ground. Sometimes it sat there not taking pictures at all because the memory card was full or the battery was dead. Some of the pictures were blurred because the lens had fogged up and needed to be cleaned manually in order for the pictures to be discernible again. To visit the camera, she relied on rides from her boyfriend, or her roommate, or the harbor seal monitoring coordinator, or Sarah Allen, or some other member of the park staff who was headed that way. First, however, for some of the rides she'd need to get all the way out to Point Reyes from where she lived in San Francisco. Sometimes she was able to borrow a car from someone, but not frequently. When she got a ride, she would often have to wait out in the seashore for hours after she completed her tasks, exposed to the elements, before someone could pick her up again. The camera was left on its own for weeks or even months at a time. It was hard to tell if it was aimed at the right spot, and sometimes she got the framing a little off. The sandbar and the seals and any boats going near them were pretty far away, and it was difficult to see what actually turned up in the photos. Was that a boat? A glare on the lens? A trick of the light? Something else?

"I don't see anything in the pictures," the harbor seal monitoring coordinator wrote to REDACTED on February 17, 2010, when REDACTED's observation notes and the images did not match up, "which makes me wonder if maybe the camera is not pointed at the right sandbar and it might need to move over to the right a little." The coordinator said she had gone ahead and moved the camera.

"My roommate is taking me out to the site so that should be fun," REDACTED replied that same day. "I am glad the camera might be on track now."

A week later she wrote again with an update on her observation site.

"When I got out there, the tripod had slipped. Footage from the video card showed that it happened at night during the week (owl?)."

When she asked seashore scientist Ben Becker to write her a letter of recommendation to go along with a fellowship application, he suggested that she "be sure to closely tie anticipated study results to inform park management." In other words, one can extrapolate that if the oyster farm was disturbing seals, this study hoped to document it. However, she encountered problem after problem. In May the camera was knocked askew again, and she thought she'd fixed it, but when she went back to check the latest batch of photos she noticed that it was aimed too high and had been photographing nothing; one photograph of nothing per minute, all day every day. She emailed the monitoring coordinator to see if she could maybe go out and fix the camera, but the monitoring coordinator was busy and couldn't. Then a second camera was installed, but REDACTED had a hard time programming it. She couldn't get the card reader to work. Did it need a special computer program? Could anyone help her out?

"We're not sure why it's not working or how to install the program," the monitoring coordinator wrote to her towards the end of
May 2010. "So I think you are going to need to call Reconyx. Sorry."

On June 5th 2010, REDACTED wrote to Ben Becker with her
worst news so far.

"Hi Ben, I have some bad news. . . . I had an accident . . ."

It turned out she had fully dislocated her kneecap and after spending all day in the hospital was discharged with crutches and a leg brace.

"I can't believe this has happened," REDACTED wrote. "It has
ruined all my plans for the summer. I can't move up to Point Reyes
now. I can't do my research. I will be stuck in the city for 6 weeks and
then have physio [ . . . ] Sorry for any inconvenience."

The very next day, on Sunday, June 7, Corey Goodman was review-
ing an NPS document when he noticed a reference in one of the appen-
dixes to what the *Light* referred to as "a renaissance camera." The
next day he announced the discovery during a meeting with seashore
officials and Tim Ragen of the MMC, whose report was not out yet.

"We were stunned to learn that the park has been secretly
photographing oyster farm activities, using a camera hidden in
thorns and bushes," Kevin Lunny told the *Light* that week. Corey
Goodman demanded that park staff dismantle the cameras immediately. Superintendent Don Neubacher had recently been transferred
to Yosemite National Park, and Point Reyes had a new chief, a local
woman from Sausalito named Cicely Muldoon. She was forty-four,
with a brown, face-framing bob. Corey said the park needed to "rebuild
trust with the community" and that Cicely must assure the public that
"on her watch, there will never be hidden cameras or listening devices
spying on ranchers and farmers within the seashore."

Wildlife cameras for the purpose of research, set to record both animals and the possibility of humans interacting with them, are fairly common in national parks and other protected areas around the country. Plus, if the public had complained that NPS did not have enough data on whether or not the oyster farm was bothering seals, then in theory at least this seemed like a reasonably effective way to remedy that. Here was an attempt to collect concrete data. Nevertheless, the media picked up on the "hidden camera" story, and locals were outraged. The *San Francisco Chronicle* said the cameras were "trained on workers in Drakes Estero." ABC News said there were three hundred thousand "hidden camera" photographs "showing Drakes Bay Oyster Company over three years." A *Harper's* article refers to them as "hidden surveillance cameras." Corey later referred to it as a "hidden camera system." At least locally, it was a public relations disaster for the park.

A reporter for the *West Marin Citizen* wrote to Sarah Allen and other park scientists hoping to get an inside scoop. When and why was the camera set up in the estero? Why wasn't the public informed? She wanted Sarah's personal point of view on the matter.

"It's important considering the other paper is now run by Dr. Goodman," the reporter wrote.

Corey sent Cicely a long email. "[ . . . ] I have some advice and a request concerning the secret camera photographing Lunny's oyster beds and oyster workers [in the estero] for the past 2? years," he wrote, seven paragraphs in.

If you simply say that this camera is aimed at wildlife, you will regret such a statement as the photographs themselves, and their use in the May 1, 2009 "Briefing Statement," reveal the true intent—the focus is on the lateral channel and the oyster beds, and is not optimized to get as many harbor seal haul-out sites as possible. I would recommend that you say that the hidden nature of the cameras disturbs you—as is the fact that Lunny was never told—and that you will investigate its purpose and history, and that you will assure the agricultural community that you will not allow spying on ranchers and farmers.

He requested that the park service email him the photo files. Cicely replied:

> You talked at the Monday meeting about how divisive this issue has been in the community. I agree, and believe we all have a real opportunity to change the tone of the discussion, acknowledge where we disagree, and doing so [sic] without rancor or malice. I confess the tenor of your message concerns me, as it seems to perpetuate the divisive tone that we are all committed to moving beyond. I look forward to discussing this further with you.

Next came a slew of emails about whether or not REDACTED, still laid up with her busted knee, would be able to get her boyfriend to go out and check the camera for her. Corey wrote to Cicely again, expressing concern about the way she was running the Seashore, in a message that was over 1,700 words long and peppered with detailed questions. Again he said that if the goal of the camera was to observe wildlife, he could think of "a half dozen" better locations from which to do so.

Corey would not be the only person to find the park's science lacking. In November he requested that the Department of the Interior conduct yet another investigation into the park's science with regard to Drakes Estero, determined as he was to prove that Sarah and her colleagues had committed scientific misconduct. Attorney-advisor Gavin Frost of the Department of the Interior submitted his report in March of 2011 on "Allegations of Scientific Misconduct at Point Reyes National Seashore"—what was called "the Frost report." While Frost was clearly unimpressed with the rigor of the science in question, he did not issue a guilty verdict.

"The factual record firmly supports conclusions that there was no criminal violation or scientific misconduct, but that NPS, as an organization and through its employees, made mistakes which may have contributed to an erosion of public confidence," Frost wrote. Indeed, one can even read a whiff of weariness into the amount of quotation marks Frost places around Corey's ("the informant's") chosen language, especially the prevalence of the word "false," as in "false claims," and "false science." (In fact, after reading through the Frost report I encountered the word "false" so many times that I started picturing the character Dwight Schrute from the television show *The Office*, who likes to refute statements by first loudly declaring *"False!"*) Frost paints a rather unflattering portrait of the Drakes Estero science, and makes it seem like the wildlife camera was exclusively Sarah Allen's project, rather than the half-committed student affair of REDACTED's that it seems to have been upon closer examination. While Sarah may have instigated the research, she did not conduct it or directly supervisor the graduate student who did. Frost noted the problems plaguing the camera research, but managed to make it sound like these deficiencies were all Sarah's fault. He notes that Sarah did manage to analyze more than five thousand photographs, although this was a relatively low percentage of the overall volume.

It seemed that outrage over the state of research at the National Park Service had eclipsed the conversation about environmental policy, and supporters of the oyster farm had changed the conversation completely. It was no longer about policy, but about science. Fred Smith and others in the environmental camp would argue that the debate about "false" science was a straw man argument. Besides, the park service was not the only one finding environmental fault with the oyster farm.

Tom Baty is a local fisherman, beachcomber and forager who had lived in Point Reyes for the past fifty-two years. When I finally met him, he reminded me of the sort of man you might encounter on a ship a hundred years ago, shouting something about jibs and forestays in the middle of a gale while other men scrabbled to do his bidding. He has a keen look in his eye and a firm handshake, and I want to say there is something vaguely ursine about him, but I don't know what. He is tall, handsome and darkish, and when we met it was at a luncheon where he'd brought salmon he caught himself, so maybe that had something to do with it. I know he caught the salmon on his own boat with a fishing rod, and not in a stream with his bare hands, but nevertheless that was the image that came to mind when he said it. In any case, Tom was fed up with the oyster farm and wanted to do something about it.

He wrote to the California Coastal Commission in September of 2011 under the subject heading "the stream of plastic debris flowing from the Drakes Bay Oyster Company," and said that in a single month he decided to walk nearly all of the beaches in the seashore with a handheld GPS unit, to record where he found debris from the oyster farm. He says he collected 726 pieces of mariculture debris, in 607 locations. Although DBOC claimed the debris was old, left over from the Johnson Oyster days, Baty asserted that much of the debris was obviously new and used exclusively by the new operation. He said that over the space of a year he had picked up literally thousands of pieces of mariculture debris, including mesh bags and PVC tubes. He even brought bags of the garbage to a Board of Supervisors hearing, echoing the avalanching arrival of Save Our Seashore petition letters in 1969, as orchestrated by Katy Miller, Congressman Clem Miller's widow. While Kevin acknowledged that the items had indeed come from his farm and promised to institute a "zero tolerance" policy, Baty said he'd since seen more debris, not less.

In 2010, Fred had decided to take a break from West Marin and go back to grad school to get a business degree. He was replaced at the EAC by a pretty woman in her thirties named Amy Trainer, with long brown hair, a history of teaching yoga, and a serene golden retriever named Henry (after Thoreau) who went with her most places. She was also a lawyer, and came in with a much more hard-line attitude with regard to the oyster farm. However, despite her efforts it seemed like the pro-wilderness side was already losing in the court of public opinion.

After the park published the draft Environmental Impact Statement for Drakes Bay Oyster Company in the fall of 2011, Corey Goodman gave a lecture at a Point Reyes Station community center called the Dance Palace to take a public look at the science in the 722-page report. He stood behind a wooden podium wearing jeans and a black T-shirt, and noted with disappointment that members of the park service were not present.

"You know, I grew up in a scientific culture," he said, "in bio-medical research where you are quite used to having to defend science. Now what I mean by that is we go constantly to scientific meetings where people who think you made a mistake or think you've said or done something wrong are always asking you tough questions." He expressed frustration that he could not seem to get that kind of scientific debate going in West Marin.

"Excuse me," he said, "the scientific community is one where we debate and we probe, and we try to actually shoot down dogma." He went on to explain that in science, you never actually "prove" something to be correct, but rather you make hypotheses and models and then see if you can disprove them. "You're always looking to ask what's wrong," he said. "I know there are lots of legislative and regulatory and policy issues. I don't consider myself an expert on those. People here know a lot more about those than I do." He scanned the room with his palms facing up and out, as if in surrender to what he didn't know. "So I'm going to try and stay focused on what is the environmental impact. Because after all, if we're going to keep or get rid of the oyster farm, or rather, if Ken Salazar, the Secretary of the Department of the Interior is going to, it should be based on environmental impacts."

He related the story of being asked to get involved, and how Steve Kinsey told him that Kevin Lunny could face jail time over the alleged environmental "felonies" being committed in Drakes Estero. He explained how blown away he was by the "Sheltered Wilderness Estuary" report, finding in his estimation that the conclusions of the source material were in fact the opposite of those stated in the brochure. His style was friendly and professorial, and a comment about

oyster feces got a giggle from the audience. He then went on to eviscer-
ate the Draft Environmental Impact Statement.

"Now mind you, this is all spending our money," he said, casting a
side-eye around the room. "This is taxpayer money. This stuff doesn't
come cheap. These are half-million and million-dollar studies."

He said that when Feinstein wrote her rider to give the option of
an extension, she added language that "legislatively instructed" NPS
to base their Environmental Impact Statement on the conclusions of
the report put out in 2009 by the National Academy of Sciences, the
highest scientific body in the United States—of which Corey is a well-
respected member. In his mind, this meant that the DEIS should have
reached the same conclusion reached in that report.

"Well, we don't need a seven-hundred-page EIS if it's going to be
based on those conclusions, because that was a pretty simple sentence,
wasn't it? 'There is a lack of strong scientific evidence that shellfish
farming has major adverse ecological effects on Drakes Estero.'"

In fact, the DEIS had, in a sense, dismissed the NAS report, because
as Corey put it "they don't define the word 'major.'" As I see it personally and as NPS scientists have also argued, it isn't the absence of the
definition of the *word* "major" that poses a problem, but rather the
failure to establish what was meant by a "major impact" or the lack
of "strong" scientific evidence. Was there perhaps *moderate* evidence
of major adverse ecological impact? Or *strong* evidence of moderate
impact? There is no universal understanding of what a "major" impact
entails, either with regard to a wilderness area or a federally protected
animal. Therefore, defining those terms was of fundamental importance.

Corey broke the report down into word frequency, saying that the
word "potential" occurred 514 times. He said the word "data" also

appeared frequently, but that most of the instances were not "relevant for today." He said the only "piece of data" came from the Becker report, which he then also dismissed.

"Five hundred and fourteen 'potentials' and one actual piece of data," he said. "[ . . . ] we've spent millions of dollars, taxpayer money, the oyster farm's been there for eighty years, and what I'm struck by is—no data. Seven hundred pages and no data."

The DEIS detailed potential impacts to seven endangered species that live in the estuary including the Myrtle's silverspot butterfly, the Western Snowy Plover and the California Least Tern, and Corey decided to tackle the possibility of harm with regard to the endangered California red-legged frog.

> First of all, I'm an environmentalist, and I hope all of you are environmentalists. We live in an incredible place—I mean, one of the most beautiful places in the world—and it's, you know, it's an honor for all of us to live here and we want to preserve it. We all know about endangered species all over the world, and we want to keep endangered species, we want to maintain biodiversity, keep species, we don't want things to go extinct. And we've seen lots of extinctions. So anytime someone raises the word about an endangered species, we should all be alarmed. And I'll show you that those words have been used to alarm people here.

He got a chuckle from the audience when he pointed out that the reason the frogs could potentially be threatened was by getting run over by oyster workers' or visitors' vehicles on land. This didn't make sense to him, since the road to the farm runs along a salt marsh, and frogs are averse to saltwater. There was also a drainage pond right next to the oyster worker housing where frogs have been observed, but he didn't mention this.

"How do you become endangered if you don't live in saltwater?" he asked. "Maybe the oyster workers, you guys, are gonna catch frogs and throw frogs in saltwater. [ . . . ] You'll find out the word is, ah, direct quote is 'increased risk of vehicle strikes.'" The audience laughed. "Driving at fifteen miles an hour over that dirt road—half a mile road—you guys are gonna run over red-legged frogs." More laughter. "Please no laughing here—this is what the EIS says." The audience laughed louder.

"For many of you who I believe live in the Inverness area, I have to tell you the fate of your homes," he went on.

And I'm really sorry. Because the biologist in me says if it's legitimate to call the red-legged frog being endangered by a half-mile piece of road right along saltwater, um, where you have to drive about fifteen miles an hour, if you have 2.6 million visitors to this park each year running around fifty miles of roads, um, I think we have to ban all motor vehicles. I think we have to cut out Inverness. We might let you stop at Point Reyes and you can walk your groceries over—I mean, I, I, I don't, I just simply don't get it. And you can go through each one of the endangered species this way, but I'll suggest to you that the endangered species simply—they become code words for us to say "My God, there's something wrong." There is no impact on endangered species. There wasn't in 1998, there isn't now.

Later, oyster farm advocates would find even more to critique with regard to the park science. In an attempt to illustrate other possible impacts, such as noise, the decibel level of a Jet Ski was used as a stand-in for the farm's much quieter oyster boats. In the absence of very much hard data on environmentally harmful effects, the biggest strike against the shellfish grower seemed to be that the presence of the farm impacted the "wilderness experience." Many seemed to find this laughable, given the neighboring dairy farms—or, at the very least, easy to dismiss.

IN OCTOBER 2012, a month before Secretary Salazar arrived in the Seashore to make his decision, celebrity food writer Michael Pollan wrote to Dianne Feinstein to express his support for the farm.

"I've followed the saga for several years now, with a mounting sense of wonder and disappointment in the behavior of the Park Service," he wrote, in a letter on UC Berkeley Graduate School of Journalism letterhead.

> Drakes Bay is an important thread in the local sustainable food community, and it would be a shame—in fact an outrage—if the company were closed down as a result of the Park Service's ideological rigidity and misuse of science.

Pollan said that an "all or nothing" ethic that pitted man against nature, wilderness against agriculture, might be useful in other instances, but not here. He said the park was twisting history and science to promote a "fantasy" of wilderness restoration in what was really a "beautiful semi-domesticated landscape." He hoped that Feinstein would be able to persuade Salazar to offer an extension of the Special Use Permit, but that was not to be.

IN NOVEMBER, SALAZAR flew out to California. He visited Point Reyes and Drakes Estero, spoke with the Lunnys and with their cattle ranching neighbors. But while he vowed to make a more substantial commitment to the ranches and dairies in the pastoral zone, he decided not to offer an extension for the oyster farm. This was the opportunity that Feinstein had fought to give the Lunnys, and now it had passed them by. Kevin said his family was beset with "disbelief and excruciating sorrow." Thinking back to the ecological design that architect Sim Van der Ryn created, I can understand just a fraction of how strong their hope must have been that they'd be able to put those dreams into action. Now, just eight years after purchasing the farm, they were being told they had to go. But Kevin was not prepared to go quietly, and right away filed a lawsuit against the United States Secretary of the Interior.

# 14

## RECKONING

I N THE FINAL legal battle over the oyster farm, two warring theories seemed to reign: the "first domino" versus the "dangerous precedent." If the oyster farm went, the "first domino" faction argued, it would herald the end of the ranches inside the seashore, and maybe in the region as a whole. The oysters would be pulled out of the water, fecal coliform in runoff from cows on the surrounding ranches would cease to be filtered by the oysters, water quality would suffer, and the ranches would be evicted by their federal landlord in order to "protect park resources." This hypothesis was not based on any particular scientific study, nor had such a thing occurred in any other location, but still the idea gained local traction. Dairy farming is especially dependent on a certain amount of critical mass, so that if one farm goes out of business, it can impact surrounding operations and jeopardize them. The same can be true of ranches raising beef cattle, which depend on the availability of a local slaughterhouse to make their business profitable. If there aren't enough ranches to support a local slaughterhouse, cattlemen are forced to spend more money on trucking their animals further afield for slaughter. Thus, the worst fear on the part of the oyster farm supporters was that without DBOC, the seashore ranches would be evicted and the whole region's celebrated local agricultural industry would collapse. On the other hand, wilderness supporters feared that reversing a wilderness designation through an act of Congress would create a "dangerous precedent" and leave all protected lands vulnerable to the interests of private business. If removing wilderness designation could be done once, they argued, it could and would be done again.

On December 3, 2012, Drakes Bay Oyster Company announced its intent to sue the federal government, represented by a team of lawyers from Cause of Action and three different law firms: Stoel Rives LLP, which focuses on environmental law; SSL Law Firm LLP, focused on real estate; and Briscoe Ivester & Bazel LLP, specializing in land use and natural resources.

"The National Park Service has not just shut down our business, but has misrepresented the law, our contracts with the State of California, and the results of scientific studies," Kevin Lunny said in a statement. "Our family business is not going to sit back and let the government steam roll [sic] our community, which has been incredibly supportive of us."

That same day, Cause of Action executive director Dan Epstein said his group fought federal agencies "every day" that abused power, ignored the law and wasted taxpayer dollars. "We aim to hold the National Park Service accountable for their treatment of the Lunny family and the Drakes Bay Oyster Company as we view their actions as a disregard for law and precedent that demands accountability," he said.

On December 12, the Lunnys' legal team of seven lawyers filed a motion for a temporary restraining order and order to show cause against Secretary Salazar, parks director Jonathan Jarvis, the Department of the Interior, the National Park Service, and various park employees. The motion claimed that the defendants had violated the Administrative Procedure Act of 1946, the National Environmental Policy Act of 1969, and the Data Quality Act of 2001. Without such a restraining order, the motion argued, the Lunnys would suffer "grave and irreparable harm" due to the closure of their business, which would result in the loss of thirty-one jobs and affordable housing for fifteen people, would damage the environment, and cause "impacts to the State of California" by terminating the "interpretative and educational value" of the oyster farm.

"We have about eight to ten million oysters still in the bay being farmed at different stages of growth," Kevin said in a media conference call on December 4, 2012. "And because we've only been given ninety days to wind down and get off the property, essentially, not maybe all but almost all of those oysters are going to have to be destroyed and the food is going to be lost and the investment for that inventory will be lost. And this all happened with one day's notice. We heard on the 29th, and our agreement expired on the 30th. So as we stated before, you know, we're not going to walk away. Instead we have incredible community support, so we're fighting for our community, our employees and our family against a federal bureaucracy here that seems to value lies, you know, over the truth, and special interests over the welfare of a whole community."

He said that the farm was a public resource and provided a public service. He did not argue that this was the case despite the fact that the farm was a private business.

"Cause of Action decided to get involved in this because Cause of Action is concerned any time arbitrary government action harms American free enterprise, and that's what this issue is about," said Dan Epstein during the same conference call. "Cause of Action first became interested in this because what we saw was the Department of Interior, through its National Park Service, was using scientific data, in what we viewed as flawed scientific data, to ultimately justify a draft Environmental Impact Statement that has now informed a decision to deny a supplemental use permit. And we think that this tells a story about how flawed agency decision-making and flawed science can have an impact upon everyday Americans. And it also tells a story about how flawed science can actually lead to real-world impacts in terms of expanding discretion of federal agencies and allowing them to engage in arbitrary and capricious action. That's why Cause of Action has decided to fight this. It's as simple as that. This is how the federal government has used its authority to shut down small business, and it's something that—if Cause of Action and others don't fight against it, it's going to be something that allows the federal government to expand its authority at the detriment to those hard workers in this economy who are trying to keep jobs and ultimately help consumers."

Epstein certainly had previous experience "fighting the federal government," as he put it. From 2009 to 2011 he worked for the U.S.

House Committee on Oversight and Government Reform, headed by California Republican congressman Darrell Issa, which mounted a series of investigations into the Obama administration. Prior to that, Epstein worked for the Charles G. Koch Charitable Foundation, and was an alumnus of the Koch Associate Program—run by the foundation—which seeks to train professionals in "the importance of economic freedom." One of the issues that the Committee on Oversight and Government Reform investigated was the National Park Service's handling of the DBOC case. Epstein then left the committee's employ in August 2011 to become the executive director of the newly formed Cause of Action. Although purportedly nonpartisan, all of Cause of Action's seed money—close to $1 million—came from the Koch family of industries via the right-wing nonprofit organization Donors Trust, operated by the former director of fundraising for the Cato Institute, which was founded as the Charles Koch Foundation in 1974. In Cause of Action's first year, Epstein was paid a salary of $74,500. In the next year that amount leapt to nearly $200,000, with bonus, and the group's revenue had climbed to over $3 million, also from Koch sources, with $1.2 million listed for "other salaries and wages," not including that of Epstein and chief legal counsel Amber Abbasi ($136,534 with bonus). According to the 990 form provided by GuideStar.org, in 2012 the group spent $38,168 on "travel." Cause of Action also solicits donations on its website.

Ten days after the media conference call with Dan Epstein to announce the lawsuit, Kevin appeared on the Fox News television show *Fox & Friends*. Titled "Shell Shock," the segment began with a dramatic animated zoom through a deserted city street and into a graveyard, landing on the all-caps title THE DEATH OF

FREE ENTERPRISE floating amidst sepulchral mists and looming headstones.

"Whoa!" said cohost Gretchen Carlson as the shot returned to the studio. "That graphic should be nominated for . . . some sort of award. That's nice! After nearly one hundred years in business the federal government is forcing them to shut down. We're talking about Drakes Bay Oyster Farm in California, [which] was recently informed that they would not be allowed to renew their federal park lease. The Interior Department plans to turn the land into a marine wilderness area, and as a result the oyster company and its thirty employees are now out of work."

(This was not actually the case, as the farm was continuing to harvest and plant its oysters.) Beside her, a screen showed footage of DBOC's employees at work before cutting to a live shot of Kevin sitting in front of a high-rise window with a view of the San Francisco Bay. He wore a light-colored button-down shirt with a small microphone clipped to the collar, and his silver hair was combed back neatly from his tanned face.

"Kevin Lunny is the owner of Drakes Bay," Carlson continued, "and he is now suing for an injunction to keep his business open. Good morning to you, Kevin!"

"Good morning, Gretchen," he replied, before explaining the local support for his operation. "The community, and our county, and the San Francisco Bay Area loves us, but that didn't resonate with Washington, D.C."

"So the Interior Department wants to shut you down," Carlson said. "Why?" Her tone was upturned with incredulity.

"Well, um," said Kevin, "actually a small handful of folks who are really wilderness activists, who care deeply about getting people off the land, I think, is the best we can tell, want to give up something so [as] to create a humanless landscape. And it's a little strange, because Point Reyes National Seashore was *created* as a working landscape. The oyster farm is completely surrounded by working ranches, and so to remove the oyster farm from the middle of the historic ranching lands is odd."

"But aren't the oysters part of the landscape?" Carlson asked.

"Well," said Kevin, "they have been for a very long time. As a matter of fact the National Academy of Sciences says that Drakes Estero where the oysters live is probably healthier with the oyster farm because of the ecosystem services. It's the reason we see oysters being planted in the Chesapeake and San Francisco Bay, and now we have an Interior Department that wants to remove them."

"So let me ask you this, the Board of Supervisors—and let's face it, this is not a conservative part of the country—the Board of Supervisors, Senator Dianne Feinstein, *Democrat*—they looked at the claims and they also became outraged at what's happening to you?"

THERE WAS NO mention of the Wilderness Act or the 1976 designation of Drakes Estero as a potential wilderness area in the *Fox & Friends* appearance at all, but it would not go unexamined in other media. On May 1, 2013, after the oyster farm's closure was postponed again due to legal action, *PBS NewsHour* aired a segment on DBOC called "Strange

Bedfellows Join Fight to Keep Oyster Farm in Operation." It noted the battle's "unlikely cast of characters" and made it clear that Salazar's decision was due to the incompatibility of a commercial operation within a wilderness area. The footage showed Kevin standing among his workers on the dock, speaking with PBS reporter Spencer Michels, a thirty-year veteran of the station. Kevin's small dog, a white Chihuahua mix with a black head, ran up to Kevin and jumped into his arms.

"This lease has an explicit renewal clause," Kevin told Michels in the video. "It was always anticipated that it could be renewed by special use permit. It says it right in the original document." In voiceover, Michels stated that Kevin bought the farm knowing the lease would expire in 2012, but that he "tried to change that."

"This is exactly what was planned for the seashore and the oyster farm is part of the working landscape," Kevin said, his blue eyes bright under the shade of a Drakes Bay Oyster Company baseball cap. "It's part of the agriculture, it's really part of the fabric, part of the history, part of the culture, that was always expected to be preserved."

But the *NewsHour* crew turned then to Fred Smith's successor at the Environmental Action Committee of West Marin, Amy Trainer, who presented a different side of the story.

"Under the 1964 Wilderness Act, commercial operations and motor boats are not allowed, they are expressly prohibited, so this operation is wholly incompatible with this national park wilderness area," she said. She stood talking to Michels on a ridge with a sweeping view of the bay behind her. "This is a very dangerous precedent. Drakes Estero is considered the ecological heart of Point Reyes National Seashore, and it absolutely should be protected for future generations, without commercial uses."

Michels also noted that the fight had become a "conservative cause" in Washington, D.C., and mentioned that Cause of Action's executive director, Dan Epstein, once worked for one of the Koch brothers. That connection was first uncovered by *Mother Jones* reporter Gavin Aronsen back in December 2012, but because the organization was so young, the 990 forms were not yet available to prove that funding came from the Koch brothers as well. After hearing Epstein's take on how the oyster farm's plight could affect American small businesses, the camera cut to former Department of the Interior official and attorney Tom Strickland in his Washington office.

"I think this situation has been hijacked by interest groups with different agendas who have spun out narratives that have no relationship to the facts," Strickland said.

The *NewsHour* crew also interviewed Phyllis Faber, a beloved eighty-five-year-old local environmental activist who was on the board of the *Point Reyes Light* and had been one of the staunchest supporters of the oyster farm.

"I look at them as being sort of backward-looking, yearning for something that can't possibly exist," Faber said of the wilderness activists. "It's almost like a religion."

"Yet she is not happy to be on the same side as Cause of Action," Michels said in voiceover, as Faber's expression changed to one of concern, seemingly while Michels explained the connection between DBOC's powerful new ally and Koch Industries.

"I am very disturbed by that and I don't agree with it at all," she said. "I think what they're headed for is trying to use a commercial operation in a park; they want to establish that on other public lands, and I think that's terribly unfortunate."

Michels remarked that the controversy had overwhelmed the residents of Point Reyes, where "Lunny and his oysters are popular," and said that many people refused to comment on the record for fear of alienating their neighbors.

He also mentioned one of the oyster farm's most worrying associations of all: its inclusion in a bill to expedite the building of the Keystone XL Pipeline, an oil and gas pipeline system in Canada and the United States that would transport tar sands oil to the Midwest and the Gulf of Mexico from up north. According to an October 2013 article in the *Huffington Post*, the Koch brothers stood to make $100 billion from the project, effectively doubling their net worth. *Forbes* columnist Tim Worstall pointed out, however, that $100 billion was an overstatement; an estimate based on gross revenue rather than profit. The pipeline was going to cost $7 billion to build, after all. Besides, even if the estimated $100 billion *was* correct, Worstall argued, this would be a good thing, since that's another $100 billion of wealth that "has been added to the stock available to us, the human race."

"Sure," Worstall wrote, "maybe the Kochs will have it for some period of time. But it's still $100 billion of wealth that has been newly created." He did not offer an alternate sum he deemed more realistic.

The bill, known as the Energy Production and Project Delivery Act of 2013, was introduced by Louisiana republican David Vitter that February. The final portion of the bill, Section 310 ("Drakes Bay Oyster Company"), which directly followed a section on "Keystone XL permit approval," stated that DBOC would be granted a renewing ten-year reservation of use and occupancy, and that "Drakes Estero in the State of California shall not be converted to a designated wilderness."

The bill is, quite frankly, a terrifying document. It proposed to repeal any agreement seeking to limit or reduce greenhouse gas emissions, including international agreements with Russia, China and India, and also included several amendments to the Endangered Species Act, such as prohibiting consideration of the impact of "greenhouse gases and climate change" when seeking to protect endangered plants or animals.

While the *PBS NewsHour* segment did give Kevin the chance to state his case, the overall presentation was less than flattering to the oyster farm, what with its allusions to Koch money and dirty tar sands oil. Cause of Action was not happy, and two weeks later sent a threatening fourteen-page Freedom of Information Act request to Michael Getler, ombudsman of PBS. The letter complained that Dan Epstein was unfairly represented, and demanded that the station release all of the footage taped for the segment so that Cause of Action could decide whether the story had been presented accurately or not, and make that footage available to the public. In the letter, Cause of Action claimed that mentioning Epstein's Koch connections was not "balanced" reporting, since PBS had described Tom Strickland without mentioning his "long track record in Democratic politics and lobbying" or Amy Trainer's "litany of left-leaning organizations and clients." The letter also suggested that Phyllis Faber's negative reaction to Cause of Action was manipulated, and expressed annoyance that *NewsHour* had strayed from the scripted description of Cause of Action's activities provided by Epstein himself in an interview. There were no factual inaccuracies in the PBS segment, but Epstein and his associates still felt their portrayal was unjust.

"Cause of Action is concerned that the *NewsHour* piece misconstrued key facts, withheld material information, and misled the audience and an interviewee," the letter stated.

In the interests of public education, Cause of Action believes that PBS must release the full video recordings involved in the preparation of the May 1, 2013 *NewsHour* story so that the public may understand the full factual picture of the issues involved and judge the facts and questions raised by the content of the video.

The letter then went on to attack PBS's integrity, invoking the Public Broadcasting Act of 1967 and alleging that PBS was failing to adhere to the required objectivity and balance. Cause of Action demanded that all video and sound footage of the interviews, including those passersby who had been willing to appear on camera, be delivered free of charge within twenty business days. While the materials of the Public Broadcasting Service would not typically be thought of as government agency records, the letter said, Cause of Action argued that "several factors exist that motivate disclosure," such as a "moral and mission-related obligation" to do so.

Kevin, his wife Nancy, and Corey Goodman were, by all appearances, horrified by the tactic, and sent a letter of their own to the station, saying that they had severed their relationship with the government watchdog. Cause of Action's letter was a clear instance of intimidation and interference with the freedom of the press, they admitted: Epstein's group had gone too far.

"We recently learned of the May 17, 2013 letter and Freedom of Information Act (FOIA) request to you from Cause of Action," Kevin, Nancy and Corey wrote in their joint letter to PBS executives. "Regrettably, all three of our names were cited in the Cause of Action letter as if we condoned it, which we did not, and as if it was submitted on our behalf, which it was not."

Yet while the Lunny-Goodman letter made it clear that they "steadfastly defend the freedom of the press," they nevertheless stood by the assertion that the *NewsHour* segment was "biased."

"The piece by Spencer Michels which aired on the PBS *NewsHour* on May 1 uncritically repeated the false accusations that we have '. . . spun out narratives that have no relationship to the facts,'" the letter stated. "On the contrary, our 'narratives'—the virtue of a small family farm, the absence of any scientific evidence of harm to the environment, and misrepresentations of science made by a federal agency in its obsession to eliminate the farm—are indisputably true."

The quote about spinning narratives had not been Michels's but Strickland's, but by then it was common practice for DBOC and its supporters to conflate a quote by their opposition with a show of opposition from the journalist presenting that quote. Goodman and the Lunnys encouraged PBS to be "more balanced" in future coverage, and asked PBS executives to get together with them again, in order to better understand their side of the story and once more hear their tales of scientific misconduct. The executives declined.

LINGUISTICALLY, AGRICULTURE AND wilderness are antonyms. In the 1500s, the English word 'wild' meant an uncultivated or desolate region. Its roots lie in words for wild beasts and untamed places. *The wild* meant woodlands, but also evolved from the word *welt*, meaning *world*. This sprang from a time when *the world* was largely unknown to the men and women living in it, or rather, in their own cultivated corners of it. The wider world was a mystery. It was undomesticated, uncontrolled and seemingly endless, ceasing as they imagined it must with a waterfall into space, a steep and sudden drop into darkness. Civilization, the cleared fields and tamed hillsides, was the exception while the wild was the rule. Barring heaven, hell, and what culture humanity could carve out for itself, the wild was all there was.

I always assumed that *estero* was a Spanish word, but if so it must have been a dialect, because the Spanish for "estuary" is not *estero* but *estuario*. In Italian, the word *estero* means "foreign." The language in which *estero* actually means "estuary" is Esperanto, the international auxiliary language first created in the nineteenth century to help foster world peace (*esperanto* means "one who hopes").

SPEAKING OF HOPE, when Joey Mendoza lost his cows in the summer of 2009 due to financial hardship within the dairy industry, he vowed that one way or another he would put his family back in business again. Jarrod, his son, had not seemed too interested in taking over the family farm, at least by Joey's initial estimation. The young man was studying criminal justice at Chico State University, but wound up getting a job near campus at an organic dairy. He was fascinated by what he learned, and realized that gaining an organic certification for the Mendoza dairy could be what saved the day. However, in the beginning of 2010, when he started to look into the idea seriously, the organic dairy industry around Point Reyes was already saturated.

"We had talked to Organic Valley, Straus, Horizon, a lot of these big organic companies, kind of pleading our case to let us back in," Jarrod told the *Point Reyes Light*. "And they were all pretty much, 'We are so full of organic milk right now that we can't take anyone else on.'" Then in June another local dairy agreed to sell the Mendozas 120 certified organic cows, as well as an existing contract with Sierra Organic, a boutique dairy company with distribution in Southern California. As had been the case with the Lunny ranch, it was not difficult to get the family's parkland pastures certified organic. By 2012, the Mendoza herd was up to two hundred animals.

Jarrod told the *Light* that organic farming was something he was still working to perfect, with the need to rotate pastures and keep a keen watch for illnesses in the animals. "I've definitely made some dumb mistakes along the way—moments when it was like, 'What the hell are you thinking?'" he told the paper.

His father, on the other hand, was proud. "He's doing a good job, getting his cows bred on time and producing a really good quality of milk," Joey said. His son was now the fourth Mendoza man to farm the land that Zena Mendoza insisted they buy.

For their neighbors the Lunnys however, the legal battle continued. Famed chef Alice Waters wrote an amicus brief in support of the oyster farm, as did many local businesses and agricultural operations. West Marin's Alliance for Local Sustainable Agriculture (ALSA) organized painting parties to make signs to give out to supporters to display in front of their homes or businesses. The signs were uniform, virtually identical. They pictured an expanse of blue water and a white sky above with a yellow sun in it, and all read "SAVE OUR DRAKES BAY OYSTER FARM" with either "AlsaMarin.com" or "SaveOurShellfish .com" written below—a whole new "SOS" campaign, with *shellfish* having replaced the *seashore*. Volunteers made more than eight hundred of these signs, ranging in size from twenty-four inches square to four by eight feet. The ALSA signs appeared on the sides of barns

in Point Reyes and on terraces in San Francisco. They were nailed to
telephone poles and propped on hillsides. They were placed next to
official signs for the Point Reyes National Seashore, hung on garden
gates and printed out and tacked to bulletin boards in coffee shops and
supermarkets and laundromats all over the Bay Area. Volunteers made
them en masse, assembly line style, with kids helping to paint, too. The
group's website showed photos of the signs drying in the sun in varying
stages of completion. One shot shows a group of painters standing in
front of a massive sign affixed to the side of a barn. They are covering
their faces with hats, bandanas or their hands, because they know that
the sign is too big to be legally displayed on the roadside. (It is, in fact,
the kind of thing that the original members of the Marin Conservation
League fought to forbid in the 1930s, when they didn't want the view
cluttered up with advertising or political messages for those driving
out to the beach.) Anyone could request a sign through the website,
and someone from ALSA would deliver it. Some homes and businesses
displayed many signs—the gas station in Point Reyes, for example, had
at least five at one point.

Not everyone was a fan of the signs, though. Some were vandal-
ized. Some disappeared in the night. Some were squiggled over with
spray paint while others had their message changed. On one, displayed
prominently near downtown Point Reyes Station, someone crossed out
the "Our" in "Save Our Drakes Bay Oyster Farm" and replaced it
with "His." The desire to make such a distinction was not entirely
isolated to a single vandal, either. More than one resident wrote in to
the local papers saying that even if they wanted the farm to continue,
it wasn't really *their* farm, it was Lunny's. At times it seemed that all

of West Marin had been roped into the cause, whether everyone liked it or not.

Drakes Bay Oyster Company remained open throughout 2013, as a tangle of lawsuits played out in the California courts. One of the judges on the U.S. Court of Appeals for the Ninth Circuit, Margaret McKeown, likened the case to a Rubik's cube, or Russian nesting dolls, as each aspect of the case seemed to circle back or fold in on itself, much the same way the scientific reports had done.

Throughout the trial, Kevin seemed to retain an ironclad conviction that what he was doing was right.

"We're confident that the courts have jurisdiction and that they're going to correct this mistake," he told the *Point Reyes Light* in May 2013. "We didn't know that we'd ever have to go through a political battle, not only to protect our way of life but to protect sustainable agriculture in West Marin from government abuse and misuse of science driving some sort of agenda for a human-less landscape that we think is going to benefit very few people."

In September 2013, the Ninth Circuit Court of Appeals denied the request for an injunction with a ruling of 2–1, although the dissenting opinion gave the oyster farm fuel to keep going. In January 2014, the courts granted DBOC a motion allowing it to remain open, and the planting and harvesting of oysters in Drakes Estero continued. In April, DBOC petitioned the U.S. Supreme Court for a writ of certiorari to review the Ninth Circuit Court's judgment, but on June 30 that request was declined, and July 31, 2014, was set as the closure date for Drakes Bay Oyster's retail portion of the company. In other words, there would be no more Oyster Shack.

During that July, Kevin used his position on the Point Reyes Seashore Ranchers Association to submit a request to NPS and various politicians on behalf of himself and his neighbors, asking that the Oyster Shack building be repurposed for selling other goods, like vegetables or dairy products. He did this without getting the approval or consent of the association, however. In response, twelve of the twenty-three Point Reyes Seashore Ranchers Association members signed and submitted a letter of mass resignation.

"It has become increasingly evident that our styles of communication in matters pertinent to the Point Reyes National Seashore are very different," the resigning ranchers wrote. "This was most recently evidenced by the letter dated July 21, 2014, which was sent on behalf of the Association to Superintendent Muldoon and various elected officials. We felt that we had inadequate time to review and respond and consider the implications of such a letter being sent."

Among the signatories was Little Joey Mendoza. His children, Jarrod and Jolyn, both of whom had followed their father in the Point Reyes dairying business, declined to comment at the time on whether or not they were still members. The others offering their resignation were Betty Nunes of A and E Ranches, Daniel and Dolores Evans of H Ranch, Robert McClure of I Ranch, Tim, Thomas and Mike Kehoe of J Ranch, Julie Rossotti of K Ranch, Dave Evans of Rogers Ranch (and owner of Bay Area favorite Marin Sun Farms), Elmer Leroy Martinelli of Martinelli Ranch, and Bob Giacomini, whose children now run the celebrated Point Reyes Farmstead Cheese Company. Although he is a member of the association, Giacomini's cows and dairy are not located inside the national park, but are inside the Golden Gate National Recreation Area, administered by the Seashore.

"We think we're stronger if we can be unified, and we were," Kevin Lunny told the *Point Reyes Light* of the split. He said the intent of the letter that the twelve members had objected to was "to underscore to the park service that we know that the oyster farm is getting kicked out, but remember, we want a place to sell our products." It was a plea to keep the buildings from the oyster farm standing after the closure. After all, the land-based site was not inside the wilderness area, just the water.

"We respect their decision to resign and we will obviously continue to work with every rancher and the ranchers association," a park representative said of the split.

A bundle of local food-based businesses attempted to bring their own lawsuit to stop the closure of DBOC, claiming the closure would cause *them* economic hardship. But Judge Yvonne Gonzalez Rogers, who had ruled against the Lunnys the previous year, dismissed the lawsuit with no small amount of contempt, saying it was "frivolous," "nonsensical," and "strains credulity."

The oyster farm and the National Park Service finally reached a settlement agreement that fall: the Lunnys would cease their operations on December 31, 2014. After almost ten years fighting the federal government, with millions spent on both sides, the Drakes Bay Oyster Company had lost.

# 15

# IN SEARCH OF AN ORIGINAL WILD

O N THE FIRST day of the New Year, the oyster farm stood empty, doors gaping, tarps fluttering in the breeze. The shacks and sheds were still present on shore and the surface of the estuary nearby was flecked with hundreds of bits of wood and plastic foam. The old oyster barge had to be broken up into pieces so it could be removed from the water. In the coming weeks the buildings would be torn down too and their rubble scraped from the shell-encrusted ground with bulldozers. The Lunnys' permit had called on them to remove all traces of their operation from the premises, on land and in the water, however the family had argued in court that doing so would bankrupt them. Therefore, a settlement was reached by which the oyster farm's owners were required to remove all of the oysters themselves from Drakes Estero, leaving the rest of the cleanup to the National Park Service, with the taxpayers footing the bill. The first three weeks of work cost more than $200,000 alone, and the cleanup was expected to take up to a year.

Hopeful until the very last, the Lunnys had kept planting their oysters until as late in the game as possible, so that many of the bivalves were forced to go to waste. Unable to be sold, they were packed out of the seashore by the truckload, destined for the landfill. Even after the New Year, and despite the settlement, many bags and strings of oysters remained. In January, park employees pulled up fifteen tons of oysters in hundreds of bags and a staggering amount of oystering paraphernalia from the water bottom. Still more remained. Underwater video shot by local conservationists while snorkeling showed still more oysters in bags sunk on the bottom throughout the estuary, their shells edged with orange *Didemnum lahillei,* and plenty of debris. There were empty black mesh bags, and rods, and wires, and treated lumber, not to mention the five miles of treated redwood that the Johnsons' racks were made of, which would require strong equipment to pull out.

The story I have written here is not the story I thought I would find when I set out to write it. I began my investigations wholly sympathetic to the oyster farm, but that sympathy eroded over time as the evidence I found did not support the arguments I had heard in favor of the farm staying. I was told that the Lunnys were given the impression, if not the promise, that they could stay past 2012, but this was not the case. Even though no such evidence was supplied during any of the court proceedings, the idea that the oyster farm was told it could stay past 2012 was so entrenched locally that I had a hard time believing it wasn't true. At the eleventh hour I found myself pressing anyone I could think of who had lent vocal support to DBOC, to the point of hounding them, asking them to help me strengthen their case. I wrote to the fifteen people who had been most involved—Kevin, and his main lawyer at the end, Peter Prows, and citizen allies who ran websites in support of DBOC, and others including journalists and academics. I asked for any evidence or documentation at all that Kevin was told he would be able to renew, thinking that there could have been some scrap of evidence that was somehow overlooked or inadmissible in court. But no one was able to come up with anything. I could not even find any on-the-record instance of Kevin saying that he was confused or misled about the lease and the wilderness designation. I wrote to Kevin repeatedly, asking him if I had gotten it wrong. I asked him to explain it to me, and to go on the record saying he was told he could renew, even though there is documentation that NPS told him otherwise.

For all I knew there had been mixed signals or a gentleman's agreement of some kind, but he declined all of my invitations to give an alternative story in his defense. I exchanged many emails over several weeks with Sarah Rolph, a woman who had offered her public relations and communications services to the Lunnys in support of their cause. The message I got was that, *No*, nobody with NPS told Kevin he could renew *per se*. Both Tom Johnson and Don Neubacher had in fact told him that NPS did *not* plan to renew; he just didn't agree with that decision and hoped he could change it. He felt that the weight of the farm's legacy would win out in the end.

As for the function of the oysters in the estuary and the argument that the commercial Japanese oysters were replacing the ecosystem services of a large and thriving population of native Olympia oysters, I am convinced that this was not the case, either. There is no convincing evidence to support this assumption, and rather strong historical and scientific evidence to suggest otherwise. Similarly, if the absence of the oysters would cause Drakes Estero to become a "cesspool" due to cattle runoff, as one Internet commenter on a *Los Angeles Times* article put the common conspiracy theory, then those oysters should not have been for consumption. In places where oysters are used to clean the water, such as with native oyster reef restoration projects for ecological reasons, those oysters themselves are too polluted to eat. Oysters do not make toxins or other pollutants magically vanish from the water, they merely take them into their own bodies. When fertilizers and treated sewage cause elevated levels of nitrogen in a waterway, this can result in algae blooms. And since oysters eat algae, an oyster population can mitigate overabundant algae and help prevent the increase in carbon dioxide produced underwater when those blooms inevitably die off and decompose—a process called eutrophication, or ocean acidification from within. But oysters do not eat fecal coliform, other animal waste, or untreated sewage. Pollutants won't be extracted from an ecosystem until the oysters that have absorbed those pollutants are removed and disposed of. Edible oysters are only grown where the water is already clean enough to grow food.

THE STORIES I heard that the park had once planned to build a gleaming new and permanent "oyster palace" were also untrue. One can argue that the historical value of the farm should have been enough to allow it to stay; that its role in the community spoke for itself and should not have been removed. This I can understand. As for the original intentions for the oyster farm, the opinions discussed in the House Report that accompanied the 1976 Point Reyes Wilderness Act were varied. Some thought the farm was not compatible in a wilderness area while some did. Some argued that even allowing the forty-year lease to continue would erode the strength of wilderness designation everywhere. Some called for its removal and others for its continuation. It also seems clear that if the government decided to allow the oyster farm to stay past 2012, that an adaptive management approach could have been developed to minimize impact to the seals. At the very least, the millions of dollars spent in the course of the legal battle could have been better spent on real, original studies to find out what was best for the estuary and its non-human inhabitants, rather than rehashing old data gathered for other purposes. Some felt that the presence of the farm took away from the "wilderness experience," and others found it to be an asset.

I suppose then, in the end, I agreed with the "dangerous precedent" argument. I don't think it is a coincidence that a Koch-backed group chose to fund the fight for the farm, and that to pry open a wilderness area for commercial use would indeed put wilderness everywhere at risk. I do not see how a government solicitor could recommend renewing the lease of a commercial operation inside wilderness when that lease was set to expire, especially when that business's environmental practices were so very much less than stellar. Still, there was a false dichotomy set up, pitting wild landscapes against cultivated ones. Wallace Stegner himself even wrote that a carefully managed landscape with grazing animals on it could offer the same kind of solace as an empty and uncultivated field. Despite arguments to the contrary, the removal of this particular oyster farm did not threaten other agriculture in the area, or oyster farms generally, which are fighting hard battles and doing wonderful things all over the country, helping with research and illustrating the stark reality of ocean acidification and what we stand to lose if we do not begin addressing climate change more actively.

The more I researched and wrote or thought about this case, the more it seemed like a Rorschach inkblot test, with people seeing within its sprawling little mess whatever monsters they already found most frightening. Depending on who was doing the looking, it was a story about "big" government, or about sloppy science, or about the vanishing nature of small-scale farms, or the struggle of the "little guy" against corrupt and unseen forces beyond his control. It was about how we have largely become separated from how our food is grown, to the detriment of both ourselves and the environment. It was a story about how stories can be twisted and histories changed, simply by repeating selective or erroneous information, whether on purpose or by accident. To some it was really a story about gentrification, with urban elite kayakers and day trippers displacing blue-collar farmers and immigrant oyster workers—people who really *used* the land for practical purposes rather than something as abstract as spiritual renewal. It was a tale of bogeymen, like the Koch brothers, and what their money could (almost) accomplish. Most of all, I think, it was a story about loss and the seeping panic we feel at that loss—whether it be the loss of nature or the loss of a way of being in the world that feels sane, where men and women pull sustenance out of the lands and water. The natural world is everywhere under attack, as we enter a new geological age influenced by man: the Anthropocene, the age of humans. Even within protected areas, ecosystems are still vulnerable and many cannot be left to their own devices in order to flourish—invasive species must be removed, and predators added or supplemented via culling programs. Acidic water washes in, destroying shellfish and other organisms. It is too late for a hands-off approach. Humans and our waste are a part of nature, and our impacts must be actively mitigated. Based on the available science, drastic changes lie ahead of us as stewards of this planet. We do not know exactly how climate change will manifest, or how quickly.

As for the people who fought in the oyster war, most would rather put it behind them. Sarah Allen has a desk job now, leading the Ocean and Coastal Resources Program for the National Park Service's Pacific West region. "I'm a bureau-ologist now," she joked over the phone. She works on mitigating and studying marine debris, among other initiatives. Kevin Lunny and his family have lost their oyster farm but still have their cattle ranch, compost business and quarry. With the funding help of their many supporters, they planned to open a restaurant on Tomales Bay in Inverness, so the family could still all work together. Brigid, the Lunnys' daughter, married the son of one of the farm's longest-tenured employees and they now have a child together. Oscar, the worker who was fired for showing me around the oyster farm in 2013, was forced to return to Mexico where he struggles to find enough work. He lives with his family in coastal Jalisco again, and his Facebook feed shows cell phone pictures of his young son, smiling under the shade of a too-big cowboy hat, or perched on the edges of colorful wooden boats. Still, he has written to me asking me to help him return to America, although there is nothing I can do. Corey Goodman continues his work as a neuroscientist and venture capitalist. Fred Smith works as a business consultant on environmental issues and sustainable agriculture. The Mendoza family continues to run their dairy.

Even at the very end, I wondered if there was some way I had gotten it all wrong. People on both sides had passionately accused me of bias—declaring that I was alternately biased in favor of the oyster farm or that I was biased against it. It is true that I have presented the facts I found to be most pertinent, and that not every incident made it into my telling of the story. Ultimately, I had to walk away, knowing I'd gotten as close to the truth as I could reasonably be expected to come.

Pursuing that truth felt, in the end, somewhat like pursuing the white stag of legend: even if we can never catch it, it is the pursuit of it that matters, as the mythical beast leads us ever onward through the fog and towards transformation.

# ACKNOWLEDGMENTS

W RITING THIS BOOK has been an exercise in humility and gratitude the likes of which I had never before imagined, let alone
experienced. I could not have done it without the support and work
of many, many people—family members, friends, colleagues, historians, reporters, authors, marine biologists, archaeologists, ranchers,
oyster farmers, strangers, librarians, people on Twitter, food writers,
politicians and one nineteenth-century sea captain kind enough to leave
behind a detailed account of his life.

Before anyone else, I want to extend my profound gratitude to
Megan and Tom Ryan, handsdown the most generous people I have
ever encountered, for giving me a room of my own (and pizza) when
I needed it most.

Many thanks to my agent Elizabeth Evans for taking an interest in
me and in this book, and for all the patience and guidance she provided
along the way. She and everyone else at the Jean V. Naggar Literary
Agency were a godsend. I am also eternally grateful to my esteemed
editor, Jack Shoemaker, and the wonderful staff at Counterpoint Press,
including Sharon Wu, Claire Shalinksy, Corinne Kalasky and Kelly
Winton.

Special thanks to the dynamite staff of the California Room at the
Marin County Civic Center Library for their help and interest (and one

ride home!), especially co-sleuths Carol Acquaviva, Laurie Thompson and Dave Williams. Special thanks also to the patient archivists at the magical and thrilling UC Berkeley Bancroft Library; I'll never forget the days I spent in your bright reading room and darkened microfilm cubicles, or eating sandwiches on the grass outside while pondering what I'd just discovered. Thanks as well to the staff of the New York Historical Society, even though the name of a certain strapping sailor remains a mystery.

Writing this book would have been absolutely impossible were it not for the wealth of primary research carried out by other people about California, West Marin, and the Drakes Bay Oyster Company controversy. For details about the Point Reyes area and its denizens, I am particularly indebted to the work of writer Jacoba Charles, whose ear for poetic and emotional detail in her journalism and radio stories proved indispensable. Equally vital were the comprehensive texts of historians Dewey Livingston and Carola DeRooy. Other writing about Point Reyes that provided key details, insight and inspiration came from Jules Evens and Paul Sadin, as well as late authors Laura Nelson Baker and Arthur Quinn. I also received assistance and advice from local West Marin publishers and journalists George Clyde, Mark Dowie, Matt Gallagher, Jim Kravets, Steve Quirt, Linda Peterson, Mary Olsen, Robin Carpenter and the late and much-missed David Bunnett. Although we interacted less directly, I would be remiss not to thank former *Point Reyes Light* editors Robert Plotkin and David Mitchell. Thanks as well to other journalists, both local and national, who covered the issues examined in this book, and whose work I reference or mined for clues, particularly: Michael Ames, Lynn Axelrod, Linda Berlin, Jeremy Blackman, P.J. Bremier, Lander Burr, Julie Cart,

Kyle Cashulin, Andrew DeFeo, Jim Doyle, Peter Fimrite, Robert Gammon, John Hulls, Peter Jamison, Debra Kahn, Leslie Kaufman, Sasha Khokha, Samantha Kimmey, Amy Littlefield, Justin Nobel, Kelly O'Mara, Christopher Peak, Paul Peterzell, Jeannette Pontacq, Mark Prado, James Salzman, Marian Schinske, Maura Thurman, Wes Venteicher, Thomas Yeatts and others. (Although I must note that acknowledgment does not necessarily equal an endorsement of editorial stance, in either direction.) I am also very grateful to Calin Van Paris, who worked as a stringer for me and contributed reporting for chapters eleven and fifteen, and whose detailed notes pretty much saved my assets. This book also benefited greatly from my reading of several germane works, especially *The Big Oyster: History on the Half Shell* by Mark Kurlansky and *A Rage for Justice: The Passion and Politics of Phillip Burton* by John Jacobs.

This book is about real people, some of whom graciously granted me interviews while others did not. I am immensely grateful to all of them, since those who would not speak to me still managed to put their versions of events out into the public sphere in one way or another. It is regrettable that Kevin Lunny stopped responding to my emails and phone calls after 2013, but I am grateful for what he shared with me before that time, and for being so vocal about his motivations, feelings and beliefs in other media at every stage of the conflict.

I am grateful as well to Corey Goodman for his early encouragement that I write a book about this issue, and for being so generous with his time and words, even if we ultimately didn't agree on what the "story of the story" turned out to be. Thanks as well to oyster farm advocates David Weiman, Peter Prows, Sarah Rolph, Jane Gyorgi and Peggy Day for their input. Sarah Rolph in particular was kind enough to debate the issue with me at length over email at the eleventh hour, with Kevin Lunny cc'ed throughout. Others who did not grant me interviews or comment included Amy Trainer, Tom Baty, Don Neubacher and Gordon Bennett. I am grateful for their public input on the matter, regardless.

Thanks as well to Steve Kinsey for his kind verification of quotes attributed to him by a third party, and for his long dedication to the community I hold dear. Extra special thanks to the estimable congressman Pete McCloskey and his beautiful wife, Helen.

I'm also grateful to Tess Elliott, editor of the *Point Reyes Light*, for suggesting I try small-town reporting full time (even if, during the course of said reporting, we didn't always see eye to eye). Many sincere thanks as well to the talented *Light* staff members I worked alongside, especially photographer David Briggs and intern Shane Scott.

I could not have written this book without the input and support of Fred Smith, who kept talking to me even when we disagreed about the topic at hand. He consistently showed remarkable compassion for everyone involved, even those who would consider themselves his opponents. (Fred: I'll keep the needs of the seagulls in mind if you spare a thought for the crabs.) I am especially grateful to longtime Point Reyes rancher Joseph Mendoza Jr., a thoroughly honorable man with an impressive family legacy, which I hope I was able to do justice to in these pages. Long may his family's cows graze. I am also forever grateful to Burr Heneman for allowing me to interview him about the Point Reyes Bird Observatory (now called Point Blue Conservation Science) and for helping me to fact-check parts of the manuscript. I am also very grateful to Greg Sarris for making time to speak with me, and for sharing his stories. Many thanks as well to Sarah Allen for her kind and helpful feedback on chapter two and on harbor seals generally, as well as her current work on climate change and marine debris. Thanks also to Point Reyes National Seashore staff members Melanie Gunn, Cicely Muldoon, John Dell'Osso, Ben Becker, Dave Press and others for always being courteous and as informative as duty permitted. Many thanks as well to Tim Ragen, former Executive Director of the Marine Mammal Commission, for his input in 2012. I am also particularly grateful to scientists Steven D. Emslie, McCrea Cobb and Ellen Hines for speaking to me about their respective areas of expertise.

Many people in West Marin provided invaluable support, leads or just a reason to smile—more than I could possibly mention here. I will surely miss some vital person in my attempt to list their names. I do however especially want to thank Donna Sheehan and Paul Reffell, the most beautiful couple I've ever met, for their love, nourishment, the loan of a Westfalia camper van, and a number of very nice breakfasts. (Between first writing these acknowledgments and turning them in, our lovely Donna passed peacefully from this life. So I will take this opportunity to send my love to Paul, and to Donna I will say this: Donna! Thank you! I love you! I promise I will work to do good things in your memory and remember that "the giving is the getting.") I am also grateful to another wise couple, booksellers Steve Costa and Kate Levinson of Point Reyes Books, for creating and maintaining one of the loveliest bookstores in the world. Many thanks to my friend Alex Fradkin, fellow Brooklynite with West Marin roots, for being especially heroic at key points. I am likewise very grateful to everyone who chatted with me about local issues at the Blackbird Café, Pine Cone Diner, Vladimir's Czechoslovakian Restaurant, Station House

Café, Old Western Saloon, Saltwater Oyster Depot, Bovine Bakery, Nick's Cove and other hangouts. The kindness and/or helpfulness of Christian Anthony, Alden Bevington, Eden Canon, Luc Chamberland, Donna Clavaud, Matt Cuyler, John Eleby, Burton Eubank, Paul Fenn, Ken Fox, Chris Kennedy, Marc Matheson, Matt McCloskey, June McCrory, Michael Mery, Hugo Soto Perez, Julia Peters, Alex Porrata, Jude Robinson, the Smith brothers, Brian Tatta, Sim Van der Ryn, Nick Whitney, Joel Whitney, Xerxes Whitney and Elizabeth Whitney is particularly noted.

I was sustained in my research through the generous contributions of eighty-one people via the crowdfunding site Indiegogo, including friends, colleagues, Twitter buddies and complete strangers. We raised $3,541, without which my research and writing would have ceased, and you would not now be holding this book in your hands. It may not seem like much, but it made an important difference. This cannot be overstated. Thank you.

Although I started working on this project in the spring of 2012, it would never have come to light were it not for the generous guidance in 2013 of poet, Chelsea Green editor and fellow Bennington College alum Michael Metivier, who helped me with early drafts of the first chapter and the proposal. Thanks as well to another Bennington alum, Jim Cairl, for free emergency computer repair on his lunch hour when the need for it was most dire. Thanks to David Pearsall for reading my first draft of chapter one and giving honest feedback.

I also want to thank friends and United Nations colleagues Radmilla Suleymanova and Melissa Gorelick, for our time spent in international territory and out of it. Also at the UN, I am very much indebted to both my longtime editor Beth Flanders, and mercifully understanding administrator Emelie Hellborg. I am grateful to all of my Press Office colleagues past and present, but especially to Doug Hand, Omar Musni, Chris Cycmanick and Christiaan Lampinen. I must also extend my heartfelt gratitude to our francophone counterparts Aurelian Colly, Jean-Eric Boulin, Fabrice Robinet, Eric Wastiaux, Diophante Tomo, Nadia Sraieb-Koepp and the rest of the gang, especially for suggesting that I take a break for lunch once in a while. Extra thanks to UN colleague and former partner on the Special Political and Decolonization Committee, the talented Shahnaz Habib, for her much-needed encouragement in the autumn of 2013 and for putting me up for a few crucial nights in March of 2012. Much gratitude to Anna Shen and Dorothea Senechal for similar reasons. Thanks as well to Farsan Ghassim (aka the R of H) for reminding me about adventure, and for his willingness to be the first line of defense against terrifying phantom creatures in the Mexican jungle.

If you'll indulge me some additional personal expressions of gratitude, I also wish to thank some of the teachers who encouraged me over the years in one way or another, including Susannah Woods, David g. Smith, Sheila Girton, Mary Oliver, Gladden Schrock, Ann Pibal, Carol Diehl, Temple Smith, Carol Wilson and Deborah Chamberlin-Taylor. I'll also thank Catherine Stapleton, a teacher of sorts, who put me back together at the darkest point of the year.

(Weirdly sincere thanks also to whoever set up the live web cams at the Monterey Bay Aquarium, the Monterey Bay Aquarium generally, David Tennant, Catherine Tate, Russell T. Davies, Stars of the Lid, Neil deGrasse Tyson, Trevor Corson, Rebecca Solnit, Zadie Smith, Susan Orlean, Carl Safina, Erik Larson, the Haribo confectionery company, the focus booth on the 15th floor of the United Nations, whoever towed my car last year, and K. Also, one more person. You know who you are, and why.)

Additionally, there are a few friends who did not have much to do with the creation of this book, but whom I will thank anyway, out of love. They are Elena Odessa Ray (née Schmidt), Brianna Young, Sanam Hasan, Jasmine Balgobin and Jasmine Hamedi. No matter how far we may drift in the world, your names are always written on my heart.

And finally, my family. Dear reader: If, in the late 1980s, you happened to see a gawky nine-year-old refusing to leave the Shadow Room at the San Francisco Exploratorium, or begging to stay for just one more night/day cycle of the watering hole diorama in the Tusher African Hall at the California Academy of Sciences, that was probably me. This book has been dedicated to my father, Patrick Brennan, for many reasons, but especially for taking me to aquariums and science museums so often as a child. (And for chocolate pudding in blue mugs, and *Graceland*, and *The Lord of the Rings*, and for trying to become a Whovian, and, and, and . . .) It is also for the rest of my family. To my mother, Victoria Bloom, who was strong enough to fight history and win, and whose laugh is better than anyone's. To my sister Lea: for Meatloaf, that time she thought there was a goblin in her room, my nieces, and the world's ugliest car. To my brother Zachary: for flower crowns and Winnie the Pooh. To my nieces June and Sienna, who are precious unicorn babies, and to Stefan Ritter, their devoted Papa. To my aunt Melody, fellow creative spirit, with love. Thanks also to Dan Carr, stepdad extraordinaire, for reading a draft of an early chapter, and for the repeated loan of an automobile so that I could get out in nature for inspiration to write the next one.

Thank you all.

# SELECTED BIBLIOGRAPHY

—. "Feinstein breaks stalemate on oyster farm permits." *Point Reyes Light*, July 7, 2008.

—. "NPS pulls controversial web docs." *Point Reyes Light*, July 26, 2008.

—. *Autobiographical dictation, biographical sketch, notes etc. of John Stillwell Morgan*. Hubert Howe Bancroft and D.R. Sessions, 1888. Bancroft Library, University of California, Berkeley. Microfilmed 1992. 52 pages.

—. House Report 94-1680, 1976.

—. *Letters from A.L.A.A to H.A Avery*. Bancroft Library, University of California, Berkeley. Letters dated October 12 and 13, 1852, San Francisco.

—. Point Reyes National Seashore General Management Plan, 1980.

—. Public Law 94-544, 1976.

—. Public Law 94-567, 1976.

—. "NAS report to be reviewed." *Point Reyes Light*, July 16, 2009.

—. "Older cameras on Drakes Estero." *Point Reyes Light*, June 24, 2010.

—. "Oyster panel expanded." *Point Reyes Light*, October 9, 2008.

—. "Seal expert visits estero." *Point Reyes Light*, November 6, 2008.

—. "Second camera pointed at estero." *Point Reyes Light*, June 17, 2010.

—. "Senate leaves oysters' fate to Jarvis, new head of parks." *Point Reyes Light*, October 1, 2009.

Abbey, Edward. *Desert Solitaire: A Season in the Wilderness*. Ballantine Books, 1984. Originally published 1968.

—. *The Monkey Wrench Gang*. Harper Perennial, 2006. Originally published 1975.

Allen, Sarah Gardner. "The distribution and abundance of marine birds and mammals in the Gulf of the Farallones and adjacent waters, 1985–1992." PhD dissertation, University of California, Berkeley, 1994.

Allen, Sarah, Jules Evens and John Kelly. "The Naturalist: Coastal wilderness." *Point Reyes Light*, April 26, 2007.

Allen, Teresa. "Herd makes a solid comeback: Tule elk's bellow returns to Marin." *Marin Independent Journal*, August 23, 1986.

Arm, Alfred M. "Charlie Johnson Farms the Sea." *Marin Independent Journal,* February 2, 1976.

Baker, Will. "Lunny consents to cease and desist order." *Point Reyes Light,* December 13, 2007.

Barrett, Stephen. "18 tule elk culled from Limantour." *Point Reyes Light,* May 27, 1999.

Baty, Tom. "Sarah Allen rules!" *Point Reyes Light*, January, 2007.

—. Letter to California Coastal Commission "Re: the stream of plastic debris flowing from the Drakes Bay Oyster Company." September 1, 2011.

Beardsley, Richard K. "Temporal and areal relationships in central California archeology." PhD dissertation. Department of Anthropology, University of California, Berkeley, 1947.

Benet, Jane. "The oyster farm." *San Francisco Chronicle*, February 8, 1978.

Bennett, Gordon. "An inconvenient local truth: Dispelling the careless rhetoric about Drakes Estero." *Point Reyes Light*, June 28, 2007.

—. "Re-save Drakes Estero." *Point Reyes Light*, April 26, 2007.

Berenson, Alex. "Pfizer hires 2 top scientists to expand drug pipeline." *New York Times*, October 5, 2007.

Berlin, Linda. "Elk would be safer with contraceptive." *Point Reyes Light*, October 1, 1992.

—. "Environmentalists spar with hunters over tule elk." *Point Reyes Light*, October 1, 1992.

—. "New contraceptive would work on elk, scientist says." *Point Reyes Light*, October 8, 1992.

—. "Park service supports shooting elk herd." *Point Reyes Light*, September 10, 1992.

Blackman, Jeremy. "John Sansing, 1925–2012." *Point Reyes Light*, March 8, 2012.

Borodic, Frank. "Workers in Drakes Bay." *Point Reyes Light*, June 19, 2008.

Bostrom, Judi. "Estero review seeks members." *Point Reyes Light,* May 1, 2008.

Bremier, P.J. "The Oyster War: The National Park Service and an organic rancher battle over the future of Drakes Estero." *Marin* magazine, November 2008.

Brennan, Summer. "Elk growth threatens seashore zoning." *Point Reyes Light,* July 19, 2012.

—. "Vanishing landscapes, captured in art." *Point Reyes Light*, June 21, 2012.

Broddrick, L. Ryan. Letter from Director, California Department of Fish and Game, Office of General Council to Superintendent, Point Reyes National Seashore Re: Drakes Bay Oyster Company lease status. May 15, 2007.

—. Memorandum from Director, California Department of Fish and Game, to Executive Director, Fish and Game Commission, Re: Agenda Item for June 24–25 Fish and Game Commission Meeting Re: Request of Johnson Oyster Company, Inc, for Lease Renewal of State Water Bottom Lease Agreements for Numbers M-438-01 and M-438.02, Drakes Estero, Marin County. June 14, 2004.

Bryant, Stewart. "Lunnys should stay." *Point Reyes Light*, May 15, 2009.

Burnham, T.J. "Sea rancher gives oysters new start." *Sacramento Bee*, June 14, 1983.

Burr, Lander. "Lunny's bill hits a snag." *Point Reyes Light*, September 24, 2009.

—. "Park service data under new scrutiny." *Point Reyes Light*, August 20, 2009.

Callicott, J. Baird, and Michael P. Nelson. *The Great New Wilderness Debate.* University of Georgia Press, 1998.

Carroll, John. "In biotech trifecta, startup lassos $31M, a CEO and a lead drug from Pfizer." *Fierce Biotech*, January 3, 2013.

—. "Promising stem cell start-ups merge, add $11.5M." *Fierce Biotech*, July 8, 2009.

Carson, Rachel. *Silent Spring.* Houghton Mifflin, 1962.

Cart, Julie. "National Park Service seeks to ease tensions with Point Reyes farmers." *Los Angeles Times*, May 26, 2014.

—. "Oyster farm dispute roils Marin County." *Los Angeles Times*, December 27, 2009.

Cashulin, Kyle. "After 30 million deaths, farmer seeks new seed." *Point Reyes Light*, July 29, 2010.

—. "Hidden camera shoots oyster workers in estero." *Point Reyes Light*, June 10, 2010.

Champion, Dale. "Helicopter cowboy rounds up herd of island's elk." *San Francisco Chronicle,* July 30, 1986.

Charles, Jacoba. "Ambrose Gondola, who trucked the first white deer to West Marin, dies at 91." *Point Reyes Light*, October 23, 2014.

—. "Chasing salmon and driving deer." *The Story Shed* radio program, KWMR 90.5 FM, November 21, 2013.

—. "Commission fines oyster farm for ditch." *Point Reyes Light*, May 13, 2008.

—. "Drakes Bay vs. Open Space." *Point Reyes Light*, May 15, 2008.

—. "Fourteen Gates from Home." *The Story Shed* radio program, KWMR 90.5 FM, February 16, 2012.

—. "Joe Mendoza, lifelong Point Reyes dairy rancher." *Point Reyes Light*, November 6, 2008.

—. "Park signs permit for Drakes Bay." *Point Reyes Light*, April 24, 2008.

—. "Scientists duel over oyster data." *Point Reyes Light*, September 11, 2008.

—. "Scuffle over oyster trip." *Point Reyes Light*, September 4, 2008.

Clyde, George. "How Rep. Phillip Burton and a Magic Marker Hijacked Tomales Bay into the Golden Gate National Recreation Area." *West Marin Review*, Vol. 4, 2012.

Cohelan, Jeffrey. Letter to Pete McCloskey, October 9, 1969.

Compas, Lynn, and Adrian Praetzellis. "Archeological Site Recording and Site Record Updating of Twenty-one Tomales Bay Archaeological Sites in Point Reyes National Seashore, Marin County, California." *Report to the National Park Service*, 1994.

Conomos, T.J. *San Francisco Bay: An Urbanized Estuary/Investigations into the Natural History of San Francisco Bay and Delta with Reference to the Influence of Man.* American Association for the Advancement of Science, Pacific Division, 1979.

Couzin-Frankel, Jennifer. "Corey Goodman, Post-Pfizer, On the Allure of Enterprise." *Science* magazine, May 2009.

Cox, David. "Lunny versus Congress." *Point Reyes Light*, July 31, 2008.

Creque, Jeffrey. "Inconvenient local truths revisited." *Point Reyes Light*, July, 2007.

—. "Letters: Drake's Estero." *Point Reyes Light*, April, 2007.

Cruz, Anne J. *Material and Symbolic Circulation Between Spain and England, 1554–1604.* Ashgate Publishing Ltd., 2008.

Curry, Marshall. *If a Tree Falls: A Story of the Earth Liberation Front.* Documentary film, 2011.

DBOC Boat Tracking Data, DBOC Boat Use. Drakes Bay Oyster Company Environmental Impact Statement.

DeFeo, Andrew. "Fish and Game to Neubacher: Oh, clam up!" *Point Reyes Light*, December 17, 2009.

——. "MMC to start seal study." *Point Reyes Light*, January 28, 2010.

——. "NPS, CCC to Lunny: Move those clams!" *Point Reyes Light*, December 10, 2009.

——. "Oyster farm to fight fine." *Point Reyes Light*, January 14, 2010.

——. "Park critiques NAS report." *Point Reyes Light*, November 12, 2009.

——. "Park denies native oysters." *Point Reyes Light*, October 8, 2009.

——. "Salazar sends deputy to park, ranchers talk." *Point Reyes Light*, February 11, 2010.

DeRooy, Carola, and Dewey Livingston. *Point Reyes Peninsula: Olema, Point Reyes Station and Inverness*. Arcadia Publishing, 2008.

Desai, Neal. "NAS should seek leak." *Point Reyes Light*, March 19, 2009.

Dietz, Betty. "Land Beneath Oyster Company Up for Auction." *Marin Independent Journal*, September 14, 1989.

——. "Tomales Bay to get 4 new oyster companies." *Marin Independent Journal*, January 20, 1989.

Digitale, Robert. "North Coast dairy cows sold to slaughter as milk prices fall." *Press Democrat*, July 19, 2009.

DOI Office of the Inspector General. *Report of Investigation—Point Reyes National Seashore*, Case Number OI-CA-07-0297-I, July 21, 2008.

Donaldson, Milford Wayne. "National Register of Historic Places Registration Form: Johnson Oyster Company." Office of Historic Preservation, Parks and Recreation. August 2011.

Doss, Margot Patterson. "Elk country." *San Francisco Chronicle,* August 10, 1986.

Dowie, Mark. "Commerce is a central purpose in parks." *Point Reyes Light*, September 26, 2013.

——. *Conservation Refugees*. MIT Press, 2011.

Doyle, Jim. "Elk's population boom: Point Reyes plan includes birth control for tule elk." *San Francisco Chronicle*, December 5, 1997.

Duddleson, William J., and Ann Lage. *Saving Point Reyes National Seashore, 1969–1970: An Oral History of Citizen Action in Conservation*. University of California, Berkeley, 1993.

Edwards, Jim. "Pfizer Biotech Chief Signs Vow of Silence for $1.7 Million." *CBS Moneywatch*, April 28, 2009.

Elliott-Fisk, Deborah. *Drakes Estero Assessment of Oyster Farming Final Completion Report*. Point Reyes National Seashore, March 2005 (revised May 2005).

Elliott, Tess. "A citizen, the Pope and Jon Jarvis walk into a bar . . ." *Point Reyes Light*, October 29, 2009.

—. "Is the Estero deal sealed?" *Point Reyes Light*, February 25, 2010.

—. "It's voyeurs versus oysters on the table." *Point Reyes Light*, September 11, 2008.

—. "Oyster farm urged to sell and relocate." *Point Reyes Light*, January 8, 2009.

—. "Park ducks charges, NAS disavows note." *Point Reyes Light*, February 4, 2010.

—. "Scientific Integrity Lost on America's Parks." *The Nation*, September 28, 2009.

—. "The point of misconduct." *Point Reyes Light*, March 26, 2009.

—. "Tidal experiment raises questions about park seal data." *Point Reyes Light*, January 8, 2009.

Environmental Action Committee of West Marin and the Sierra Club. "On the future of oyster farming in the Point Reyes National Seashore." *Point Reyes Light*, October 11, 2007.

Evans, Jules. *A Natural History of Point Reyes Peninsula*. University of California Press, 1988.

Fisher, Jon K. "Future bright for California elk." *Outdoor California*, May–June 1994.

Fisher, M.F.K. *Consider the Oyster*. North Point Press, 1988. Originally published 1941.

Fost, Dan. "West Marin's elk get checked." *Marin Independent Journal*, November 29, 1995.

Frisch, Wolfgang, Martin Meschede and Ronald C. Blakey. *Plate Tectonics: Continental Drift and Mountain Building*. Springer, 2010.

Frost, Gavin. *Public Report on Allegations of Scientific Misconduct at Point Reyes National Seashore, California*. United States Department of the Interior, Office of the Solicitor, March 22, 2011.

Galletto, Beth. "Holidays on the half shell." *Pacific Sun*, December 6, 1985.

Gilliam, Harold. *San Francisco Bay*. Doubleday, 1957.

Ginsberg, Jo. Letter from California Coastal Commission Enforcement Analyst to Drakes Bay Oyster Company Re: compliance with Consent Cease and Desist Order CCC-07-CD-11 (Drakes Bay Oyster Company)—Drakes Bay Oyster Company out of compliance with terms and conditions specified within the letter. September 16, 2009.

—. Letter from California Coastal Commission Enforcement Analyst to Drakes Bay Oyster Company Re: compliance with Consent Cease and Desist Order CCC-07-CD-11 (Drakes Bay Oyster Company)—Notice of violation related to placement of Manila clams in harbor seal exclusion area. December 7, 2009.

Goodman, Corey. "A lesson in journalistic ethics." *Point Reyes Light*, November 19, 2009.

—. "National Park Service harbor seal claims versus data." *Point Reyes Light*, September 30, 2007.

—. "Opinion: Neubacher's false science: One year later." *Point Reyes Light*, April 3, 2008.

—. "Sandbars and debates: Proposal to the EAC." *Point Reyes Light*, April 24, 2008.

GPS INFO: Attachment 12c to the letter from Drakes Bay Oyster Company to Point Reyes National Seashore on November 15, 2010, regarding maps of racks (oyster rack GPS information).

Graves, Ted. "Drakes Estero is not wilderness." *Point Reyes Light*, August 21, 2008.

Greenberg, Michael. "Apology is due." *Point Reyes Light*, August 14, 2008.

—. "Enviros at large." *Point Reyes Light*, February 5, 2009.

—. "Is Sarah Allen objective?" *Point Reyes Light*, 2007.

Greengo, Robert E. "Molluscan species in California Shell Middens." *University of California, Berkeley, University of California Archaeological Survey Reports*, 1951.

Halstead, Richard. "Park recommends killing deer." *Marin Independent Journal*, August 22, 2006.

Harden, Deborah. *California Geology*. Prentice Hall, 2003.

Harris, Liz. "Point Reyes' crowd control: Volunteers and biologists help maintain elk." *San Francisco Chronicle*, August 17, 2001.

Hart, John. *An Island in Time: 50 Years of Point Reyes National Seashore*. Pickleweed Press, 2012.

HARVEST AREA TYPE: Attachment 10d to the letter from Drakes Bay Oyster Company to Point Reyes National Seashore on November 15, 2010, regarding oyster production (harvest area).

Hill, Julia Butterfly. *The Legacy of Luna: The Story of a Tree, a Woman, and a Struggle to Save the Redwoods*. HarperOne, 2001.

Horowitz, Donna. "Solving Tomales elk population problem." *San Francisco Examiner*, April 20, 1997.

Hulin, Tod. Letter to Robert Mayo, September 18, 1969.

Hulls, John. "NAS leak." *Point Reyes Light*, March 19, 2009.

—. "No rules at the top." *Point Reyes Light*, August 28, 2008.

—. "Somewhat logically: Park tells Feinstein to shuck off." *Point Reyes Light*, August 8, 2007.

—. "Somewhat logically: Deep Oyster reveals outraged Academy reviewers." *Point Reyes Light*, March 5, 2009.

—. "Somewhat logically: No seal of approval." *Point Reyes Light*, October 16, 2008.

—. "Somewhat logically: Reflections on the Inspector General's report." *Point Reyes Light*, April 7, 2008.

—. "Somewhat logically: Shellfish motives." *Point Reyes Light*, April 23, 2009.

—. "Somewhat logically: They're either FOIA or they're aginst ya." *Point Reyes Light,* July 26, 2008.

—. "The Inspector General report on Drakes Estero." *Point Reyes Light*, July 17, 2008.

Jacobs, John. *A Rage for Justice: The Passion and Politics of Phillip Burton*. University of California Press, 1995.

Jamison, Peter. "Native oyster research in Drakes Estero will not go forward." *Point Reyes Light*, May 25, 2006.

—. "Rancher Lunny buys Johnson Oyster Company." *Point Reyes Light,* January 20, 2005.

Johnson, Rick. "Letters: Drake's Estero." *Point Reyes Light,* June 7, 2007.

Johnston, Verna R. "The Return of the Tule Elk." *Pacific Discovery,* Jan/Feb 1978.

Jones, Natalie. "No parity and equality for oyster farm." *Point Reyes Light*, February 26, 2009.

Kahn, Debra. "Ag interests, enviros spar over Calif. wilderness plan." *New York Times*, May 7, 2009.

Kahn, Lynnette. "Down with the liars." *Point Reyes Light*, August 14, 2008.

Kaufman, Leslie. "Debate Flares on Limits of Nature and Commerce in Parks." *New York Times*, October 31, 2009.

Kaufman, Miranda. "Out & About: History Explorer: Africans in Tudor and Stuart Britain." *BBC History Magazine*, April 2014.

Kelleher, Brian. *Drakes Bay: Unraveling California's Great Maritime Mystery*. Kelleher & Associates, 1997.

Ketcham, Brannon. Email to Tricia Wingard, Tracy Hamm and Melissa Stedeford Re: Escrow account for DBOC. Point Reyes National Seashore, May 27, 2011.

Khokha, Sasha. "Are Dairy Farmers a Dying Breed?" NPR, July 24, 2009.

Kling, Jim. "Corey Goodman: Meet the man behind Pfizer's recent decision to bet its entire R&D effort on the biotech model." *Nature Biotechnology*, April 2009.

Konzak, Michael, and Adrian Praetzellis. "Archaeology of *Ostrea Lurida* in Drakes Estero, Point Reyes National Seashore." Anthropological Studies Center, Sonoma State University, 2011.

Kovner, Guy. "'Marine vomit' can smother other species, including oyster beds." *Press Democrat*, October 14, 2012.

Krakauer, Jon. *Into the Wild*. Anchor Books, 1997.

Krogh, Bud. Memorandum to Doug Hofe, September 26, 1969.

—. Memorandum to Tod Hulin, September 29, 1969.

Kurlansky, Mark. *The Big Oyster: History on the Halfshell*. Ballantine Books, 2006.

La Forge, Paul. "Destroy All Monsters." *The Believer*, September 2006.

Leuty, Ron. "Goodman to leave Pfizer biotech unit." *San Francisco Business Times*, April 28, 2009.

—. "Labrys Biologics, founded by Corey Goodman, snags Pfizer migraine drug, $31 million." *San Francisco Business Times,* January 3, 2013.

Lewis, C.S. *The Lion, the Witch and the Wardrobe*. Geoffrey Bles, 1950.

Leydecker, Mary. "Oyster lovers gather to gorge themselves." *Marin Independent Journal*, August 9, 1984.

Libby, Granville. *Collection of 29 autograph letters of California historical interest, written to his mother and brother in Portland, Maine*. Edward Laurence Doheny Memorial Library, letters dated March 7, 1852–March 2, 1858.

Liberatore, Paul. "Booming bivalves are grown in Marin." *Marin Independent Journal*, January 12, 1995.

Littlefield, Amy. "Legislation would extend oyster operation in Bay Area national park." *Los Angeles Times*, June 24, 2009.

Livingston, Dewey. *Discovering Historic Ranches at Point Reyes*. Point Reyes National Seashore Association, 2009.

London, Jack. *John Barleycorn*. Century Company, 1913.

—. *Tales of the Fish Patrol*. BookSurge Classics, 2004. Originally published 1905.

Longstreth, Carolyn. "Muddles estero." *Point Reyes Light*, May 8, 2008.

Lunny, Kevin. Letter from Drakes Bay Oyster Company to permitting agencies Re: Drakes Bay Oyster Farm Emergency Repair Project Description. April 4, 2011.

——. Letter from Drakes Bay Oyster Company to permitting agencies Re: Emergency Repair Permit Applications for Damages Caused by the March 19 & 20, 2011, Windstorm. March 25, 2011.

——. Letter from Drakes Bay Oyster Company to Point Reyes National Seashore Re: boat parking and floating dock area dredging. March 5, 2011.

——. Letter to Cassidy Teufel, California Coastal Commission Re: Coastal Development Permit Application No: 2-06-003. Drakes Bay Oyster Company, October 5, 2009.

——. Letter to Cassidy Teufel, California Coastal Commission Re: Coastal Development Permit Application No: 2-06-003—Response to CCC letter of March 9, 2010. Drakes Bay Oyster Company, March 16, 2010.

——. Letter to Christine Chestnut, California Coastal Commission Statewide Enforcement Unit Re: CCC-07-CD-04. Drakes Bay Oyster Company. January 30, 2008.

——. Letter to Christine Chestnut, California Coastal Commission Statewide Enforcement Unit Re: CCC-07-CD-04. Drakes Bay Oyster Company. January 31, 2008.

——. Letter to Cicely Muldoon, Superintendent, Point Reyes National Seashore [Re: request to modify boundaries of CDFG lease and to cultivate Olympia oysters and purple-hinged rock scallops]. Drakes Bay Oyster Company, July 22, 2010.

——. Letter to Cicely Muldoon, Superintendent, Point Reyes National Seashore Re: Drakes Bay Oyster Company Comments on National Park Service Scoping Letter for Special Use Permit Environmental Impact Statement. Drakes Bay Oyster Company, November 24, 2010.

——. Letter to Don Neubacher, December 29, 2009.

——. Letter to Jo Ginsberg, California Coastal Commission Re: Consent Cease & Desist Order No. CCC-07-CD-II. Drakes Bay Oyster Company, November 14, 2008.

——. Letter to Jo Ginsberg, California Coastal Commission Re: CCC-07-CD-II Drakes Bay Oyster Company. Drakes Bay Oyster Company, December 21, 2009.

——. Letter to John Carlson Jr., Executive Director, Department of Fish and Game Re: Lease No. M-438-01. Drakes Bay Oyster Company, April 27, 2010.

——. Letter to John Carlson Jr., Executive Director, Department of Fish and Game Re: Lease No. M-438-0—Boundary Revision. Drakes Bay Oyster Company, May 10, 2010.

——. Letter to Natalie Gates, National Park Service. November 10, 2010.

——. Letter to Natalie Gates, National Park Service Re: Housing. Drakes Bay Oyster Company, November 15, 2010.

——. Letter to Natalie Gates, Point Reyes National Seashore Re: 1—Vessel Transit Plan. Drakes Bay Oyster Company, November 15, 2010.

——. Letter to Natalie Gates, National Park Service. November 15, 2010.

——. Letter to Natalie Gates, Point Reyes National Seashore Re: New cultured species request. March 4, 2011.

——. Letter (with attachments) to Natalie Gates, Point Reyes National Seashore Re: supplemental scoping information. Drakes Bay Oyster Company, March 4, 2011.

——. Letter (with attachments) to Natalie Gates, Point Reyes National Seashore Re: alternate building design. Drakes Bay Oyster Company, March 5, 2011.

——. Letter to Natalie Gates, Point Reyes National Seashore Re: Lease No. M-438-01 lease line adjustment. Drakes Bay Oyster Company, March 15, 2011.

——. Letter to Susan Roberts, Executive Director, Ocean Studies Board, National Academy of Sciences. February 11, 2009.

Lytz, Karl S. Letter to Secretary of the Interior Ken Salazar Re: Special Use Permit for Drakes Bay Oyster Company. Latham & Watkins LLP, July 6, 2010.

MAP: Attachment 10c to the letter from Drakes Bay Oyster Company to Point Reyes National Seashore on November 15, 2010, regarding oyster production (November 2007 map).

Markowitz, Hal. "Sarah's science rules." *Point Reyes Light*, July 31, 2008.

Martin, Glen. "When nature and profit thrive." *San Francisco Chronicle*, December 27, 1993.

Mason, Clark. "Tribal roots dispute erupts among Dry Creek Pomo." *Press Democrat*, November 18, 2012.

McCamman, John. Letter from Acting Director, California Department of Fish and Game, to Assembly Member Jared Huffman Re: California Department of Fish and Game position on Drakes Bay Oyster Farm. March 25, 2008.

McCloskey, Pete. Congressional testimony before the Subcommittee on National Parks and Recreation at the Committee on Interior and Insular Affairs, May 13, 1969.

——. Letter to John Ehrlichman, September 16, 1969.

—. Letter to Tod Hulin, October 10, 1969.

McLeod, Christopher, Glenn Switkes and Randy Hayes. *Glen Canyon Damn* (film). Distribution: Earth First! Roadshow, Summer 1982.

McNaughton, Kora. "A chance to save elk lives by helping count them." *Point Reyes Light*, April 1, 1993.

Melchior, Jillian Kay. "Raw Deal: Bad science and contempt for the law allow the government to destroy a family oyster farm." *National Review Online*, December 10, 2012.

Mery, Michael. "Editorial or article?" *Point Reyes Light*, January 15, 2009.

Mihan, Ralph. Letter to Point Reyes National Seashore Superintendent Re: Point Reyes Wilderness Act. February 26, 2004.

Miller, R.L. "Dear Progressive Bay Area, Please STFU about Drakes Bay Oyster Farm." *Daily Kos*, December 7, 2012.

Miller, Sarah Allen. "Movement and activity patterns of harbor seals at the Point Reyes Peninsula." Master's thesis, University of California, Berkeley, 1988.

Mitchell, Dave. "Park has only three years to solve elk problem." *Point Reyes Light*, July 3, 1986.

—. "Scientists irked by park." *Point Reyes Light*, September 4, 2008.

—. "Several people carry water for the park." *Point Reyes Light*, September 11, 2008.

—. "What witnesses told investigators about the park." *Point Reyes Light*, August 28, 2008.

Moore, Thomas O. Letter to Tom Johnson of Johnson Oyster Company. Department of Fish and Game Marine Region Laboratory, February 2, 2004.

National Park Service. *Drakes Estero: A Sheltered Wilderness Estuary*. Version I. Department of the Interior. Point Reyes National Seashore, September 2006.

—. *Drakes Estero: A Sheltered Wilderness Estuary*. Version II. Department of the Interior. Point Reyes National Seashore, May 2007.

National Research Council. "Best Practices for Shellfish Mariculture and a Scientific Review of Ecological Efforts in Drakes Estero, Pt. Reyes National Seashore, California." National Academy of Sciences, 2009.

Neil, Alex. "Decision near on booming elk herd." *Marin Independent Journal*, September 2, 1993.

Neubacher, Donald. Letter to California Fish and Game Commission Re: Consent Item #15 for the December 9, 2009, Fish and Commission Meeting regarding expansion of Manila Clams to Drakes Estero Aquaculture Lease M-438-01. National Park Service, December 8, 2009.

—. Letter to Kevin Lunny. United States Department of the Interior, National Park Service, December 22, 2009.

—. Letter to Robert Treanor, Executive Director, State of California Fish and Game Commission Re: Consent Item #32, Request of Tom Johnson, Johnson Oyster Company (JOC), Inc. for Lease Renewal of State Water Bottom Lease Agreements for M-438-01 and M-438-02, Drakes Bay, Marin County, June 24, 2004 Fish and Game Commission Meeting. National Park Service, June 18, 2004.

—. Letter to Tom Moore, California Department of Fish and Game Marine Region Laboratory. March 15, 2004.

Nobel, Justin. "Fishermen debate marine protection." *Point Reyes Light*, February 7, 2008.

—. "Oysters or marine reserve?" *Point Reyes Light*, February 14, 2008.

O'Mara, Kelly. "It's Not Just About the Oysters." *California Lawyer*, March 2014.

Packard, E.L. *The Molluscan Fauna from San Francisco Bay*. University of California Publications in Zoology, Vol. 14, No. 2, 1918.

Patterson, Missy. "Ask Missy." *Point Reyes Light*, June 19, 2008.

Perry, Pat. "New Method at Shell Fish Farm." *Marin Independent Journal*, September 15, 1966.

Peterzell, Paul. "County sues Johnson Oyster Co. Suit cites 'health and safety risk.'" *Marin Independent Journal*, October 14, 1995.

Phelan, Deborah. "'Fairytale' deer enchant West Marin." *Marin Independent Journal*, September 25, 1993.

Polansky, Barbara. "A prehistoric archaeological settlement pattern model for the Point Reyes peninsula." Master's thesis, Sonoma State University, 1998.

Pontacq, J. "Ollie 'Erster versus Smokey the Bear." *Coastal Post*, April 2007.

Potter, Will. *Green Is the New Red: An Insider's Account of a Social Movement Under Siege*. City Lights Publishers, 2011.

Prado, Mark. "Elk rebounding: Point Reyes study tracks animals once nearly extinct." *Marin Independent Journal*, January 14, 2005.

—. "Elk rescue: Good deed or bad decision?" *Marin Independent Journal*, June 23, 2005.

—. "Few non-native deer remain." *Marin Independent Journal*, December 5, 2010.

—. "Marin's deer dilemma: Local herd threatened by non-native population in Point Reyes seashore." *Marin Independent Journal*, April 28, 2002.

—. "Plan to kill fallow, axis deer runs into opposition." *Marin Independent Journal,* February 6, 2006.

—. "Woolsey sets sights on sparing invasive deer." *Marin Independent Journal,* July 25, 2007.

Ptak, Louis. "Learn more about Sarah Allen." *Point Reyes Light,* January, 2007.

Quinn, Arthur. *The Broken Shore: The Marin Peninsula.* Smith, Gibbs Publisher, 1981.

Quirt, Steve. "Artichokes and Grass at G Ranch: Diversification is underway at Lunny Ranch." *Grown in Marin: Farm and Crop Diversification Newsletter,* University of California Cooperative Extension, July 2004.

Ramey, Kirsten. Email to Brannon Ketcham, Point Reyes National Seashore Re: Escrow account for DBOC. California Department of Fish and Game, Aquaculture and Bay Management Project, May 26, 2011.

Reutinger, Joan. "Birth Control Alternative to Hunting Deer Being Considered." *Coastal Post,* February 13, 1984.

Riley, Laura. "Oysters and champagne in West Marin." *Point Reyes Light,* January 3, 1986.

Riley, Tom. "Tomales Tom's." *Point Reyes Light,* February 12, 1987.

Rilla, Ellie and David Lewis et al. *M.B. Boissevain, Marin's First Farm Advisor.* Regents of the University of California, 2012.

Rogers, Rob. "West Marin oyster grower makes deal, but future is still uncertain." *Marin Independent Journal,* April 26, 2008.

Ruch, Jeff. "Park Service rudely blamed." *Point Reyes Light,* July 31, 2008.

Rudo, Mark O. "Little Archeological Evidence of the Olympia oyster (*Ostrea lurida*) at Drakes Estero, Point Reyes National Seashore California." National Park Service, Pacific West Region, September 2009.

Sadin, Paul. *Managing a Land in Motion: An Administrative History of the Point Reyes National Seashore.* National Park Service, 2007.

Salzman, James E. "Scientists as Advocates: The Point Reyes Bird Observatory and Gill Netting in Central California." *Conservation Biology* Vol. 3, June 1989.

Sarris, Greg. "Fidel's Place." *Bay Nature,* April 2012.

—. "Maria Evangeliste." www.greg-sarris.com, 2013.

—. "On Sacred Places." *Bay Nature,* April 2003.

—. "The Last Woman from Petaluma." www.greg-sarris.com, 2013.

Schinske, Marian. "Park advisors OK relocating some elk." *Point Reyes Light,* April 2, 1998.

—. "30 more elk on Pierce Point injected with contraceptive." *Point Reyes Light*, June 25, 1998.

—. "Copter gives elk rides at Pierce Point." *Point Reyes Light*, December 3, 1998.

—. "Park tries contraception on tule elk." *Point Reyes Light*, August 7, 1997.

Schwendinger, Robert J. *International Port of Call: An Illustrated Maritime History of the Golden Gate*. Smithmark, 1986.

Seredy, Kate. *The White Stag*. Viking Press, 1937.

Shapiro, Nina. "Toby Bradshaw, Target of Famous Arson, Hunts Elk, Praises Vegetarianism, and Defends Genetic Engineering." *Seattle Weekly*, June 21, 2012.

Skinner, John E. *An Historical Review of the Fish and Wildlife Resources of the San Francisco Bay Area*. Water Projects Branch Report No. 1, June 1962.

Slobig, Zachary. "Easy Target/There's a plan afoot to eradicate the white fallow deer in Point Reyes—but could there be another way to keep rangers, ranchers, animal lovers, Hindus and venison diners on the same side?" *San Francisco Chronicle*, May 6, 2007.

Smith, Frederick. "EAC supports ranchers." *Point Reyes Light*, February 5, 2009.

—. "Letter: Help prevent land grab at national park." *Santa Cruz Sentinel*, October 8, 2009.

—. "Slated for wilderness." *Point Reyes Light*, April 10, 2008.

—. "Why Drakes Bay Oyster Company must go in 2012." *Point Reyes Light*, January 22, 2009.

Smith, Scott. "Indian casinos embroiled in turmoil." Associated Press, November 22, 2014.

Smith, Susan E., and Susumu Kato. *The Fisheries of San Francisco Bay: Past, Present and Future*. National Marine Fisheries Service, 1979.

Snyder, George. "Racking up profit at Drake's Bay: A fat farm for 7 million oysters." *San Francisco Chronicle*, April 26, 1976.

Solnit, Rebecca. *Savage Dreams: A Journey into the Landscape Wars of the American West*. University of California Press, 1994.

Sonoma State University. "Federated Indians of Graton Rancheria Donate $1.5 Million to Sonoma State for Endowed Chair in Native American Studies." Press release, December 8, 2003.

Speet, Tibbett L. "Once scarce elk may be endangering itself." *Marin Independent Journal*, May 4, 1991.

Staff. "Tule elk to find two new homes." *Marin Independent Journal*, November 8, 1976.

Stienstra, Tom. "Glorious resurgence of tule elk." *San Francisco Examiner*, September 29, 1991.

Studdert, Robert. Letter to Robert Treanor, California Fish and Game Re: Water Bottom Lease No. M-438-01 Johnson Oyster Company. August 9, 1993.

Suri, Jeremi. "The Nukes of October: Richard Nixon's Secret Plan to Bring Peace to Vietnam." *Wired*, February 25, 2008.

Sutherland, John. "Drakes red herring." *Point Reyes Light*, April 10, 2008.

Taylor, Kate. "Birth control bullets may be used on elk herd at Point Reyes." *San Francisco Chronicle*, July 6, 1993.

Teufel, Cassidy. Letter to John Dell'Osso, Acting Superintendent, Point Reyes National Seashore Re: Coastal Development Permit Application for Drakes Bay Oyster Company. March 30, 2010.

Thayer, Paul. Letter to Michael Greenberg, Alliance for Local Sustainable Agriculture. California State Lands Commission, July 26, 2007.

Thompson, John. "Fighting nature: What are we doing?" *Animal Chronicles: A Marin Humane Society Publication*, spring 2006.

Thoron, Samuel. "Allen character assassination." *Point Reyes Light*, January, 2007.

——. "Kevin Lunny's orchestra." *Point Reyes Light*, July 31, 2008.

Thuermer, Angus M. "Photographers sue to stop Grand Teton elk hunt." *WyoFile*, October 21, 2014.

Thurman, Maura. "Big hopes for fewer tule elk births: birth control test may curb Point Reyes fast growing herd." *Marin Independent Journal*, May 24, 1998.

——. "Point Reyes elk: Up close and personal. Researchers put radio collars on 19." *Marin Independent Journal*, November 6, 1996.

——. "Too many tule." *Marin Independent Journal*, August 3, 1997.

——. "W. Marin tule elk herd to be reduced." *Marin Independent Journal*, September 24, 1992.

Tizard, Will. "Protestors, elk hunters face off at Suisun Bay." *San Francisco Examiner*.

Tompkins, Barry. "Warning to West Marin deer: Run!" *Marin Independent Journal*, July 29, 2007.

Treganza, Adan E. "The examination of Indian shellmounds in the Tomales and Drakes Bay areas with reference to sixteenth century history contacts." Report to the California Department of Parks and Recreation, 1959.

Turnbull, George. Letter to Kevin Lunny. National Park Service, Pacific West Region, December 4, 2009.

Turner, Wallace. "Rep. Phillip Burton, Democratic Liberal, Dies on Visit to California." *New York Times,* April 11, 1983.

Upshaw, Jennifer. "Hobbled fawn on the mend." *Marin Independent Journal,* August 12, 2008.

Van der Ryn, Sim. "Community forum on the future of the Seashore." *Point Reyes Light,* March 19, 2009.

Van der Ryn, Sim, and Buddy Williams. Drakes Estero Aquaculture Center Concept Design, April 29, 2009. Ecological Design Collaborative, April 29, 2009.

—. Drakes Estero Aquaculture Center Site Design Comparisons. Ecological Design Collaborative, May 27, 2009.

Van Paris, Calin. "How exactly do you farm oysters?" *The Bold Italic,* March 28, 2014.

—. "Shell Games." *Marin* magazine, July 2014.

Venteicher, Wes. "Feinstein bill gives Lunny a decade more." *Point Reyes Light,* June 25, 2009.

—. "Supes endorse longer lease." *Point Reyes Light,* July 16, 2009.

Von der Porten, Edward P. "Drakes Bay Shell Mound Archeology 1951–1962." Drake Navigators Guild, 1963.

Watt, Laura. "What you may not know about the laws governing Drakes Estero." *Point Reyes Light,* November 18, 2010.

Whitaker, John C. Memorandum to George Murphy and Don Clausen. November 18, 1969.

—. Memorandum to John Ehrlichman, November 13, 1969.

White, Richard. "Back to the wild in Point Reyes." *Los Angeles Times,* November 27, 2012.

Wigert, Bill. "Drakes oysters, California's treasure in a half-shell." *Point Reyes Light,* April 24, 2008.

Williams, Woody. "Like Shellfish? Two 'Farms' Flourish in Marin: Raising Oysters for Commercial Sale." *Marin* magazine, August 1949.

Wilson, Bill. "Down on the Oyster Farm." *Sacramento Bee,* March 19, 1981.

Wilson, Doug, and Gordon Bennett for Sierra Club Marin Group. "In support of the Estero." *Point Reyes Light,* April 17, 2008.

Wyss, Dennis. "The hunt is on at Point Reyes: Rangers 'cull' non-native deer to protect park." *Marin Independent Journal,* January 26, 1992.

Yeatts, Thomas. "A worker's life on Drakes Bay Oyster Farm." *Point Reyes Light*, April 5, 2007.

—. "Lunnys forced to remove cows from G Ranch." *Point Reyes Light*, 2007.

—-. "Supervisors back Lunny against Park." *Point Reyes Light*, May 10, 2007.

APPENDICES

# APPENDIX A
## TIMELINE

| | |
|---|---|
| c. 8000 BC–4000 BC | Humans settle near Point Reyes |
| 1579 | Sir Francis Drake lands, likely at Drakes Beach |
| 1776 | Spanish establish Misión San Francisco de Asís |
| 1849 | California Gold Rush |
| 1858 | Shafter brothers begin dairy farming empire on Point Reyes |
| 1869 | Completion of the transcontinental railroad |
| 1932 | First lease issued to farm oysters in Drakes Estero |
| 1957 | Johnson Oyster Company begins operating in the estero |
| 1962 | Creation of Point Reyes National Seashore |
| 1964 | United States Wilderness Act |
| 1972 | Johnson sells oyster farm land to the park, signs forty-year lease |
| 1976 | Point Reyes Wilderness Act, declaring Drakes Estero "potential wilderness" |
| 2005 | Lunny family buys oyster farm, renames it Drakes Bay Oyster Company |

# APPENDIX B
## KEY SCIENTIFIC AND INVESTIGATIVE REPORTS

1. Drakes Estero Assessment of Oyster Farming Final Completion Report, by Deborah Elliott-Fisk et al. for the National Park Service (2005), aka "the Elliott-Fisk report"

2. Drakes Estero: A Sheltered Wilderness Estuary, by Sarah Allen et al. for the National Park Service (version #1 2006, version #2 2007), aka "the Sheltered Wilderness Estuary report"

3. Department of the Interior Inspector General's Report (2008), aka "the IG report"

4. Shellfish Mariculture in Drakes Estero, Point Reyes National Seashore, California, by the National Academy of Sciences National Research Council (2009), aka "the NAS report"

5. Modeling the effects of El Niño, density-dependence, and disturbance on harbor seal (*Phoca vitulina*) counts in Drakes Estero, California: 1997–2007, by Ben Becker et al. for the National Park Service (version #1 2008, version #2 2009, version #3 2011), aka "the Becker report"

6. Public Report on Allegations of Scientific Misconduct at Point Reyes National Seashore, California, by Gavin Frost for the Department of the Interior Office of the Solicitor (2011), aka "the Frost report"

7. Mariculture and Harbor Seals in Drakes Estero, California, by the Marine Mammal Commission (2011), aka "the MMC report"

8. Draft Environmental Impact Statement for the Drakes Bay Oyster Company Special Use Permit, by the National Park Service (2011), aka "the DEIS"

9. Environmental Impact Statement for the Drakes Bay Oyster Company Special Use Permit, by the National Park Service (2012), aka "the EIS"

# APPENDIX C
## LAWS AND OTHER DOCUMENTS

## I. WALLACE STEGNER'S WILDERNESS LETTER

Los Altos, Calif.

December 3, 1960

David E. Pesonen

Wildland Research Center

Agricultural Experiment Station

243 Mulford Hall

University of California

Berkeley 4, Calif.

Dear Mr. Pesonen:

I believe that you are working on the wilderness portion of the Outdoor Recreation Resources Review Commission's report. If I may, I should like to urge some arguments for wilderness preservation that involve recreation, as it is ordinarily conceived, hardly at all. Hunting, fishing, hiking, mountain-climbing, camping, photography, and the enjoyment of natural scenery will all, surely, figure in your report. So will the wilderness as a genetic reserve, a scientific yardstick by which we may measure the world in its natural balance against the world in its man-made imbalance. What I want to speak for is not so much the wilderness uses, valuable as those are, but the wilderness idea, which is a resource in itself. Being an intangible and spiritual resource, it will seem mystical to the practical minded—but then anything that cannot be moved by a bulldozer is likely to seem mystical to them. I want to speak for the wilderness idea as something that has helped form our character and that has certainly shaped our history as a people. It has no more to do with recreation than churches have to do with recreation, or than the strenuousness and optimism and expansiveness of what the historians call the "American Dream" have to do with recreation. Nevertheless, since it is only in this recreation survey that the values of wilderness are being compiled, I hope you will permit me to insert this idea between the leaves, as it were, of the recreation report. Something will have gone out of us as a people if we ever let the remaining wilderness be destroyed; if we permit the last virgin forests to be turned into comic books and plastic cigarette cases; if we drive the few remaining members of the wild species into zoos or to extinction; if we pollute the last clear air and dirty the last clean streams and push our paved roads through the last of the silence, so that never again will Americans be free in their own country from the noise, the exhausts, the stinks of human and automotive waste. And so that never again can we have the chance to see ourselves single, separate, vertical and individual in the world, part of the environment of trees and rocks and soil, brother to the other animals, part of the natural world and competent to belong in it. Without any remaining wilderness we are committed wholly, without chance for even momentary reflection and rest, to a headlong drive into our technological termite-life, the Brave New World of a completely man-controlled environment. We need wilderness preserved—as much of it as is still left, and as many kinds—because it was the challenge against which our character as a people was formed. The reminder and the reassurance that it is still there is good for our spiritual health even if we never once in ten years set foot in it. It is good for us when we are young, because of the incomparable sanity it can bring briefly, as vacation and rest, into our insane lives. It is important to us when we are old simply because it is there—important, that is, simply as an idea.

We are a wild species, as Darwin pointed out. Nobody ever tamed or domesticated or scientifically bred us. But for at least three millennia we have been engaged in a cumulative and ambitious race to modify and gain control of our environment, and in the process we have come close to domesticating ourselves. Not many people are likely, any more, to look upon what we call "progress" as an unmixed blessing. Just as surely as it has brought us increased comfort and more material goods, it has brought us spiritual losses, and it threatens now to become the Frankenstein that will destroy us. One means of sanity is to retain a hold on the natural world, to remain, insofar as we can, good animals. Americans still have that chance, more than many peoples; for while we were demonstrating ourselves the most efficient and ruthless environment-busters in history, and slashing and burning and cutting our way through a wilderness continent, the wilderness was working on us. It remains in us as surely as Indian names remain on the land. If the abstract dream of human liberty and human dignity became, in America, something more than an abstract dream, mark it down at least partially to the fact that we were in subdued ways subdued by what we conquered. The Connecticut Yankee, sending likely candidates from King Arthur's unjust kingdom to his Man Factory for rehabilitation, was over-optimistic, as he later admitted. These things cannot be forced, they have to grow. To make such a man, such a democrat, such a believer in human individual dignity, as Mark Twain himself, the frontier was necessary, Hannibal and the Mississippi and Virginia City, and reaching out from those the wilderness; the wilderness as opportunity and idea, the thing that has helped to make an American different from and, until we forget it in the roar of our industrial cities, more fortunate than other men. For an American, insofar as he is new and different at all, is a civilized man who has renewed himself in the wild. The American experience has been the confrontation by old peoples and cultures of a world as new as if it had just risen from the sea. That gave us our hope and our excitement, and the hope and excitement can be passed on to newer Americans, Americans who never saw any phase of the frontier. But only so long as we keep the remainder of our wild as a reserve and a promise—a sort of wilderness bank. As a novelist, I may perhaps be forgiven for taking literature as a reflection, indirect but profoundly true, of our national consciousness. And our literature, as perhaps you are aware, is sick, embittered, losing its mind, losing its faith. Our novelists are the declared enemies of their society. There has hardly been a serious or important novel in this century that did not repudiate in part or in whole American technological culture for its commercialism, its vulgarity, and the way in which it has dirtied a clean continent and a clean dream. I do not expect that the preservation of our remaining wilderness is going to cure this condition. But the mere example that we can as a nation apply some other criteria than commercial and exploitative considerations would be heartening to many Americans, novelists or otherwise. We need to demonstrate our acceptance of the natural world, including ourselves;

we need the spiritual refreshment that being natural can produce. And one of the best places for us to get that is in the wilderness where the fun houses, the bulldozers, and the pavement of our civilization are shut out.

Sherwood Anderson, in a letter to Waldo Frank in the 1920s, said it better than I can. "Is it not likely that when the country was new and men were often alone in the fields and the forest they got a sense of bigness outside themselves that has now in some way been lost. . . . Mystery whispered in the grass, played in the branches of trees overhead, was caught up and blown across the American line in clouds of dust at evening on the prairies. . . . I am old enough to remember tales that strengthen my belief in a deep semi-religious influence that was formerly at work among our people. The flavor of it hangs over the best work of Mark Twain. . . . I can remember old fellows in my home town speaking feelingly of an evening spent on the big empty plains. It had taken the shrillness out of them. They had learned the trick of quiet. . . ."

We could learn it too, even yet; even our children and grandchildren could learn it. But only if we save, for just such absolutely non-recreational, impractical, and mystical uses as this, all the wild that still remains to us. It seems to me significant that the distinct down-turn in our literature from hope to bitterness took place almost at the precise time when the frontier officially came to an end, in 1890, and when the American way of life had begun to turn strongly urban and industrial. The more urban it has become, and the more frantic with technological change, the sicker and more embittered our literature, and I believe our people, have become. For myself, I grew up on the empty plains of Saskatchewan and Montana and in the mountains of Utah, and I put a very high valuation on what those places gave me. And if I had not been able periodically to renew myself in the mountains and deserts of western America I would be very nearly bughouse. Even when I can't get to the back country, the thought of the colored deserts of southern Utah, or the reassurance that there are still stretches of prairies where the world can be instantaneously perceived as disk and bowl, and where the little but intensely important human being is exposed to the five directions of the thirty-six winds, is a positive consolation. The idea alone can sustain me. But as the wilderness areas are progressively exploited or "improve," as the jeeps and bulldozers of uranium prospectors scar up the deserts and the roads are cut into the alpine timberlands, and as the remnants of the unspoiled and natural world are progressively eroded, every such loss is a little death in me. In us.

I am not moved by the argument that those wilderness areas which have already been exposed to grazing or mining are already deflowered, and so might as well be "harvested." For mining I cannot say much good except that its operations are generally short-lived. The extractable wealth is taken and the shafts, the tailings, and the ruins left, and in a dry country such as the American West the wounds men make in the earth do not quickly heal. Still, they are only wounds; they aren't absolutely mortal. Better a wounded wilderness than none at all. And as for grazing, if it is strictly controlled so that it does not destroy the ground cover, damage the ecology, or compete with the wildlife it is in itself nothing that need conflict with the wilderness feeling or the validity of the wilderness experience. I have known enough range cattle to recognize them as wild animals; and the people who herd them have, in the wilderness context, the dignity of rareness; they belong on the frontier, moreover, and have a look of rightness. The invasion they make on the virgin country is a sort of invasion that is as old as Neolithic man, and they can, in moderation, even emphasize a man's feeling of belonging to the natural world. Under surveillance, they can belong; under control, they need not deface or mar. I do not believe that in wilderness areas where grazing has never been permit- ted, it should be permitted; but I do not believe either that an otherwise untouched wilderness should be eliminated from the preservation plan because of limited existing uses such as grazing which are in conso- nance with the frontier condition and image.

Let me say something on the subject of the kinds of wilderness worth preserving. Most of those areas contemplated are in the national forests and in high mountain country. For all the usual recreational purposes, the alpine and the forest wildernesses are obviously the most important, both as genetic banks and as beauty spots. But for the spiri- tual renewal, the recognition of identity, the birth of awe, other kinds will serve every bit as well. Perhaps, because they are less friendly to life, more abstractly nonhuman, they will serve even better. On our Saskatchewan prairie, the nearest neighbor was four miles away, and at night we saw only two lights on all the dark rounding earth. The earth was full of animals—field mice, ground squirrels, weasels, fer- rets, badgers, coyotes, burrowing owls, snakes. I knew them as my little brothers, as fellow creatures, and I have never been able to look upon animals in any other way since. The sky in that country came clear down to the ground on every side, and it was full of great weath- ers, and clouds, and winds, and hawks. I hope I learned something from looking a long way, from looking up, from being much alone. A prairie like that, one big enough to carry the eye clear to the sinking, rounding horizon, can be as lonely and grand and simple in its forms as the sea. It is as good a place as any for the wilderness experience to happen; the vanishing prairie is as worth preserving for the wilderness idea as the alpine forest. So are great reaches of our western deserts, scarred somewhat by prospectors but otherwise open, beautiful, waiting, close to whatever God you want to see in them. Just as a sample, let me suggest the Robbers' Roost country in Wayne County, Utah, near the Capitol Reef National Monument. In that desert climate the dozer and jeep tracks will not soon melt back into the earth, but the country has a way of making the scars insignificant. It is a lovely and terrible wilderness, such wilderness as Christ and the prophets went out into; harshly and beautifully colored, broken and worn until its bones are exposed, its great sky without a smudge of taint from Technocracy, and in hidden corners and pockets under its cliffs the sudden poetry of springs. Save a piece of country like that intact, and it does not matter in the slightest that only a few people every year will go into it. That is precisely its value. Roads would be a desecration, crowds would ruin it. But those who haven't the strength or youth to go into it and live can simply sit and look. They can look two hundred miles, clear into Colorado: and looking down over the cliffs and canyons of the San Rafael Swell and the Robbers' Roost they can also look as deeply into themselves as anywhere I know. And if they can't even get to the places on the Aquarius Plateau where the present roads will carry them, they can simply contemplate the idea, take pleasure in the fact that such a timeless and uncontrolled part of earth is still there.

These are some of the things wilderness can do for us. That is the reason we need to put into effect, for its preservation, some other principle than the principles of exploitation or "usefulness" or even recreation. We simply need that wild country available to us, even if we never do more than drive to its edge and look in. For it can be a means of reassuring ourselves of our sanity as creatures, a part of the geography of hope.

Very sincerely yours,
Wallace Stegner

## II. THE 1962 POINT REYES NATIONAL SEASHORE ACT

Public Law 87-657

87th Congress, 2nd Session

September 13, 1962

AN ACT

To establish the Point Reyes National Seashore in the State of California, and for other purposes.

Be it enacted by the Senate and House of Representatives of the United States of America in Congress assembled. That in order to preserve, for purposes of public recreation, benefit, and inspiration, a portion of the diminishing seashore of the United States that remains undeveloped, the Secretary of the Interior (hereinafter referred to as the "Secretary") is hereby authorized to take appropriate action in the public interest toward the establishment of the national seashore set forth in section 2 of this Act.

Sec. 2. (a) The area comprising that portion of the land and waters located on Point Reyes Peninsula, Marin County, California, which shall be known as the Point Reyes National Seashore, is described as follows by reference to that certain boundary map, designated NS-PR-7001, dated June 1, 1960, on file with the Director, National Park Service, Washington, District of Columbia.

Beginning at a point, not monumented, where the boundary line common to Rancho Punta de los Reyes (Sobrante) and Rancho Las Baulines meets the average high tide line of the Pacific Ocean as shown on said boundary map;

Thence southwesterly from said point 1,320 feet offshore on a prolongation of said boundary line common to Rancho Punta de los Reyes (Sobrante) and Rancho Las Baulines;

Thence in a northerly and westerly direction paralleling the average high tide line of the shore of the Pacific Ocean; along Drakes Bay, and around Point Reyes;

Thence generally northerly and around Tomales Point, offshore a distance of 1,320 feet from average high tide line;

Thence southeasterly along a line 1,320 feet offshore and parallel to the average high tide line along the west shore of Bodega Bay and Tomales Bay to the intersection of this line with a prolongation of the most northerly tangent of the boundary of Tomales Bay State Park;

Thence south 54 degrees 32 minutes west 1,320 feet along the prolongation of said tangent of Tomales Bay State Park boundary to the average high tide line on the shore of Tomales Bay;

Thence following the boundary of Tomales Bay State Park in a southerly direction to a point lying 105.4 feet north 41 degrees east of an unimproved road heading westerly and northerly from Pierce Point Road;

Thence south 41 degrees west 105.4 feet to a point on the north right-of-way of said unimproved road;

Thence southeasterly along the north right-of-way of said unimproved road and Pierce Point Road to a point at the southwest corner of Tomales Bay State Park at the junction of the Pierce Point Road and Sir Francis Drake Boulevard;

Thence due south to a point on the south right-of-way of said Sir Francis Drake Boulevard;

Thence southeasterly along said south right-of-way approximately 3,100 feet to a point;

Thence approximately south 19 degrees west approximately 300 feet;

Thence south approximately 400 feet;

Thence southwest to the most northerly corner of the Inverness watershed area;

Thence southerly and easterly along the west property line of the Inverness watershed area approximately 9,040 feet to a point near the intersection of this property line with an unimproved road as shown on said boundary map;

Thence southerly along existing property lines that roughly follow said unimproved road to its intersection with Drakes Summit Road and to a point on the north right-of-way of Drakes Summit Road;

Thence easterly approximately 100 feet along the north right-of-way of said Drakes Summit Road to a point which is a property line corner at the intersection with an unimproved road to the south;

Thence southerly and easterly and then northerly, as shown approximately on said boundary map, along existing property lines to a point on the south right-of-way of the Bear Valley Road, approximately 1,500 feet southeast of its intersection with Sir Francis Drake Boulevard;

Thence easterly and southerly along said south right-of-way of Bear Valley Road to a point on a property line approximately 1,000 feet west of the intersection of Bear Valley Road and Sir Francis Drake Boulevard in the village of Olema;

Thence south approximately 1,700 feet to the northwest corner of property now owned by Helen U. and Mary S. Shafter;

Thence southwest and southeast along the west boundary of said Shafter property to the southwest corner of said Shafter property;

Thence approximately south 30 degrees east on a course approximately 1,700 feet to a point;

Thence approximately south 10 degrees east on a course to the centerline of Olema Creek;

Thence generally southeasterly up the centerline of Olema Creek to a point on the west right-of-way line of State Route Numbered 1;

Thence southeasterly along westerly right-of-way line to State Highway Numbered 1 to a point where a prolongation of the boundary line common to Rancho Punta de los Reyes (Sobrante) and Rancho Las Baulines would intersect right-of-way line of State Highway Numbered 1;

Thence southwesterly to and along said south boundary line of Rancho Punta de los Reyes (Sobrante) approximately 2,900 feet to a property corner;

Thence approximately south 38 degrees east approximately 1,500 feet to the centerline of Pine Gulch Creek;

Thence down the centerline of Pine Gulch Creek approximately 400 feet to the intersection with a side creek flowing from the west;

Thence up said side creek to its intersection with said south boundary line of Rancho Punta de los Reyes (Sobrante);

Thence southwest along said south boundary line of Rancho Punta de los Reyes to the point of beginning, containing approximately 53,000 acres. Notwithstanding the foregoing description, the Secretary is authorized to include within the Point Reyes National Seashore the entire tract of land owned by the Vedanta Society of Northern

California west of the centerline of Olema Creek, in order to avoid a severance of said tract.

(b) The area referred to in subsection (a) shall include also a right-of-way, to be selected by the Secretary, of not more than 400 feet in width to the aforesaid tract from the intersection of Sir Francis Drake Boulevard and Haggerty Gulch.

Sec. 3. (a) Except as provided in section 4, the Secretary is authorized to acquire, and it is the intent of Congress that he shall acquire as rapidly as appropriated funds become available for this purpose or as such acquisition can be accomplished by donation or with donated funds or by transfer, exchange, or otherwise the lands, waters, and other property, and improvements thereon and any interest therein, within the areas described in section 2 of this Act or which lie within the boundaries of the seashore as established under section 5 of this Act (hereinafter referred to as "such area"). Any property, or interest therein, owned by a State or political subdivision thereof may be acquired only with the concurrence of such owner. Notwithstanding any other provision of law, any Federal property located within such area may, with the concurrence of the agency having custody thereof, be transferred without consideration to the administrative jurisdiction of the Secretary for use by him in carrying out the provisions of this Act. In exercising his authority to acquire property in accordance with the provisions of this subsection, the Secretary may enter into contracts requiring the expenditure, when appropriated, of funds authorized by section 8 of this Act, but the liability of the United States under any such contract shall be contingent on the appropriation of funds sufficient to fulfill the obligations thereby incurred.

(b) The Secretary is authorized to pay for any acquisitions which he makes by purchase under this Act their fair market value, as determined by the Secretary, who may in his discretion base his determination on an independent appraisal obtained by him.

(c) In exercising his authority to acquire property by exchange, the Secretary may accept title to any non-Federal property located within such area and convey to the grantor of such property any federally owned property under the jurisdiction of the Secretary within California and adjacent States, notwithstanding any other provision of law. The properties so exchanged shall be approximately equal in fair market value, provided that the Secretary may accept cash from or pay cash to the grantor in such an exchange in order to equalize the values of the properties exchanged.

Sec. 4. No parcel of more than five hundred acres within the zone of approximately twenty-six thousand acres depicted on map numbered NS-PR-7002, dated August 15, 1961, on file with the director, National Park Service, Washington, District of Columbia, exclusive of that land required to provide access for purposes of the national seashore, shall be acquired without the consent of the owner so long as it remains in its natural state, or is used exclusively for ranching and dairying purposes including housing directly incident thereto. The term "ranching and dairying purposes," as used herein, means such ranching and dairying, primarily for the production of food, as is presently practiced in the area.

In acquiring access roads within the pastoral zone, the Secretary shall give due consideration to existing ranching and dairying uses and shall not unnecessarily interfere with or damage such use.

Sec. 5. (a) As soon as practicable after the date of enactment of this Act and following the acquisition by the Secretary of an acreage in the area described in section 2 of this Act, that is in the opinion of the Secretary efficiently administrable to carry out the purposes of this Act, the Secretary shall establish Point Reyes National Seashore by the publication of notice thereof in the Federal Register.

(b) Such notice referred to in subsection (a) of this section shall contain a detailed description of the boundaries of the seashore which shall encompass an area as nearly as practicable identical to the area described in section 2 of this Act. The Secretary shall forthwith after the date of publication of such notice in the Federal Register (1) send a copy of such notice, together with a map showing such boundaries, by registered or certified mail to the Governor of the State and to the governing body of each of the political subdivisions involved; (2) cause a copy of such notice and map to be published in one or more newspapers which circulate in each of the localities; and (3) cause a certified copy of such notice, a copy of such map, and a copy of this Act to be recorded at the registry of deeds for the county involved.

Sec. 6. (a) Any owner or owners (hereinafter in this subsection referred to as "owner") of improved property on the date of its acquisition by the Secretary may, as a condition to such acquisition, retain the right of use and occupancy of the improved property for noncommercial residential purposes for a term of fifty years. The Secretary shall pay to the owner the fair market value of the property on the date of such acquisition less the fair market value on such date of the right retained by the owner.

(b) As used in this Act, the term "improved property" shall mean a private noncommercial dwelling, including the land on which it is situated, whose construction was begun before September 1, 1959, and structures accessory thereto (hereinafter in this subsection referred to as "dwelling"), together with such amount and locus of the property adjoining and in the same ownership as such dwelling as the Secretary designates to be reasonably necessary for the enjoyment of such dwelling for the sole purpose of noncommercial residential use and occupancy. In making such designation the Secretary shall take into account the manner of noncommercial residential use and occupancy in which the dwelling and such adjoining property has usually been enjoyed by its owner or occupant.

Sec. 7. (a) Except as otherwise provided in this Act, the property acquired by the Secretary under this Act shall be administered by the Secretary, subject to the provisions of the Act entitled "An Act to establish a National Park Service, and for other purposes," approved August 25, 1916 (39 Stat. 535), as amended and supplemented, and in accordance with other laws of general application relating to the national park system as defined by the Act of August 8, 1953 (67 Stat. 496), except that authority otherwise available to the Secretary for the conservation and management of natural resources may be utilized to the extent he finds such authority will further the purposes of this Act.

(b) The Secretary may permit hunting and fishing on lands and waters under his jurisdiction within the seashore in such areas and under such regulations as he may prescribe during open seasons prescribed by applicable local, State, and Federal law. The Secretary shall consult with officials of the State of California and any political subdivision thereof who have jurisdiction of hunting and fishing prior to the issuance of any such regulations, and the Secretary is authorized to enter into cooperative agreements with such officials regarding such hunting and fishing as he may deem desirable.

Sec. 8. There are authorized to be appropriated such sums as may be necessary to carry out the provisions of this Act, except that no more than $14,000,000 shall be appropriated for the acquisition of land and waters and improvements thereon, and interests therein, and incidental costs relating thereto, in accordance with the provisions of this Act.

Approved September 13, 1962.

## III. THE 1964 WILDERNESS ACT

Public Law 88-577 (16 U.S. C. 1131-1136)
88th Congress, Second Session
September 3, 1964

AN ACT

To establish a National Wilderness Preservation System for the permanent good of the whole people, and for other purposes.

Be it enacted by the Senate and House of Representatives of the United States of America in Congress assembled.

SHORT TITLE

Sec. 1. This Act may be cited as the "Wilderness Act".

WILDERNESS SYSTEM ESTABLISHED—STATEMENT
OF POLICY

Sec. 2. (a) In order to assure that an increasing population, accompanied by expanding settlement and growing mechanization, does not occupy and modify all areas within the United States and its possessions, leaving no lands designated for preservation and protection in their natural condition, it is hereby declared to be the policy of the Congress to secure for the American people of present and future generations the benefits of an enduring resource of wilderness. For this purpose there is hereby established a National Wilderness Preservation System to be composed of federally owned areas designated by the Congress as "wilderness areas," and these shall be administered for the use and enjoyment of the American people in such manner as will leave them unimpaired for future use as wilderness, and so as to provide for the protection of these areas, the preservation of their wilderness character, and for the gathering and dissemination of information regarding their use and enjoyment as wilderness; and no Federal lands shall be designated as "wilderness areas" except as provided for in this Act or by a subsequent Act.

(b) The inclusion of an area in the National Wilderness Preservation System notwithstanding, the area shall continue to be managed by the Department and agency having jurisdiction thereover immediately before its inclusion in the National Wilderness Preservation System unless otherwise provided by Act of Congress. No appropriation shall be available for the payment of expenses or salaries for the administration of the National Wilderness Preservation System as a separate unit nor shall any appropriations be available for additional personnel stated as being required solely for the purpose of managing or administering areas solely because they are included within the National Wilderness Preservation System.

DEFINITION OF WILDERNESS

(c) A wilderness, in contrast with those areas where man and his own works dominate the landscape, is hereby recognized as an area where the earth and its community of life are untrammeled by man, where man himself is a visitor who does not remain. An area of wilderness is further defined to mean in this Act an area of undeveloped Federal land retaining its primeval character and influence, without permanent improvements or human habitation, which is protected and managed so as to preserve its natural conditions and which (1) generally appears to have been affected primarily by the forces of nature, with the imprint of man's work substantially unnoticeable; (2) has outstanding opportunities for solitude or a primitive and unconfined type of recreation; (3) has at least five thousand acres of land or is of sufficient size as to make practicable its preservation and use in an unimpaired condition; and (4) may also contain ecological, geological, or other features of scientific, educational, scenic, or historical value.

## NATIONAL WILDERNESS PRESERVATION SYSTEM— EXTENT OF SYSTEM

Sec. 3. (a) All areas within the national forests classified at least 30 days before September 30, 1964, by the Secretary of Agriculture or the Chief of the Forest Service as "wilderness," "wild," or "canoe" are hereby designated as wilderness areas. The Secretary of Agriculture shall:

(1) Within one year after September 30, 1964, file a map and legal description of each wilderness area with the Interior and Insular Affairs Committees of the United States Senate and the House of Representatives, and such descriptions shall have the same force and effect as if included in this Act: Provided, however, That correction of clerical and typographical errors in such legal descriptions and maps may be made.

(2) Maintain, available to the public, records pertaining to said wilderness areas, including maps and legal descriptions, copies of regulations governing them, copies of public notices of, and reports submitted to Congress regarding pending additions, eliminations, or modifications. Maps, legal descriptions, and regulations pertaining to wilderness areas within their respective jurisdictions also shall be available to the public in the offices of regional foresters, national forest supervisors, and forest rangers.

(b) The Secretary of Agriculture shall, within ten years after September 30, 1964, review, as to its suitability or nonsuitability for preservation as wilderness, each area in the national forests classified on September 3, 1964, by the Secretary of Agriculture or the Chief of the Forest Service as "primitive" and report his findings to the President. The President shall advise the United States Senate and House of Representatives of his recommendations with respect to the designation as "wilderness" or other reclassification of each area on which review has been completed, together with maps and a definition of boundaries. Such advice shall be given with respect to not less than one-third of all the areas now classified as "primitive" within three years after September 3, 1964, not less than two-thirds within seven years after September 3, 1964, and the remaining areas within ten years after September 3, 1964. Each recommendation of the President for designation as "wilderness" shall become effective only if so provided by an Act of Congress. Areas classified as "primitive" on September 3, 1964, shall continue to be administered under the rules and regulations affecting such areas on September 3, 1964, until Congress has determined otherwise. Any such area may be increased in size by the President at the time he submits his recommendation to the Congress by not more than five thousand acres with no more than one thousand two hundred and eighty acres of such increase in any one compact unit; if it is proposed to increase the size of any such area by more than five thousand acres or by more than one thousand two hundred and eighty acres in any one compact unit the increase in size shall not become effective until acted upon by Congress. Nothing herein contained shall limit the President in proposing, as part of his recommendations to Congress, the alteration of existing boundaries of primitive areas or recommending the addition of any contiguous area of national forest lands predominantly of wilderness value. Not withstanding any other provisions of this Act, the Secretary of Agriculture may complete his review and delete such area as may be necessary, but not to exceed seven thousand acres, from the southern tip of the Gore Range-Eagles Nest Primitive Area, Colorado, if the Secretary determines that such action is in the public interest.

(c) Within ten years after September 3, 1964, the Secretary of the Interior shall review every roadless area of five thousand contiguous acres or more in the national parks, monuments and other units of the national park system and every such area of, and every roadless island within, the national wildlife refuges and game ranges, under his jurisdiction on September 3, 1964, and shall report to the President his recommendation as to the suitability or nonsuitability of each such area or island for preservation as wilderness. The President shall advise the President of the Senate and the Speaker of the House of Representatives of his recommendation with respect to the designation as wilderness of each such area or island on which review has been completed, together with a map thereof and a definition of its boundaries. Such advice shall be given with respect to not less than one-third of the areas and islands to be reviewed under this subsection within three years after September 3, 1964, not less than two-thirds within seven years of September 3, 1964, and the remainder within ten years of September 3, 1964. A recommendation of the President for designation as wilderness shall become effective only if so provided by an Act of Congress. Nothing contained herein shall, by implication or otherwise, be construed to lessen the present statutory authority of the Secretary of the Interior with respect to the maintenance of roadless areas within units of the national park system.

(d) (1) The Secretary of Agriculture and the Secretary of the Interior shall, prior to submitting any recommendations to the President with respect to the suitability of any area for preservation as wilderness:

(A) give such public notice of the proposed action as they deem appropriate, including publication in the Federal Register and in a newspaper having general circulation in the area or areas in the vicinity of the affected land;

(B) hold a public hearing or hearings at a location or locations convenient to the area affected. The hearings shall be announced through such means as the respective Secretaries involved deem appropriate, including notices in the Federal Register and in newspapers of general circulation in the area: Provided, That if the lands involved are located in more than one State, at least one hearing shall be held in each State in which a portion of the land lies;

(C) at least thirty days before the date of a hearing advise the Governor of each State and the governing board of each county, or in Alaska the borough, in which the lands are located, and Federal departments and agencies concerned, and invite such officials and Federal agencies to submit their views on the proposed action at the hearing or by not later than thirty days following the date of the hearing.

(2) Any views submitted to the appropriate Secretary under the provisions of (1) of this subsection with respect to any area shall be included with any recommendations to the President and to Congress with respect to such area.

(e) Any modification or adjustment of boundaries of any wilderness area shall be recommended by the appropriate Secretary after public notice of such proposal and public hearing or hearings as provided on subsection (d) of this section. The proposed modification or adjustment shall then be recommended with map and description thereof to the President. The President shall advise the United States Senate and the House of Representatives of his recommendations with respect to such modification or adjustment and such recommendations shall become effective only on the same manner as provided for in subsections (b) and (c) of this section.

## USE OF WILDERNESS AREAS
Sec. 4. (a) The purposes of this Act are hereby declared to be within and supplemental to the purposes for which national forests and units of the national park and national wildlife refuge systems are established and administered and:

(1) Nothing in this Act shall be deemed to be in interference with the purpose for which national forests are established as set forth in the Act of June 4, 1897 (30 Stat. 11), and the Multiple Use Sustained-Yield Act of June 12, 1960 (74 Stat. 215).

(2) Nothing in this Act shall modify the restrictions and provisions of the Shipstead-Nolan Act (Public Law 539, Seventy-first Congress, July 10, 1930; 46 Stat. 1020), the Thye-Blatnik Act (Public Law 733, Eightieth Congress, June 22, 1948; 62 Stat. 568), and the Humphrey-Thye-Blatnik-Andersen Act (Public Law 607, Eighty-fourth Congress, June 22.1965; 70 Stat. 326), as applying to the Superior National Forest or the regulations of the Secretary of Agriculture.

(3) Nothing in this Act shall modify the statutory authority under which units of the national park system are created. Further, the designation of any area of any park, monument, or other unit of the national park system as a wilderness area pursuant to this Act shall in no manner lower the standards evolved for the use and preservation

of such park, monument, or other unit of the national park system in accordance with the Act of August 25, 1916, the statutory authority under which the area was created, or any other Act of Congress which might pertain to or affect such area, including, but not limited to, the Act of June 8, 1906 (34 Stat. 225; 16 U.S.C. 432 et seq.); section 3(2) of the Federal Power Act (16 U.S.C. 796 (2)); and the Act of August 21, 1935 (49 Stat. 666; 16 U.S.C. 461 et seq.).

(b) Except as otherwise provided in this Act, each agency administering any area designated as wilderness shall be responsible for preserving the wilderness character of the area and shall so administer such area for such other purposes for which it may have been established as also to preserve its wilderness character. Except as otherwise provided in this Act, wilderness areas shall be devoted to the public purposes of recreational, scenic, scientific, educational, conservation, and historical use.

## PROHIBITION OF CERTAIN USES

(c) Except as specifically provided for in this Act, and subject to existing private rights, there shall be no commercial enterprise and no permanent road within any wilderness area designated by this Act and, except as necessary to meet minimum requirements for the administration of the area for the purpose of this Act (including measures required in emergencies involving the health and safety of persons within the area), there shall be no temporary road, no use of motor vehicles, motorized equipment or motorboats, no landing of aircraft, no other form of mechanical transport, and no structure or installation within any such area.

SPECIAL PROVISIONS

(d) The following special provisions are hereby made:

(1) Within wilderness areas designated by this Act the use of aircraft or motorboats, where these uses have already become established, may be permitted to continue subject to such restrictions as the Secretary of Agriculture deems desirable. In addition, such measures may be taken as may be necessary in the control of fire, insects, and diseases, subject to such conditions as the Secretary deems desirable.

(2) Nothing in this Act shall prevent within national forest wilderness areas any activity, including prospecting, for the purpose of gathering information about mineral or other resources, if such activity is carried on in a manner compatible with the preservation of the wilderness environment. Furthermore, in accordance with such program as the Secretary of the Interior shall develop and conduct in consultation with the Secretary of Agriculture, such areas shall be surveyed on a planned, recurring basis consistent with the concept of wilderness preservation by the Geological Survey and the Bureau of Mines to determine the mineral values, if any, that may be present; and the results of such surveys shall be made available to the public and submitted to the President and Congress.

(3) Not withstanding any other provisions of this Act, until midnight December 31, 1983, the United States mining laws and all laws pertaining to mineral leasing shall, to the extent as applicable prior to September 3, 1964, extend to those national forest lands designated by this Act as "wilderness areas"; subject, however, to such reasonable regulations governing ingress and egress as may be prescribed by the Secretary of Agriculture consistent with the use of the land for mineral location and development and exploration, drilling, and production,

and use of land for transmission lines, waterlines, telephone lines, or facilities necessary in exploring, drilling, producing, mining, and processing operations, including where essential the use of mechanized ground or air equipment and restoration as near as practicable of the surface of the land disturbed in performing prospecting, location, and, in oil and gas leasing, discovery work, exploration, drilling, and production, as soon as they have served their purpose. Mining locations lying within the boundaries of said wilderness areas shall be held and used solely for mining or processing operations and uses reasonably incident thereto; and hereafter, subject to valid existing rights, all patents issued under the mining laws of the United States affecting national forest lands designated by this Act as wilderness areas shall convey title to the mineral deposits within the claim, together with the right to cut and use so much of the mature timber therefrom as may be needed in the extraction, removal, and beneficiation of the mineral deposits, if needed timber is not otherwise reasonably available, and if the timber is cut under sound principles of forest management as defined by the national forest rules and regulations, but each such patent shall reserve to the United States all title in or to the surface of the lands and products thereof, and no use of the surface of the claim or the resources therefrom not reasonably required for carrying on mining or prospecting shall be allowed except as otherwise expressly provided in this Act: Provided, That, unless hereafter specifically authorized, no patent within wilderness areas designated by this Act shall issue after December 31, 1983, except for the valid claims existing on or before December 31, 1983. Mining claims located after September 3, 1964, within the boundaries of wilderness areas designated by this Act shall create no rights in excess of those rights which may be patented under the provisions of this subsection. Mineral leases, permits, and licenses covering lands within national forest wilderness areas designated by this Act shall contain such reasonable stipulations as may be prescribed by the Secretary of Agriculture for the protection of the wilderness character of the land consistent with the use of the land for the purposes for which they are leased, permitted, or licensed. Subject to valid rights then existing, effective January 1, 1984, the minerals in lands designated by this Act as wilderness areas are withdrawn from all forms of appropriation under the mining laws and from disposition under all laws pertaining to mineral leasing and all amendments thereto.

(4) Within wilderness areas in the national forests designated by this Act, (1) the President may, within a specific area and in accordance with such regulations as he may deem desirable, authorize prospecting for water resources, the establishment and maintenance of reservoirs, water-conservation works, power projects, transmission lines, and other facilities needed in the public interest, including the road construction and maintenance essential to development and use thereof, upon his determination that such use or uses in the specific area will better serve the interests of the United States and the people thereof than will its denial; and (2) the grazing of livestock, where established prior to September 3, 1964, shall be permitted to continue subject to such reasonable regulations as are deemed necessary by the Secretary of Agriculture.

(5) Other provisions of this Act to the contrary notwithstanding, the management of the Boundary Waters Canoe Area, formerly designated as the Superior, Little Indian Sioux, and Caribou Roadless Areas, in the Superior National Forest, Minnesota, shall be in accordance with the

general purpose of maintaining, without unnecessary restrictions on other uses, including that of timber, the primitive character of the area, particularly in the vicinity of lakes, streams, and portages: Provided, That nothing in this Act shall preclude the continuance within the area of any already established use of motorboats.

(6) Commercial services may be performed within the wilderness areas designated by this Act to the extent necessary for activities which are proper for realizing the recreational or other wilderness purposes of the areas.

(7) Nothing in this Act shall constitute an express or implied claim or denial on the part of the Federal Government as to exemption from State water laws.

(8) Nothing in this Act shall be construed as affecting the jurisdiction or responsibilities of the several States with respect to wildlife and fish in the national forests.

## STATE AND PRIVATE LANDS WITHIN WILDERNESS AREAS

Sec. 5. (a) In any case where State-owned or privately owned land is completely surrounded by national forest lands within areas designated by this Act as wilderness, such State or private owner shall be given such rights as may be necessary to assure adequate access to such State-owned or privately owned land by such State or private owner and their successors in interest, or the State-owned land or privately owned land shall be exchanged for federally owned land in the same State of approximately equal value under authorities available to the Secretary of Agriculture: Provided, however, That the United States shall not transfer to a state or private owner any mineral interests unless the

State or private owner relinquishes or causes to be relinquished to the United States the mineral interest in the surrounded land.

(b) In any case where valid mining claims or other valid occupancies are wholly within a designated national forest wilderness area, the Secretary of Agriculture shall, by reasonable regulations consistent with the preservation of the area as wilderness, permit ingress and egress to such surrounded areas by means which have been or are being customarily enjoyed with respect to other such areas similarly situated.

(c) Subject to the appropriation of funds by Congress, the Secretary of Agriculture is authorized to acquire privately owned land within the perimeter of any area designated by this Act as wilderness if (1) the owner concurs in such acquisition or (2) the acquisition is specifically authorized by Congress.

## GIFTS, BEQUESTS, AND CONTRIBUTIONS

Sec. 6. (a) The Secretary of Agriculture may accept gifts or bequests of land within wilderness areas designated by this Act for preservation as wilderness. The Secretary of Agriculture may also accept gifts or bequests of land adjacent to wilderness areas designated by this Act for preservation as wilderness if he has given sixty days advance notice thereof to the President of the Senate and the Speaker of the House of Representatives. Land accepted by the Secretary of Agriculture under this section shall become part of the wilderness area involved. Regulations with regard to any such land may be in accordance with such agreements, consistent with the policy of this Act, as are made at the time of such gift, or such conditions, consistent with such policy, as may be included in, and accepted with, such bequest.

(b) The Secretary of Agriculture or the Secretary of the Interior is authorized to accept private contributions and gifts to be used to further the purpose of this Act.

## ANNUAL REPORTS

Sec. 7. At the opening of each session of Congress, the Secretaries of Agriculture and Interior shall jointly report to the President for transmission to Congress on the status of the wilderness system, including a list and descriptions of the areas in the system, regulations in effect, and other pertinent information, together with any recommendations they may care to make.

Approved September 3, 1964.

———————————

## IV. THE 1976 POINT REYES WILDERNESS ACT

Public Law 94-544

94th Congress

October 18, 1976

AN ACT

To designate certain lands in the Point Reyes National Seashore, California, as wilderness. amending the Act of September 13. 1962 (76 Stat. 538). as amended 16 U.S.C. 459e-6a). and for other purposes.

Be it enacted by the Senate and House of Representatives of the United States of America in Congress assembled, That, in furtherance of the purposes of the Point Reyes National Seashore Act (76 Stat. 538 16 U.S.C. 459c), and of the Wilderness Act (78 Stat. 890: 16 U.S.C. 1131-36), and in accordance with section 3(c) of the Wilderness Act, the following lands within the Point Reyes National Seashore are hereby designated as wilderness, and shall be administered by the Secretary of the Interior in accordance with the applicable provisions of the Wilderness Act: those lands comprising twenty-five thousand three hundred and seventy acres, and potential wilderness additions comprising eight thousand and three acres, depicted on a map entitled "Wilderness Plan. Point Reyes National Seashore," numbered 612 90,000-B and dated September 1976, to be known as the Point Reyes Wilderness.

Sec. 2. As soon as practicable after this Act takes effect, the Secretary of the Interior shall file a map of the wilderness area and a description of its boundaries with the Interior and Insular Affairs Committees of the United States Senate and House of Representatives, and such map and descriptions shall have the same force and effect as if included in this Act; Provided, however, That correction of clerical and typographical errors in such map and descriptions may be made.

Sec. 3. The area designated by this Act as wilderness shall be administered by the Secretary of the Interior in accordance with the applicable provisions of the Wilderness Act governing areas designated by that Act as wilderness areas, except that any reference in such provisions to the effective date of this Act, and, where appropriate, any reference to the Secretary of Agriculture, shall be deemed to be a reference to the Secretary of the Interior.

Sec. 4. (a) Amend the Act of September 13, 1962 (76 Stat. 538), as amended (16 U.S.C. 459c-6a), as follows:

In section 6(a) insert immediately after the words "shall be administered by the Secretary," the words "without impairment of its natural values, in a manner which provides for such recreational, educational, historic preservation, interpretation, and scientific research opportunities as are consistent with, based upon and supportive of the maximum protection, restoration, and preservation of the natural environment within the area,".

(b) Add the following new section 7 and redesignate the existing section 7 as section 8:

"Sec. 7. The Secretary shall designate the principal environmental education center within the seashore as 'The Clem Miller Environmental Education Center,' in commemoration of the vision and leadership which the late Representative Clem Miller gave to the creation and protection of Point Reyes National Seashore."

Approved October 18, 1976.

## V. SOLICITOR'S LETTER REGARDING WILDERNESS DESIGNATION IN DRAKES ESTERO

United States Department of the Interior

Office of the Solicitor

San Francisco Field Office

1111 Jackson Street, Suite 735

Oakland, California 94607

February 26, 2004

To:      Superintendent

      Point Reyes National Seashore

From:  Field Solicitor

      San Francisco Field Office

Re:     Point Reyes Wilderness Act

As requested, this memorandum opinion reviews the Point Reyes wilderness situation as it related to the Johnson Oyster Company 40-year Reservation of Use and Occupancy which expires in 2011 [sic], or might be terminated sooner for cause or other process. The Wilderness Act of 1964, and the Point Reyes Wilderness Act of 1976, provide the guidance for implementation of wilderness within the Seashore and are the basis for NPS's obligations to manage the subject land and waters toward conversion of the potential wilderness areas to wilderness status.

In conjunction with the Seashore authorization act of 1962, the State of California, by 1965 legislation (copy attached), conveyed to the United States all of the right, title and interest of the State in lands one-quarter mile seaward of the mean high tide. More precisely the

State granted "all the tide and submerged lands or other lands beneath navigable waters situated within the boundaries of the Point Reyes National Seashore . . ." to the United States. Excepted from this grant and reserved to the State were the "right to fish upon, and all oil, gas and other hydrocardons in the lands . . . together with the right to explore or prospect . . . " within the tidal and submerged lands. However, these reserved rights were not to be "exercised in such manner as to cause . . . unnecessary pollution of the coastal waters," and no "well or drilling operations of any kind shall be conducted upon the surface of such lands."

On October 18, 1976, the Point Reyes Wilderness Act designated 25,370 acres as wilderness and 8,003 acres as potential wilderness. Public Law 94-544, Oct. 18, 1976. The area designated as potential wilderness (2,811 acres) for area 2 of three areas included the waters of Drakes Estero and the adjoining inter-tidal land and upon which Johnson Oyster Farm operates a commercial oyster business. (map attached)

This Congressional designation of the wilderness and potential wilderness (see the House and State discussions of the legislation in the Congressional Record—copy attached) was made notwithstanding a September 8, 1976 letter written by John Kyl, Assistant Secretary of the Interior, to James A. Haley, Chairman of the Committee on Interior and Insular Affairs wherein he stated the Department's position on the Point Reyes Wilderness Act. While DOI was largely supportive of the Act, Mr. Kyl's letter said that the Department did not recommend the inclusion of the tidelands extending one quarter mile offshore within the boundaries of Point Reyes, as granted by the State of California as potential wilderness. According to the Kyl's letter [sic], the State's retention of mineral and fishing rights rendered this area "inconsistent with wilderness." This letter is the only record in the legislative history that raises this point in the area's wilderness and potential wilderness designation. After review of the 1965 State Act, the Wilderness Act, Point Reyes Wilderness Act, case law and present day NPS Directors' orders and Management Policies, it is the view of this office that the remarks in the Kyl letter are not only inaccurate but overridden by the Congressional action, as explained below.

The 1965 State Act is very limited in its two reservations of rights, i.e., public right to fish and severely restricted in mineral exploration access, i.e. no surface disturbance of any kind. Both reservations would not conflict with the Secretary converting the potential water area and shore land wilderness acres into designated wilderness. Further, notwithstanding the Department's letter, the Congress ultimately designated 25,370 wilderness and 8,000 potential wilderness acres which exceeded the acreage recommended by the Administration. This reflects that Congress did not heed Mr. Kyl's recommendation and conclusions and enacted its preferred wilderness act.

Addressing the potential wilderness lands and water, the House Report 94-1680, accompanying the eventually enacted Bill (RR 8002) states that it was its intent that there be "effort to steadily continue to remove all obstacles to the eventual conversion of these lands and waters to wilderness status." (copy attached) The designations are implemented by the Park Service's 2001 Management Policies on wilderness which state that "[I]n the process of determining suitability, lands will not be excluded solely because of existing rights or privileges (e.g., mineral exploration and development, commercial operations . . ."). Further, the Park Service's Management Policies clearly state that the Park Service must make decisions regarding the management of potential wilderness even though some activities may temporarily detract from its wilderness character. The Park Service is to manage potential wilderness as wilderness to the extent that existing non-conforming conditions allow. The Park Service is also required to actively seek to remove from potential wilderness the temporary, non-conforming conditions that preclude wilderness designation. 6.3.1. Wilderness Resource Management, General Policy. (selected excerpts attached)

Hence, the Park Service is mandated by the Wilderness Act, the Point Reyes Wilderness Act and its Management Policies to convert potential wilderness, i.e. the Johnson Oyster Company tract and the adjoining Estero, to wilderness status as soon as the non-conforming use can be eliminated.

Ralph G. Mihan

## VI. SECRETARY OF THE INTERIOR KEN SALAZAR'S DECISION OF NOVEMBER 29, 2012

November 29, 2012

To:         Director, National Park Service

Through:    Principal Deputy Assistant Secretary for Fish
            and Wildlife and Parks

From:       Secretary Ken Salazar

CC:         Regional Director, Pacific West Region, NPS
            Superintendent, Point Reyes National Seashore

Subject:    Point Reyes National Seashore—Drakes Bay Oyster
            Company

After giving due consideration to the request of the Drakes Bay Oyster Company ("DBOC") to conduct commercial operations within Point Reyes National Seashore in the State of California ("Point Reyes"), I have directed the National Park Service (NPS) to allow the permit to expire at the end of its current term. This decision is based on matters of law and policy including:

The explicit terms of the 1972 conveyance from the Johnson Oyster Company to the United States of America. The Johnson Oyster Company received $79,200 for the property. The Johnson Oyster Company also reserved a 40-year right of use and occupancy expiring November 30, 2012. Under these terms and considerations paid, the United States purchased all the fee interest that housed the oyster operation. In 2004, DBOC acquired the business from Johnson Oyster Company, including the remaining term of the reservation of use and occupancy and was explicitly informed "no new permit will be issued" after the 2012 expiration date.

The continuation of the DBOC operation would violate the policies of NPS concerning commercial use within a unit of the National Park System and nonconforming uses within potential or designated wilderness, as well as specific wilderness legislation for Point Reyes National Seashore.

The area within Point Reyes that Congress identified as potential wilderness includes a biologically rich estuary known as Drakes Estero, consisting of several tidal inlets tributary to Drakes bay, on the southern side of the Point Reyes peninsula. Drakes Estero encompasses approximately 2,500 acres of tideland and submerged lands and is home to one of the largest harbor seal populations in California. In 1999 the eastern portion of Drakes Estero, known as the Estero de Limantour, was converted from potential to designated wilderness, becoming the first (and still the only) marine wilderness on the Pacific coast of the United States outside of Alaska. DBOC's commercial mariculture operation is the only use in the remaining portion of Drakes Estero preventing its conversion from potential to designated wilderness.

Therefore, I direct you to:

Notify DBOC that both the Reservation of Use and Occupancy ("RUO") and the Special Use Permit ("SUP") held by DBOC expire according to their terms on November 30, 2012.

Allow DBOC a period of 90 days after November 30, 2012, to remove its personal property, including shellfish and racks, from the lands and waters covered by the RUO and SUP in order for DBOC to minimize the loss of its personal property and meet its obligations to vacate and restore all areas covered by the RUO and SUP. No commercial activities may take place in the waters of Drakes Estero after November 30, 2012.

Effectuate the conversion of Drakes Estero from potential to designated wilderness.

Because of the importance of sustainable agriculture on the pastoral lands within Point Reyes, I direct that you pursue extending permits for the ranchers within those pastoral lands to 20-year terms.

Finally, I direct you to use all existing legal authorizations at your disposal to help DBOC workers who might be affected by this decision, including assisting with relocation, employment opportunities, and training.

I have taken this matter very seriously. I have personally traveled to Point Reyes National Seashore, visited DBOC, met with a wide variety of interested parties on all sides of this issue, and considered many letters, scientific reports, and other documents. The purpose of this memorandum is to document the reasons for my decision and to direct you to take all necessary and appropriate steps to implement it.

[Author's note: "I. Factual and Legal Background" and "II. Discussion" have been omitted from the reproduction of this memorandum because the information has previously been supplied in these pages and appendices. The full text is available from www.doi.gov.]

III. Implementation

Based on the foregoing, I hereby direct that you expeditiously take all necessary and appropriate steps to implement my decision. My decision means that, after November 30, 2012, DBOC no longer will be legally authorized to conduct commercial operations within Point Reyes. Accordingly, I direct that the NPS publish in the Federal

Register the notice announcing the conversion of Drakes Estero from potential to designated wilderness. I direct that the NPS allow DBOC a period of 90 days after November 30, 2012, to remove its personal property, including shellfish and racks, from the lands and waters covered by the RUO and SUP in order for DBOC to minimize the loss of its personal property and to meet its obligations to vacate and restore all areas covered by the RUO and SUP. No commercial activities may take place in the waters of Drakes Estero after November 30, 2012. During this 90-day period, DBOC may conduct limited commercial activities onshore to the extent authorized in writing by NPS.

I am aware that allowing DBOC's existing authorizations to expire by their terms will result in dislocation of DBOC's business and may result in the loss of jobs for approximately 30 people currently employed by DBOC. I therefore direct that you use existing legal authorities to ameliorate to the extent possible the economic and other impacts on DBOC's employees, including providing information and other assistance to those employees to the full extent authorized under the Uniform Relocation Assistance and Real Property Acquisition Policies Act of 1970, codified as amended at 42 U.S.C. 4601-4655. Additionally, I direct you to develop a plan for training and to work with the local community to identify job opportunities for DBOC employees.

Finally, the Department of the Interior and the NPS support the continued presence of dairy and beef ranching operations in Point Reyes' pastoral zone. I recognize that ranching has a long and important history on the Point Reyes peninsula, which began after centuries-old Coast Miwok traditions were replaced by Spanish mission culture at the beginning of the 19th century. Long-term preservation of ranching was a central concern of local interests and members of Congress as they considered legislation to establish the Point Reyes National Seashore in the late 1950s and early 1960s. In establishing the pastoral zone (Point Reyes enabling legislation PL 87-657, Section 4) Congress limited the Government's power of eminent domain and recognized "the value to the Government and the public of continuation of ranching activities, as presently practiced, in preserving the beauty of the area." (House Report No. 1628 at pages 2503-04.) Congress amended the Point Reyes enabling legislation in 1978 to authorize the NPS to lease agriculture property that has been used for ranching or dairying purposes. (Section 318, Public Law 95-625, 92 Stat. 3487, 1978.) The House Report explained that the "use of agricultural lease-backs is encouraged to maintain this compatible activity, and the Secretary is encouraged to utilize this authority to the fullest extent possible." (House Report 95-1165, page 344.)

Accordingly, I direct that the Superintendent work with the operators of the cattle and dairy ranches within the pastoral zone to reaffirm my intention that, consistent with applicable laws and planning processes, recognition of the role of ranching be maintained and to pursue extending permits to 20-year terms for the dairy and cattle ranches within that pastoral zone. In addition, the values of multi-generational ranching and farming at Point Reyes should be fully considered in future planning efforts. These working ranches are a vibrant and compatible part of Point Reyes National Seashore, and both now and in the future represent an important contribution to the Point Reyes superlative natural and cultural resources.

IV. My decision honors Congress's direction to "steadily continue to remove all obstacles to the eventual conversion of these lands and waters to wilderness status" and this ensures that these precious resources are preserved for the enjoyment of future generations of the American public, for whom Point Reyes National Seashore was created. As President Lyndon Johnson said on signing the Wilderness Act in 1964, "If future generations are to remember us with gratitude rather than contempt, we must leave them something more than the miracle of technology. We must leave them a glimpse of the world as it was in the beginning, not just after we got through with it."

Oct. 18, 1976


Document contains footnote: "It is noted that the State continued to issue to Johnson Oyster Company commercial allotments in Drakes Estero which seem to be in conflict with the 1965 State legislative grant and 1976 Congressional mandate to convert the bays of the Estero into wilderness status. On the other hand, the continued public fishing in the Estero is consistent with the State legislative grant and the conversion to wilderness status. Further, since the United States owns the tide and submerged lands in Drakes Estero, it clearly follows that permission of NPS is appropriate for commercial activities taking place on those granted lands."

Document contains footnote: "See the District Court ruling that past commercial activities, in this case timber harvesting, do not preclude an area's wilderness designation. Minnesota Public Interest Research Group v. Butz 401 F. Supp. 1276, 1329 (1975)."

# INDEX

*Page locators for names of cities within states are not replicated under the state.*